The Organizational Life of Psychoanalysis

The Organizational Life of Psychoanalysis is a wide-ranging exploration and examination of the organizational conflicts and dilemmas that have troubled psychoanalysis since its inception. Kenneth Eisold provides a unique, detailed, and closely reasoned account of the systems needed to carry out the tasks of training, quality control, community building, and relationships with the larger professional community. He explores how the freedom to innovate and explore can be sustained in a context where the culture has insisted on certain standards being set and enforced, standards that have little to do with providing effective pathways to cure.

Each chapter in this collection addresses a specific dilemma faced by the profession, including:

- Who is to be in charge of training and who will determine those who succeed the existing leadership?
- Which theories and practices are to be approved and which proscribed and censored?
- How is the competition with alternative methods, including psychotherapy informed by psychoanalysis, to be managed?

Several chapters are devoted to exploring the reciprocal influence of Freudian psychoanalysis and Jungian analytical psychology. Others explore the specific dilemmas and difficulties affecting the field currently, stemming from the massive restructuring of the health care industry and the changes affecting all professions, as they are reshaped into massive organizations no longer marked by personal relationships and individual control.

The Organizational Life of Psychoanalysis will be essential reading for psychoanalysts, psychoanalytic psychotherapists, and anyone interested in the future of psychoanalysis as a profession. It will appeal greatly to anyone who has assumed full or partial responsibility for the management of a psychoanalytic institute or association.

Kenneth Eisold is a practicing psychoanalyst, as well as an organizational consultant, who has written extensively on the psychodynamics of large systems as well as on the organizational dimension of psychoanalysis and continues to advise and coach. He is Past President of the International Society for the Psychoanalytic Study of Organizations as well as former Director of the Organizational Program at The William Alanson White Institute, where he trained consultants in working psychodynamically with organizations. He is a Fellow of the A. K. Rice Institute.

Psychoanalysis in a New Key Book Series
Donnel Stern
Series Editor

When music is played in a new key, the melody does not change, but the notes that make up the composition do: change in the context of continuity, continuity that perseveres through change. Psychoanalysis in a New Key publishes books that share the aims psychoanalysts have always had, but that approach them differently. The books in the series are not expected to advance any particular theoretical agenda, although to this date most have been written by analysts from the Interpersonal and Relational orientations.

The most important contribution of a psychoanalytic book is the communication of something that nudges the reader's grasp of clinical theory and practice in an unexpected direction. Psychoanalysis in a New Key creates a deliberate focus on innovative and unsettling clinical thinking. Because that kind of thinking is encouraged by exploration of the sometimes surprising contributions to psychoanalysis of ideas and findings from other fields, Psychoanalysis in a New Key particularly encourages interdisciplinary studies. Books in the series have married psychoanalysis with dissociation, trauma theory, sociology, and criminology. The series is open to the consideration of studies examining the relationship between psychoanalysis and any other field – for instance, biology, literary and art criticism, philosophy, systems theory, anthropology, and political theory.

But innovation also takes place within the boundaries of psychoanalysis, and Psychoanalysis in a New Key therefore also presents work that reformulates thought and practice without leaving the precincts of the field. Books in the series focus, for example, on the significance of personal values in psychoanalytic practice, on the complex interrelationship between the analyst's clinical work and personal life, on the consequences for the clinical situation when patient and analyst are from different cultures, and on the need for psychoanalysts to accept the degree to which they knowingly satisfy their own wishes during treatment hours, often to the patient's detriment.

For a full list of all the titles in the Psychoanalysis in a New Key series, please visit the Routledge website.

RECENT TITLES IN THIS SERIES

Vol. 38 *Interpersonal Psychoanalysis and the Enigma of Consciousness* Edgar A. Levenson and Edited by Alan Slomowitz

Vol. 37 *The Organizational Life of Psychoanalysis: Conflicts, Dilemmas, and the Future of the Profession* Kenneth Eisold

Vol. 36 *Nonlinear Psychoanalysis: Notes from Forty Years of Chaos and Complexity Theory* Robert M. Galatzer-Levy

Vol. 35 *A Beholder's Share: Essays on Winnicott and the Psychoanalytic Imagination* Dodi Goldman

Vol. 34 *The Interpersonal Perspective in Psychoanalysis, 1960s–1990s: Rethinking Transference and Countertransference* Edited by Donnel B. Stern and Irwin Hirsch

The Organizational Life of Psychoanalysis

Conflicts, Dilemmas, and the Future of the Profession

Kenneth Eisold

LONDON AND NEW YORK

First published 2018
by Routledge
2 Park Square, Milton Park, Abingdon, Oxon OX14 4RN

and by Routledge
711 Third Avenue, New York, NY 10017

Routledge is an imprint of the Taylor & Francis Group, an informa business

© 2018 Kenneth Eisold

The right of Kenneth Eisold to be identified as author of this work has been asserted by him in accordance with sections 77 and 78 of the Copyright, Designs and Patents Act 1988.

All rights reserved. No part of this book may be reprinted or reproduced or utilised in any form or by any electronic, mechanical, or other means, now known or hereafter invented, including photocopying and recording, or in any information storage or retrieval system, without permission in writing from the publishers.

Trademark notice: Product or corporate names may be trademarks or registered trademarks, and are used only for identification and explanation without intent to infringe.

British Library Cataloguing in Publication Data
A catalogue record for this book is available from the British Library

Library of Congress Cataloging in Publication Data
Names: Eisold, Kenneth, author.
Title: The organizational life of psychoanalysis : conflicts, dilemmas,
and the future of the profession / Kenneth Eisold.
Description: Abingdon, Oxon ; New York, NY : Routledge, [2018] |
Series: Psychoanalysis in a new key book series ; 37 |
Includes bibliographical references and index.
Identifiers: LCCN 2017003079 | ISBN 9781138229198 (hardback : alk. paper) |
ISBN 9781138229204 (pbk. : alk. paper) | ISBN 9781315390062 (epub) |
ISBN 9781315390055 (mobipocket/kindle)
Subjects: LCSH: Psychoanalysis–History. | Psychiatry–History. |
Psychotherapy–History.
Classification: LCC BF173.E549 2018 | DDC 150.19/5–dc23
LC record available at https://lccn.loc.gov/2017003079

ISBN: 978-1-138-22919-8 (hbk)
ISBN: 978-1-138-22920-4 (pbk)
ISBN: 978-1-315-39008-6 (ebk)

Typeset in Times New Roman
by Out of House Publishing

Contents

Foreword by Jay Greenberg		ix
Acknowledgments		xiv

Introduction   1

PART ONE
Psychoanalytic History   **3**

1   Freud as Leader: The Early Years of the Viennese Society   5

2   The Splitting of the New York Psychoanalytic Society
and the Construction of Psychoanalytic Authority   32

3   Psychoanalysis and Psychotherapy: A Long and
Troubled Relationship   55

PART TWO
Organizational Analysis   **83**

4   The Intolerance of Diversity in Psychoanalytic Institutes   85

5   Psychoanalytic Training: The "Faculty System"   111

6   Institutional Conflicts in Jungian Analysis   130

7   Jung, Jungians, and Psychoanalysis   152

viii Contents

PART THREE
Problems of Professionalization   179

8 Psychoanalysis as a Profession: Past Failures and
   Future Possibilities   181

9 The Erosion of Our Profession   210

10 Succeeding at Succession: The Myth of Orestes   225

11 Psychoanalytic Training: Then and Now, The Heroic
   Age, and the Domestic Era   241

   Index   258

Foreword

Jay Greenberg

The conceptual structure of every intellectual discipline is shaped by the organizational structures within which ideas emerge, develop, and find either acceptance or rejection. This is perhaps even more true of psychoanalysis than of other disciplines, because psychoanalysis began – explosively – with the work of one man who sought to cure illness by challenging the most cherished beliefs of the culture that was in large part responsible for creating illness in the first place. From the very beginning of his clinical work and of the theory-building that emerged from it, Freud was aware of both the power and the fragility of what he was creating; if his work was to have enduring influence it would have to be protected from the many dangers that threatened it. And he was also aware that this was beyond the reach of any one leader, no matter how brilliant or charismatic. If his insights were to survive, others would have to be recruited to the cause and organizations would have to be built that would advance its purposes.

As a field of study, psychoanalysis is well equipped to explore the relationships among the ideas that define a discipline, the people who commit their professional lives to the development of those ideas, the organizations that authorize, reward, and punish those practitioners, all within the larger culture within which all this is embedded. The essential goal of psychoanalysis, after all, is to dissect the desires and the fears that shape our behavior and experience and the structures – personal and social – that we create to deal with them. However, there are not many psychoanalysts who have the expertise that is needed to implement this project, or the breadth and depth of understanding that is required. Fewer still are able to sustain the particular kind of binocular vision (extending Bion's use of the term) that allows us to see the nuanced interactions that grow from the meeting of individual aspirations and anxieties and the needs of organizations with their attendant pressures.

Kenneth Eisold is among the very few who can keep track of all the moving parts that are involved in creating, growing, and sustaining what has at various times been an intellectual discipline, a profession, and a movement; as a result, his insight informs every page of this important book. His comfort with disparate but complementary perspectives on the work we do and the structures within which we do it is contagious. Eisold brings the reader along with him as he develops his argument and we come away from every page with a new, deepened appreciation of the complexities that haunt our lives both as clinicians working privately with our patients and as members of broader communities.

Eisold is able to accomplish this because he views the organizational history of psychoanalysis with a clinician's eye, and also because he is a gifted storyteller. From one point of view this book is, throughout, a very human story, very well told. Eisold's account of the early days of psychoanalysis, the emergence of a set of ideas and practices from its isolation in the mind of its creator to public airing in the Wednesday night meetings of Freud and his first disciples, is filled with poignant descriptions of the tensions that inevitably emerged among men who were reaching – sometimes collaboratively, sometimes in competition with each other, often in reaction to perceived threats from outside the group – to develop and promote ideas that they were certain would change the world.

As the story unfolds, we see how these early tensions – modified only somewhat by the rapid growth of institutionalized psychoanalysis and by changing cultural circumstances – persist and continue to shape the character of the discipline. Freud knew that not only his theories but his movement would meet with resistance; it could not be otherwise with ideas that direct our attention to aspects of our experience that we spend a great deal of energy avoiding. But also from the beginning there was a thin, often imperceptible line between Freud's protection of psychoanalysis and his protection of his own position as founder and leader. Eisold's book is, in part, a meditation on authority and authoritarianism in psychoanalytic organizations and in clinical psychoanalysis itself. Because he is a clinician he is able to sustain a compassionate vision of the ways in which legitimate authority can devolve into authoritarianism, serving the needs of what he terms a "social defense" that protects senior members of an embattled community against the various anxieties to which their position makes them vulnerable. But because he is an organizational consultant he is also keenly aware of – and critical of – the costs of this defense not only to the institutions involved but to the discipline itself.

Despite the breadth of his vision and the sweep of the story he tells, Eisold's book speaks directly to the experience of every practicing psychoanalyst, and even more broadly to the experience of all mental health providers. With incisive clarity and with passion that draws the reader to his argument he shows us how the themes he is addressing affect issues we struggle with on a daily basis; we come away from his account with a deepened appreciation of the pressures that silently but profoundly influence our clinical work. Much of what he said struck me in much the same way that a good psychoanalytic interpretation might: I had a sense that "Yes, I know that! But why didn't I think of it until now?" Because psychotherapists of all persuasions work essentially alone we tend not to notice the larger contexts in which our work is embedded. Eisold makes a strong case that when we reflect on our professional identities we think mainly about personal, typically dyadic experience with teachers, supervisors, training analysts; rarely do we consider the enduring influence of the institutes in which we trained or of the societies of which we are members. And even more rarely do we give any thought to the impact of broad social forces: the relationship of the practice of psychotherapy to a medical system that is itself in a constant state of flux, economic forces that shape broad attitudes toward the professions and "professionalism" in general, and so on.

Eisold cautions that we ignore these forces at our peril. And, in what is certainly one of the most important lessons that he has to teach, he shows us how they give shape to many controversies that are familiar to all practicing psychoanalysts and psychotherapists but that we tend to think about deeply but somewhat narrowly in clinical and/or theoretical terms. I will mention only a few of the many issues that he addresses in surprising and illuminating ways.

First, there is the vexing problem of the distinction between psychoanalysis and psychotherapy, which has been disputed, often bitterly, for a century or more. Eisold makes it clear that we cannot appreciate the nuances of this debate without stepping outside of our more familiar frames of reference; full understanding requires that we consider what is at stake in organizational, economic, and professional terms.

Second, Eisold takes up the problem of theoretical diversity within psychoanalytic thinking. While at first glance this might appear to be purely an intellectual or academic matter – the disputes are often seen as resulting from the ambiguities inherently involved in any attempt to explain or even to describe the elusive phenomena that constitute human experience – full understanding also requires paying attention to the organizations within which controversies emerge and develop. Eisold is particularly effective in describing how institutional life provokes and sustains destructive schisms or, to put a slightly different spin on it, how potentially generative differences can become destructive when caught up in struggles over power and authority.

Third, Eisold is particularly persuasive when he addresses the tensions inherent when dyads (analyst/analysand, supervisor/supervisee) function within the structure of a larger organization that has priorities that will always be different from those of the dyad. This leads to clashing loyalties and commitments as both members of the dyad struggle to meet demands that are, or at least seem to be, mutually exclusive. A familiar example of this is supervision conducted under the auspices of a psychoanalytic institute, in which the supervisor functions simultaneously (and in some ways incompatibly) as teacher and evaluator. This creates a dilemma for the supervisee: learning requires being as honest as possible about the work that he or she is doing; but progression requires meeting criteria that have been established elsewhere. Similarly, the supervisor is caught in a dilemma: the teaching function requires working in depth with what the supervisee is bringing, but as gatekeeper he or she must also pay attention to the demands of the institute that authorized the supervision in the first place. The tensions involved in this dual role, Eisold shows, affect both the structure of the institute and the supervisory process itself.

These are only a few of the issues that are illuminated, often surprisingly, in this powerful and engaging book. It is important, I would say essential, reading for anybody who is interested in the complex, often difficult to grasp, relationships among clinical work, theory-building, and organizational structures. And that should be all of us.

Acknowledgments

Every effort has been made to contact the copyright holders for their permission to reprint selections of this book. The publishers would be grateful to hear from any copyright holder who is not here acknowledged and we will undertake to rectify any errors or omissions in future editions of this book.

Chapter 1 originally published as Eisold, K., Freud as Leader: The Early Years of the Viennese Society, *The International Journal of Psychoanalysis*, vol. 78/1 (February 1997), pp. 87–104. Reprinted by permission of John Wiley & Sons, Inc.

Chapter 2 originally published as Eisold, K., The Splitting of the New York Psychoanalytic Society and the Construction of Psychoanalytic Authority, *The International Journal of Psychoanalysis*, vol. 79/5 (October 1998), pp. 871–85. Reprinted by permission of John Wiley & Sons, Inc.

Chapter 3 originally published as Eisold, K., Psychotherapy and Psychoanalysis: A Long and Troubled History, *The International Journal of Psychoanalysis*, vol. 86 (2005), pp. 1175–95. Reprinted by permission of John Wiley & Sons, Inc.

Chapter 4 originally published as Eisold, K., The Intolerance of Diversity in Psychoanalytic Institutes, *The International Journal of Psychoanalysis*, vol. 75/4 (August 1994), pp. 785–800. Reprinted by permission of John Wiley & Sons, Inc.

Chapter 5 originally published as Eisold, K., Psychoanalytic Training: The "Faculty System," *Psychoanalytic Inquiry*, vol. 24 (2004), pp. 51–70. Reprinted by permission of Taylor & Francis, LLC.

Chapter 6 originally published as Eisold, K., Institutional Conflicts in Jungian Analysis, *Journal of Analytical Psychology*, vol. 46 (2001), pp. 335–53. Reprinted by permission of John Wiley & Sons, Inc.

Chapter 7 originally published as Eisold, K., Jung, Jungians, and Psychoanalysis, *Psychoanalytic Psychology*, vol. 19 (2002), pp. 501–24. Reprinted by permission of The American Psychological Association.

Chapter 8 originally published as Eisold, K., Psychoanalysis as a Profession: Past Failures and Future Possibilities, *Contemporary Psychoanalysis*, vol. 39 (2003), pp. 557–82. Reprinted by permission of Taylor & Francis, LLC.

Chapter 9 originally offered as a plenary talk at a conference at the Tavistock Centre, London, October 21, 2005, "Extension, Dilution and Survival." Published as Eisold, K., The Erosion of Our Profession, *Psychoanalytic Psychology*, vol. 24 (2007), pp. 1–9. Reprinted by permission of The American Psychological Association.

Chapter 10 originally published as Eisold, K., Succeeding at Succession: The Myth of Orestes, *Journal of Analytic Psychology*, vol. 53 (2008), pp. 619–32. Reprinted by permission of John Wiley & Sons, Inc.

Chapter 11 originally published as Eisold, K., Psychoanalytic Training: Then and Now, in *The Future of Psychoanalysis: The Debate about the Training Analyst System*, Psychoanalytic Ideas and Applications Series. Peter Zagermann, ed. London: Karnac, 2017, pp. 53–69. Permission granted by Rod Tweedy, Editor, Karnac Books.

Introduction

These essays, presentations, and talks on the organizational conflicts and dilemmas that have troubled psychoanalysis since its inception were published originally over the past 20 years. They address such questions as: Why has its history been so marked by schisms? How has a collection of professionals, well trained to detect unconscious motivations in others, been unable to understand and modify the assumptions that stand in the way of their own success? Why has the field been unable to adapt to the profound changes in the mental health industry in recent years?

The essays were written for psychoanalysts and published in top-tier psychoanalytic journals. They were well received, but recent years have made it more apparent that the field urgently needs to address its internal problems, and it is showing signs of being able to do so. Institutes that split apart are now merging. Our international organizations are becoming more open and inclusive. Policies that mandated hierarchical control and excluded significant sectors of our field are being changed. And there is a growing awareness that the organizations of psychoanalysis need to become more sophisticated and adroit.

Psychoanalysis historically has tended to focus almost entirely on the patient/analyst dyad, but there is a growing awareness that its focus needs to widen to include its organizations and the larger community. In June 2015, Stephano Boligningi, president of the IPA, spoke in Rome of modifying the traditional tripartite model of training to include a fourth element, organizational understanding, a recognition that the issues these essays address is increasingly vital to the future of the field. (A similar collection of my essays was recently translated and published in Italy.) Perhaps an even more important sign of the growing tolerance and flexibility of the professional associations of psychoanalysis is the frequency of discussions about their purpose and their inclusiveness, and the greater willingness to open their doors and modify their standards to include previously excluded sectors.

Should the APsaA (American Psychoanalytic Association) become a "big tent," accommodating all those interested in psychoanalysis and engaging in some form of practice? It is uncertain, of course, if this will happen, but even in considering that option many know that the field would have to develop a more sophisticated and supple conception of itself as well as an appreciation of the conflicts, dilemmas, and stress points likely to arise as a result of its increasing diversity.

The essays collected here do not address that question directly. But I believe they allow us a deeper grasp of the complex and often hidden issues that afflict the field inside the box it has constructed for itself. If we want to think outside the box, we have to be able to see it first.

Part One

Psychoanalytic History

Chapter One

Freud as Leader

The Early Years of the Viennese Society

[Originally published as Freud as Leader: The Early Years of the Viennese Society, *The International Journal of Psychoanalysis*, vol. 78/1 (February 1997), pp. 87–104.]

"Freud never lost control of the group as a whole; he proved a masterful leader," Nunberg wrote in his introduction to the *Minutes of the Vienna Psychoanalytic Society* (Nunberg & Federn, 1962, p. xxiv). But Freud's own assessment of his leadership was very different. In his "On the History of the Psychoanalytic Movement," he disparaged his ability to lead the group of Viennese supporters he had gathered around himself starting in 1902: "I could not succeed in establishing among its members the friendly relations that ought to obtain between men who are all engaged upon the same difficult work" (Freud, 1914, p. 25).

As a generalization, Freud's statement has a good deal of superficial plausibility, given the fact that the period he describes included the notorious splits with Adler and Jung. Indeed, he wrote his "History" in order to explain and justify what appeared to the larger world as sectarian schisms, damaging to the reputation of psychoanalysis as a serious scientific endeavor. In that context, it adds to his account of those conflicts, a modest confession of his inadequacy as a leader. And, I think, moreover, he truly believed he lacked such skills.

On several occasions Freud expressed his distaste for the burdens of leadership and doubts about his ability. In 1907 he wrote to Jung: "I have always felt that there is something about my personality, my ideas and manner of speaking, that people find strange and repellent," which he attributed to being an "'obsessional' type, each specimen of which vegetates in a sealed-off world of his own" (McGuire, 1974, p. 82).

And again, in 1908: "I am certainly unfit to be a chief, the '*splendid isolation*' of my decisive years has set its stamp upon my character" (Ibid., p. 141). Many times during these years, moreover, he spoke of being too old for the burdens of leadership.

But Freud's "failure to establish friendly relations" in Vienna also casts a shadow on the Viennese and alludes to what had by then become a common attitude within the psychoanalytic community. Binswanger reported Freud's discouraged remark following an early meeting: "Well, now you have seen the gang" (Binswanger, 1957). And Jones reported Jung's description of the Viennese group "as a medley of artists, decadents and mediocrities" (Jones, 1955, II, p. 33).

Much of this is attributable to competition between the locals and the visitors from abroad. Abraham wrote Eitingon, following his 1907 visit to the society, "I am not too thrilled by the Viennese adherents ... *He* is all too far ahead of the others" (Gay, 1988, p. 178). Jones, in his autobiography, wrote that the Viennese "seemed an unworthy accompaniment to Freud's genius" (Jones, 1959, pp. 159–60). Nor, I think, was Freud above stimulating rivalry as a means of encouraging his followers.

Moreover, as we shall see, relations between Freud and the Viennese group became strained and, at times, acrimonious: as the society grew in size, transformed itself into a professional organization, encountered competition from outside, and redefined its relationship with its founder and most precious member, it went through stormy times. But it has never fully escaped this early reputation as a collection of rivalrous, petty, and contentious men. Gay (1988), with seeming definitiveness, characterized their meetings as "testy, even acrimonious, as members sparred for position, vaunted their originality, or voiced dislike of their fellows with a brutal hostility masquerading as analytic frankness" (p. 176).

The other side to this story, of course, is Freud's reputation as the tyrannical father who could not let his sons grow up to become independent (Puner, 1947; Roustang, 1982). Jung, in several bitter letters during his break with Freud, accused him of "playing the father" (McGuire, 1974, p. 535). Wittels (1924) links Freud to the tyrannical father of "Totem and Taboo," and he offered the tart comment about the stifling of dissent: "Suppression makes people snappish" (p. 142). Roazen (1969), not untypically, voices the conclusion that "the best of

Freud's male pupils left because the atmosphere was too narrow and ultimately degrading" (p. 48).

The most poignant evidence of this comes from Freud himself. In April 1910, he wrote Ferenczi that he felt threatened by "falling into the role of the dissatisfied and superfluous old man" (Brabant, 1993, p. 155). In November of 1910, he complained to Jung of his growing difficulties with Adler: "He is ... forcing me into the unwelcome role of the aging despot who prevents young men from getting ahead" (McGuire, 1974, p. 373).

But, if we examine the evidence of what went on in the Viennese group more closely, these characterizations become more and more puzzling. Freud's own description of this group in his "History" is unquestionably, if somewhat grudgingly, positive: "On the whole I could tell myself that it was hardly inferior, in wealth and variety of talent, to the staff of any clinical teacher one could think of" (Freud, 1914, p. 25). Indeed, individually, many of the members of the group are viewed today as important and distinguished contributors to the development of psychoanalysis. Moreover, an examination of the minutes of the society from 1906 through 1915, carefully edited by Nunberg and Federn (1962, 1967, 1974, 1975), reveals that, in fact, those meetings were lively, obviously stimulating to the members, and productive. They may not have been in Freud's term "friendly"; indeed, they were often contentious and competitive. But by any measure they were successful and, precisely in the way that Freud had hoped, developing the ideas and practice of psychoanalysis.

The objective success of these meetings hardly needs to be dwelt upon, and Freud unquestionably played a major role in this success. There is a substantial psychoanalytic literature on the qualities of the successful leader that can help us grasp how Freud contributed to this success. Zaleznik (1989), for example, notes that the successful leader is often "twice born," distinct in his identity from others, as a result, and exceptionally purposive in pursuing his vision. (See Newton, 1995.) Similarly, Lapierre (1991) notes the importance of the personal authority of the leader, stemming from the clarity of his "inner truth," enabling him to project his desires and fantasies into his followers. Zonis and Offer (1985), working from a self-psychological perspective, identify the type of the "wise leader" who has transformed his primary narcissistic needs, on the one hand, actively pursuing his ego ideal, but, on the other, able to appraise himself realistically. All of these perspectives capture something of Freud's personal achievement, at this stage in his life, enabling him to lead the psychoanalytic movement. He became a compelling – at times, mesmerizing – leader.

And yet the story of Freud's leadership is also profoundly disappointing. In his own terms, he failed to turn over the leadership to others, as he repeatedly sought to do, and he lost the intellectual companionship of the men he loved the most. Moreover, starting with these early years, psychoanalysis became encumbered with a reputation for sectarian intolerance – a reputation subsequently reiterated and reinforced – damaging to its efforts to establish its scientific standing and inhibiting to its internal development.

Clearly, the responsibility for all this cannot be attributed to Freud. He played a vital role in bringing this about, but so did his followers. Freud was a leader in so far and in the manner that was allowed by his followers.

There is a strand of psychoanalytic thinking on this subject that begins with the pioneering observations of Bion (1969), stressing the control that groups exert over leaders. Noting that all groups are simultaneously engaged in pursuing a task as well as defending against anxiety – they are what he called "work groups" and "basic assumption groups" – he called attention to the unconscious ways in which groups manipulate leaders in the service of their defensive needs. Menzies-Lyth (1967) has elucidated the largely hidden impact of "social defenses" in social systems, affecting task performance and controlling the scope of leadership. Shapiro (1979), also working in this tradition, has suggested the impact of group regression on leadership, as has Kernberg (1980a, 1980b). Other theorists stressing the power of unconscious dynamics in groups have looked at it somewhat differently. Anzieu (1984) has studied the powerful role of unconscious fantasy in groups to subvert rational planning. Strozier (1985), working from a self-psychology perspective, has explored the constraints on the leader stemming from his role as selfobject; the increasing fragmentation of selves in groups, accompanied by narcissistic rage, produces an increasing need for an idealized leader.

I will use here Bion's framework for understanding the process of the group, although other frameworks accounting for the dynamic interplay between leaders and followers could also serve. The Viennese

The Early Years of the Viennese Society 9

Society was a relatively small group, close to the size of the groups with which Bion made his initial clinical observations, but also because his terms are descriptive and parsimonious – and they closely fit the phenomena for which we have evidence. At the same time, I follow Rice (1963) and Kernberg (1980c) in looking at such dynamics in the framework of a task system: regression leading to "basic assumption" behavior tends to occur in groups when there is a conflict between tasks or a discontinuity between task and the requisite structures for carrying out task.

A close look at the records of the society, as we shall see, strongly supports the presence of basic assumptions. Freud and his followers, feeling continually besieged by the medical and cultural establishment, could hardly avoid the basic assumption of fight/flight, i.e., the belief that their primary need was to defend themselves against external dangers. On the other hand, given the power and importance of Freud to the group, neither could they avoid the basic assumption of dependency, the belief that they needed Freud's support and protection to survive. At the same time, they all were engaged in trying to develop the organizational structures they needed to address the various tasks they faced; and, as we shall see, there was an essential conflict in their understanding of that task.

Clearly, Freud was not entirely the "masterful leader" Nunberg described. Neither was he the domineering despot he has sometimes been made out to be – nor the ineffective leader he sometimes felt he was. The Viennese, on the other hand, were not a petty and squabbling band of mediocre followers; neither were they heroes or victims. They were, at various times, to be sure, all of these as they attempted to rise to the challenges they faced and react to pressures they did not understand. Above all, they were passionately engaged in an enterprise that brought out the best and the worst in them. Together, they brought psychoanalysis into the world and, stimulated by profound anxiety, engaged in destructive unconscious defensive acts as well.

Before Salzburg

Begun in 1902, at the suggestion of Stekel, the group first came into being when Freud sent postcards to four physicians – Stekel, Adler, Kahane, and Reitler – to meet informally with him in his waiting room. The "first evenings were inspiring … We were so enthralled by these meetings that we decided new members could be added to our circle only by unanimous consent" (Stekel, 1950, p. 116). By the time minutes were first recorded in October 1906 by Rank, the group had become more structured. The decision to hire Rank and keep formal records must, in itself, have marked a decisive moment in the development of the group; after four years of meeting, it had developed a sense of its own permanence and importance. According to Rank's minutes, it now consisted of 17 members: "Prof. Dr. Freud chairs the meetings, Otto Rank acts as salaried secretary. The meetings take place, as a rule, every Wednesday evening at eight thirty o'clock at Prof. Freud's home ..." (Nunberg & Federn, 1962, p. 6).

At this stage in its development, the group had something of a hybrid character: in the words of a subcommittee formed to consider new rules in 1908, it was "something in between a group invited by Professor Freud and a society" (Nunberg & Federn, 1962, p. 315). That is, it continued to be a group of members who had ties to Freud and to whom Freud looked to carry on the enterprise of psychoanalysis he had founded. At the same time, members had ties to each other and to the enterprise on their own, ties that were increasingly formalized as rights and obligations to the society: presenting papers, participating in the discussions, paying dues, voting on new members, etc. Clearly, these overlapping structures – "a group invited by Professor Freud and a society" – were profoundly bound together: without Freud, the society would lack the guidance and support of the primary authority for the understanding and practice of its discipline; on the other hand, without the society, Freud would lack a vital means to extend the influence of his ideas. Yet, indissoluble as the two were at this point, their interests were not identical. The "group invited by Professor Freud" had as its primary purpose the development of Freud's ideas and influence; the "society" was there to further the professional development of its members (Levinson, 1994).

There are early signs of this tension, as Freud struggled to distinguish his authority from that of the group. At the start of the first meeting in the fall of 1906, for example, he retracted an earlier agreement to share decisions on publications with the group (Nunberg & Federn, 1962, pp. 6–7). Again, over the summer of 1907, he announced that he had dissolved the society, giving each member the opportunity to renew his membership. His ostensible reason was to reestablish "the personal freedom of each individual" (Nunberg & Federn, 1962, p. 203). But his deferential tactfulness also had the effect of reminding members that only Freud himself had the power to take such a step; it was his group. Moreover, framing his concern in terms of the members' "personal freedom" obscured the extent to which they possessed a formal organization of their own. Sachs (1945) recalled that Freud opened annual business meetings with the remark "Now we must play highschool fraternity" (p. 62).

This "fraternity" was becoming increasingly assertive. Binswanger (1957) had been impressed by the fact that "conflicting opinions were voiced freely, and that no one pulled his punches – Freud himself, for all the respect shown him, was often contradicted." Indeed, there were a number of occasions on which they criticized each other's dependence upon Freud. In October 1906, for example, Stekel noted that "everything in [Rank's] book is seen through spectacles colored by Freudian teachings, without going beyond Freud" (Nunberg & Federn, 1962, p. 25). In February 1907, Sadger complains that the group as a whole is "inclined to overestimate the significance of the Freudian teachings for psychology; that is to say, the importance of the sexual factor for psychology, for the unconscious" (Ibid., p. 132). Two months later, Federn "sees the error of those who, totally imbued with the Freudian way of thinking, ignore all other points of view" (Ibid., p. 165).

At the meeting of February 5, 1908, "Adler and Federn make motions and proposals concerning the reorganization of the meetings" (Nunberg & Federn, 1962, p. 298). Federn added a motion of his own to abolish the society's "'intellectual communism.' No idea may be used without the authorization of its author" (Ibid., p. 299). Subsequently, Sadger proposed: "Personal invectives and attacks should immediately be suppressed by the Chairman who shall be given authority to do so" (Ibid., p. 300). Graf commented, shortly afterwards, on the proposals and the discussion: they "stem from a feeling of uneasiness. We no longer are the type of gathering we once were. Although we are still guests of the Professor, we are about to become an organization. Therefore, he suggests the following motion ... To move the meetings from the Professor's apartment to another place" (Ibid., p. 301).

Freud's response to this upsurge of organizational activity on the part of the group was tactful and tactical. He opposed Sadger's proposal on the grounds that he found it painful to reprimand anyone, but he also warned the group that if they could not collaborate better, "then he cannot help but close down [shop]" (Ibid., p. 301). He proposed setting up a committee to make recommendations; the discussions concluded with a unanimous reaffirmation of their "intellectual communism."

At the next meeting of the society, February 12, the committee proposed by Freud made recommendations that were primarily procedural. They rejected Graf's suggestion of a change of locale. Adler proposed, however, "monthly meetings in some other locality (perhaps a small auditorium at the University), to which all those who apply should be admitted if they have been approved by a two-third majority. From this group some could be selected for membership in the more intimate Wednesday circle by the voting procedure practiced until now" (Ibid., pp. 315–16). According to the minutes: "Adler's minority motion evokes a lively discussion" (Ibid., p. 317). But Adler withdrew his motion as Freud suggested the formation of a larger group entirely separate from the Wednesday Society.

The net result of these proposals and discussions was, on the surface at least, very little. Nothing was done about the formation of a larger group. What, then, was at stake?

As Graf's comments at the February 5 meeting suggest, the group was no longer the same group; it had evolved to the point where it felt more keenly its own authority and the need to assert more control over its own functioning. In this respect, these struggles of February 1908 are extensions of the struggle over Freud's authority that we could see signs of earlier. The proposals were counterparts to Freud's subtle declaration of ownership the previous summer in "dissolving" the society. And, I think, Freud recognized this in reminding the group that he could "close down [shop]."

There is another aspect of this struggle, however, that links to the group's anxiety about its relationship with Freud. Sadger's proposal to give the chairman power to suppress personal attacks speaks to the growing dismay in the group about its own contentiousness and conflict, a situation that was referred to in the minutes of the following meeting, February 12, as "the 'ill humor in the empire' which has lately arisen" (Ibid., p. 316).

It is not difficult to trace this "ill humor" back to the meeting two months before, on December 4, 1907, at the start of which Freud "reports Jung's suggestion that in the Spring a congress of all 'followers' be held (perhaps in Salzburg)" (Ibid., p. 254). That meeting, formally devoted to the presentation and discussion of a paper by Sadger, erupted in unprecedented vitriol. "Stekel is horrified and fears that [Sadger's] work will harm our cause" (Ibid., p. 255). "Federn is indignant. Sadger has not said a single word about ... sexual development" (Ibid., p. 256). "Wittels first takes exception to the personal outburst of rage and indignation on the part of Stekel and Federn. He considers these entirely out of place" (Ibid., p. 257). In response, Freud advised moderation, obviously attempting to calm the frayed tempers, but at the end Sadger declared: "He expected to receive information and instruction, but takes home nothing but some invectives" (Ibid., p. 258).

Clearly, the precipitant for these unprecedented conflicts was Freud's announcement of Jung's plan for the congress: the group was confronted for the first time by the fact that Freud had other followers who might in fact accomplish more for him than they. Sadger became the scapegoat of the meeting on one level because, I suspect, his work aroused the immediate feeling in the group that it was not good enough to represent psychoanalysis and satisfy Freud. On another level, I suspect, he was a stand-in for Freud himself, receiving the helpless rage they dared not direct at the professor.

But, of course, the anxiety in the group could not be contained by blaming Sadger. At the January 8, 1908 meeting, when it was Stekel's turn to present, Sadger counter-attacked. Stekel rejoined: "he is horrified at the lack of understanding which he has encountered tonight" (Ibid., p. 280). March 4, Stekel attacked Adler in turn. The normal give and take of the meetings had become bitter and personal.

The society was caught in a dilemma. On the one hand, how could its members preserve it as an instrument for their own professional development, a need that was all the more apparent now as Freud was finding disciples elsewhere? This lay behind the proposals to move the meetings from Freud's waiting room, to form a separate society, and to abolish "intellectual communism." On the other hand, how could they eliminate the self-destructive conflicts that only served to further alienate Freud? The proposals to streamline the meetings and to give Freud greater authority to quell dissent were designed to accomplish this end.

The deepest fear expressed in these meetings, though, was the loss of Freud's allegiance, and that fear appears to have been most completely addressed in their submitting entirely to his recommendations for reform. The outcome reassured them and confirmed their dependence.

For Freud, the outcome was a group of adherents who more fully recognized their reliance upon him. They had worked through their panic of being abandoned, and were now prepared to present an orderly presence at the Salzburg Congress. Thus he could more fully depend upon them to take their place among the other adherents of psychoanalysis elsewhere in the world – not only Jung but also Jones, Abraham, and Ferenczi, as well as A. A. Brill and Morton Prince from America – who were preparing to join up at Salzburg.

Adler's proposal for two groups in Vienna was a last-ditch effort at the meeting to affirm the notion of an independent society as well as preserve the intimate connection with Freud. The "larger group" could continue the freewheeling discussions and foster the competition over developing original ideas and formulations that the group's renewed dedication to "intellectual communism" would only inhibit. On the other hand, Adler's proposal raised the specter of competition for access to Freud. The "lively discussion" provoked by Adler's proposal suggests that the idea must have had significant support, but Freud's counter-proposal to preserve the Wednesday group intact while creating an entirely separate larger organization, in effect, reassured the group that he was not prepared – at this point, certainly – to kick anyone out. They could all continue to meet with him – if they behaved, which is to say, if they contained their anxiety about competition with Freud's followers outside of Vienna.

But the idea of the "larger group" was inevitable. Two years later at the Nuremberg Congress, when the IPA was formed under Jung's leadership, it provoked another crisis for the Viennese.

To Nuremberg and the IPA

The minutes of the meetings before the Nuremberg Congress, at the end of March 1910, show no anticipatory anxiety as Freud apparently played his cards close to his vest; no one knew in advance what he had planned with Ferenczi and Jung. And for good reason. Ferenczi's proposal, first announced in his address "On the Organization of the

Psychoanalytic Movement" (Ferenczi, 1911), but obviously approved by Freud, called for the creation of the International Psychoanalytic Association, with Jung the designated president for life, possessing the power to censor all psychoanalytic publications. Adding insult to injury, Ferenczi, in his introductory remarks on the history of psychoanalysis, completely omitted any reference to the contributions of the Viennese; indeed, he characterized the first "heroic" age of psychoanalysis – before "the appearance of Jung and the 'Zurichers'" – as a time when Freud was "entirely alone" (Ferenczi, 1911, p. 300).

The Viennese, predictably, were outraged. According to Wittels, they met in Stekel's room, secretly, to plan their opposition, when suddenly Freud appeared: "Never before had I seen him so greatly excited. He said: 'Most of you are Jews, and therefore incompetent to win friends for the new teaching … We are all in danger.' Seizing his coat by the lapels, he said: 'They won't even leave me a coat to my back. The Swiss will save us – will save me, and all of you as well'" (Wittels, 1924, p. 140). They reached a compromise in which some of the more onerous features of Ferenczi's proposal were modified. There was to be no censorship, and Jung's term was limited to two years.

When meetings of the society resumed in Vienna on April 6, 1910, Freud pointed out that "the implementing of these resolutions will signify a new period for the activities of our society." Until now, the members of the society have been his guests: "now this is no longer feasible. The society must constitute itself and elect a president." Declining to be president of the new society, Freud proposed Adler (Nunberg & Federn, 1967, pp. 463–4).

Adler responded, as if on behalf of the Viennese group; he explained their actions in Nuremberg, calling Freud to account for his part in the conflict and blaming the "harshness" of Ferenczi's "Memorandum." He then went on to speak in a proudly affirmative, if not defiant manner: "We can therefore say today that from now on we belong to an association that chooses its president in a free election by members with equal rights, like every other association" (Ibid., p. 464).

The mood of the meeting was sad and defensive. Stekel commented that he "cannot imagine how we would exist … without Freud – who seems to harbor deep hatred towards Vienna" (Ibid., p. 466). Federn disavowed "any hostile intentions towards Zurich," blaming instead "the aloof behavior of the members from Zurich … Even though it is difficult to imagine the old patriarchal relationship ceasing to exist, surely Freud has good reasons for his decision, and to fight against them will, he supposes, be in vain" (Ibid., p. 466). Sadger "thinks that he has observed that Freud has been fed up with the Viennese for the last two years now" (Ibid., p. 465). "However, the fact is that we need him" (Ibid., p. 467).

Gradually the mood of the meeting shifted. Freud reminded them of the "many compelling reasons" for Zurich becoming the center, but more importantly reassured them of his continued presence and involvement. The group searched for a way to define Freud's continuing special role, and at his suggestion made him "scientific chairman." It then elected Adler president.

It is clear from the subsequent meetings that an effective transition was made with relative smoothness. The group got down to the business of electing an executive committee, setting up a committee to oversee the *Zentralblatt*, finding a new location for its meetings, setting new dues, establishing a library, and, by the following fall, establishing its statutes. Freud himself commented in a letter to Jung that the founding of the IPA, while perhaps premature for the development of the group in Zurich, "in Vienna it has definitely helped. The style has improved and enthusiasm is great" (McGuire, 1974, p. 321).

The relative ease with which the Viennese surmounted this crisis, I believe, can be attributed to the fact that they had been preparing for it for two years, in effect, since their recognition in February 1908 of their hybrid status. They were ready now to take the step of becoming, in Adler's proud words, "an association that chooses its president in a free election by members with equal rights" (Nunberg & Federn, 1967, p. 464). But also in the intervening two years, the group had developed in Adler a leader who was felt to be capable of taking over from Freud. Freud, of course, clearly recognized that development in proposing Adler, and the group recognized it as well in tacitly assigning him the role of its spokesman.

As Stepansky (1983) has carefully shown, Adler was far from the rebellious and difficult member of the Viennese Society he has been retrospectively identified as being throughout these years. Indeed, he was frequently approvingly cited by Freud for his thoughtful and original contributions. Moreover, unlike Stekel, Sadger, and even Federn, he refrained from comments that could incite opposition to Freud's ideas, while at the same time developing his own thoughts and, as we have seen, his own proposals for the development of the society.

At the last Scientific Meeting of the society before the summer break of 1909, for example, Adler gave a paper, "The Oneness of the Neuroses," developing ideas that clearly departed from Freud's. The minutes report Freud's judicious and extensive comments: "Prof. Freud sees little to find fault with, in the details of Adler's unusually lucid and consistent train of thought, but he must confess that in general, he has a different standpoint" (Nunberg & Federn, 1967, p. 265).

A few days later, Jung wrote Freud that he had heard through a patient that Adler "is moving away from you and is going off on his own, in the opposite direction to you, even. Is there any truth in it?" (McGuire, 1974, p. 232). To which Freud replied: "Yes, I believe there is truth in the story. He is a theorist, astute and original, but not attuned to psychology ... A decent sort, though; he won't desert in the immediate future, but neither will he participate as we should like him to. We must hold him as long as possible" (Ibid., p. 235). Throughout this period, it seems clear, neither Freud nor Adler wished to stress their differences; both chose to see their ideas as essentially compatible.

A year later, anticipating Adler's election as president of the Vienna Society, Freud wrote Ferenczi about his reasons for selecting Adler: "I will transfer the leadership to Adler, not out of inclination or satisfaction but because he is the only [prominent] personality and because in this position it will perhaps be necessary for him to share the defense of the common ground" (Brabant, 1993, p. 155). Several months later, Freud wrote Jung: "Adler is hypersensitive and deeply embittered because I consistently reject his theories" (McGuire, 1974, p. 331). But this is in the context of Freud's criticism of Jung's dilatoriness in setting up the IPA and underscores his appeal to Jung to act more promptly and collaboratively with the Viennese group. Clearly he wanted Jung to know how awkward his position had become with the Viennese as a result of his delays. "You know how jealous they all are – here and elsewhere – over your privileged position with me ... and I think I am justified in feeling that what people say against you as a result is being said against me" (Ibid., p. 330; see also Kerr, 1993).

In a similar vein, Freud exhorted Jung on October 31, 1910: "I also believe that you have not overcome your dislike of our Viennese colleagues ... You are unquestionably right in your characterization of

Stekel and Adler ... But it does not befit a superior man like you to bear a grudge against them. Take it with humour as I do except on days when weakness gets the better of me" (Ibid., p. 366).

A month later, it appears that his "weakness" is more frequently getting the better of him; he writes Jung: "My spirits are dampened by the irritations with Adler and Stekel, with whom it is very hard to get along ... Adler is a very decent and highly intelligent man, but he is paranoid ... He is always claiming priority, putting new names on everything, complaining that he is disappearing under my shadow, and forcing me into the unwelcome role of the aging despot who prevents young men from getting ahead. They are also rude to me personally, and I'd gladly get rid of them both. But it won't be possible ... And on top of it all, this absurd Viennese local pride and jealousy of you and Zurich!" (Ibid., p. 373). December 3, Freud writes again: "It is getting really bad with Adler. You see a resemblance to Bleuler; in me he awakens the memory of Fliess, but an octave lower ... The crux of the matter – and that is what really alarms me – is that he minimized the sexual drive and our opponents will soon be able to speak of an experienced psychoanalyst whose conclusions are radically different from ours" (Ibid., p. 376).

The minutes for this period, the fall of 1910, following the euphoria of the spring response to the Nuremberg Congress, show that, in fact, the Wednesday-night discussions in Vienna were increasingly crystallized around the theoretical differences between Adler and Freud. At the meeting of November 16, Hitschmann offered the proposal that "Adler's theories be for once thoroughly discussed in their interconnections, with particular attention to their divergence from Freud's doctrine" (Nunberg & Federn, 1974, p. 59). Hitschmann's proposal, ostensibly aimed at introducing clarity into the debates, set the stage for a confrontation that led three and a half months later to Adler's resignation.

Far more was at stake, obviously, than the clarification of theoretical differences. As Freud reportedly confided to Wortis (1940) years later: "personal differences – jealousy or revenge or some other kind of animosity always came first ... scientific differences came later" (p. 848). In retrospect, I believe it is possible to see that the increasing tension between Freud and Adler derived from conflicts between their roles, exacerbated by the society's new status. The developments since

The Early Years of the Viennese Society   19

Nuremberg had placed the underlying conflict about the purpose of the society and the society's relationship with Freud into greater and greater prominence.

Adler had always stood for the independence of the society, which now he formally led, as well as for the development of independent theoretical thinking within it. He had successfully rallied the members in the wake of the Nuremberg crisis and managed the transition into this new phase. But the dependence that all the members had felt as "guests of Professor Freud" – the dependence that had caused them to feel anxious and depressed in the aftermath of the Nuremberg Congress when they lost "the old patriarchal relationship" (Nunberg & Federn, 1967, p. 466) – continued to be felt in the group. Freud had reassured them that he would not withdraw, that all relationships would remain as they had been, but it must have been increasingly apparent that, in fact, this was not so.

For one thing, it must have been clear to members of the society that Freud was in fact siding with Jung in the disputes that arose between them. Neither his heart not his loyalty remained with the Viennese. Freud's letters to Jung show that he was anything but complacent about Jung's shortcomings as leader of the IPA; he not only exhorted Jung to behave better toward the Viennese and take up his role as president more aggressively, but also he offered to intervene as "go-between" with Adler and Stekel, the editors of the *Zentralblatt*: "I can put through all your demands and block anything that doesn't suit you" (McGuire, 1974, p. 367). But the minutes of the society suggest that to the Viennese he was apologetic if not merely silent; he either defended Jung casually or ignored their complaints about him. Moreover, as he himself attests in his letters to Jung, he became increasingly irritable and impatient. The Viennese could not help but wonder on whose side he was.

But things could not remain the same for another reason as well. An independent society would have to tolerate competition and differences, theoretical and otherwise. Adler's selection as its president, indeed, followed from the stature he had gained as a thinker. In this sense, the more outspoken debates of the fall of 1910 were inevitable outgrowths of the new status of the society as, in Kanzer's words, "a congregation of scientists with varying views and degrees of competence ... no longer an assemblage of students who sat at the feet of a master" (1971, p. 39). Indeed, the debates were undoubtedly meant to test the limits of this tolerance – and, of course, the limits of Freud's tolerance.

Throughout the final months of 1910, Freud's impatience mounted. Ostensibly he was irritated with Adler's behavior, as well as Stekel's, but they were only the most obvious targets for his growing irritation with the society and the increasingly difficult position he felt between the society and Jung. When Hitschmann, then, made his seemingly innocuous proposal, the group unconsciously set the stage for a showdown by pitting the two men who represented the poles of their ambivalence against each other. Adler was prodded into a more exposed position, while Freud was prodded into deciding how far he would allow such theoretical independence to be tolerated.

By the time the debate actually occurred, Freud had clearly decided that Adler had to go. The minutes for February 1, 1911, describe Adler's presentation of his paper and Freud's lengthy and detailed response in relatively straightforward terms, but there is no mistaking Freud's tone. The bulk of his criticism focused on his view that because it minimizes the power of libido and the "ego's fear of the libido" (Ibid., p. 149), Adler's is a surface psychology, merely "ego psychology, deepened by the knowledge of the psychology of the unconscious" (Ibid., p. 147). As such, Freud seemed willing to concede, it can be a useful supplement to psychoanalysis, but, he states: "This is not psychoanalysis" (Ibid., p. 146). Worse, he affirms, it will "do great harm to psychoanalysis ... It will ... make use of the latent resistances that are still alive in every psychoanalyst, in order to make its influence felt" (Ibid., p. 147).

Wittel's account, largely based on Stekel's recollections, concentrates on the drama of the occasion: the "Freudian adepts made a mass attack on Adler, an attack almost unexampled for its ferocity even in the fiercely contested field of psychoanalytic controversy ... Freud had a sheaf of notes before him, and with gloomy mien seemed prepared to annihilate his adversary" (Wittels, 1924, pp. 150–1). Graf noted that Adler "quietly and firmly" defended his point of view, but was nonetheless "banished" (Graf, 1942, pp. 472–3).

Those who spoke on behalf of Adler confined themselves, primarily, to defending his right to develop his ideas; they seem taken off guard by the coordinated detail and intensity of the attack.

The Early Years of the Viennese Society   21

"Furtmuller considers it premature to assume a *pro* or *con* attitude ... [and tries] to refute some of Prof. Freud's objections" (Ibid., p. 156). In the third meeting both Freud and Adler make efforts to temporize: "Prof. Freud considers Adler's doctrines to be wrong and, as far as the development of psychoanalysis is concerned, dangerous. But these are scientific errors ... that do great credit to their creator" (Ibid., p. 172). Adler commented that his writings "would not have been possible if Freud had not been his teacher." If he is at fault for endangering psychoanalysis, "he will not hesitate to draw the necessary conclusions" (Ibid., p. 174). Following the meeting, the minutes announce, Adler resigned as president "because of the incompatibility of his scientific attitude with his position in the society" (Ibid., p. 177).

Adler, I think, struggled to account for the ferocity of Freud's affect, by seeing it as motivated by his fear for the future of psychoanalysis, much as he and the other members of the society had seen Freud's ferocity mobilized in Nuremberg. If psychoanalysis is endangered – or, more to the point, if Freud saw it as endangered – the appropriate response would be to reassure him and soberly take stock of the danger his actions may inadvertently evoke.

"I have decided, after this unsuccessful attempt, to take the reins back into my own hands and I mean to keep a tight hold on them" (McGuire, 1974, p. 400), Freud announced to Jung in his letter of March 1, 1911. Two weeks later, he added, "Naturally, I am only waiting for an occasion to throw them both [Adler and Stekel] out, but they both know it and are being very cautious and conciliatory, so there is nothing I can do for the present" (McGuire, 1974, p. 403).

At the March 1 meeting, when Freud took over the presidency, we can see the members of the society pulling back from the consequences of the "discussion" of Adler's theories. After voting unanimously to thank both Adler and Stekel for their services, the society passed an addendum in which it refused "to acknowledge any incompatibility" (Ibid., p. 179). The editors of the minutes comment in a footnote: "It is actually rather puzzling that the majority of the members, despite the clear state of affairs, and against Freud's expressed wish, nevertheless voted in favor of the amendment" (Ibid., p. 179). But it is not so puzzling if one is willing to see in this defiant gesture the remnant of the society's independence. They would bow to Freud's wish and reinstate

22 Psychoanalytic History

themselves in his good graces by deposing Adler, but they would also remind him again of their capacity to defy him.

With the "Palace revolution in Vienna" (McGuire, 1974, p. 403) Freud seemed to turn more fully against the group he now formally led. On March 30, he writes Jung: "You have been very kind to the Viennese in your handling of the Congress question. Unfortunately they are a lot of rabble and I shall feel neither horror nor regret if the whole show here collapses one of these days" (Ibid., p. 411).

The Viennese had succeeded in preventing Freud's withdrawal from active leadership in the society; he was forced into shouldering the unwanted burden of leadership. That, in itself, may account for his irritation, especially at the point when he longed for stronger ties with Jung, not with them. But, I suspect, his contempt came from his sense he had been manipulated into becoming the object of the group's dependency, while at the same time, ambivalently, they continued to remind him of their power to thwart him. They had played upon his fears of the internal enemy, provided a scapegoat, and placed themselves once again under his care.

By October 1911, Freud decided on the expulsion of Adler's associates from the society and forced a vote. The society that defiantly refused to see incompatibility between Adler's role and beliefs in March was forced into taking the stand that no one could belong to the society as well as Adler's new group. But it seems that, by then, both sides were prepared for the break.

Stekel's resignation the following year, in October 1912, was over his refusal to cede editorial control of the *Zentralblatt*. For Freud it was unpardonable that Stekel should resign the society and yet insist that he retain the editorship of its journal. But in fact Stekel had the power to do just that – and did, forcing the society to found a new journal in its stead. Ironically, in this ultimately self-defeating gesture, Stekel affirmed the independence of his editorial role and the power of society members to thwart Freud's control. Like Adler, the year before, his gesture of independence, however, only seemed to confirm the dependence of the society upon Freud.

But curiously there is no mention of this in the minutes of the society. Indeed, virtually all references to organizational matters disappear after October 1911: elections to posts, appointments, new members.

All that is noted are the names of those in attendance, and increasingly perfunctory accounts of the discussion.

Nunberg, one of the editors of Volume 4, notes "something that is quite puzzling – namely, that Freud's most devoted followers are beginning to minimize his achievements, and on certain occasions it almost looks as if there were a mutual understanding among them to do so, one in which even Tausk, Federn, Hitschmann, Sadger – those most devoted pupils of Freud – are taking part. At times, these men seem to have forgotten Freud's teachings" (Nunberg & Federn, 1975, p. xv). It is not clear to me precisely what occasions Nunberg has in mind; I cannot find any overt minimizations of Freud's achievements, certainly none comparable to those notable in the years 1906–8. But one does find, I think, a loss of vigor and excitement in the discussions, as well as occasions in which Freud does appear to be patiently providing elementary lessons.

One sees, in effect, the presence of the "basic assumption" (Bion, 1969) of dependency. Members on occasion argue or dispute, but it does seem as if they have lost the capacity to clarify things for themselves. Grinker (1940), observing somewhat later, suggested their meetings were "like a religious ritual the meaning of which has long been forgotten and the necessity for it long passed" (p. 854). Sterba (1982) noted the atmosphere of reverence and strict hierarchy (see Rustin, 1985). Weiss confessed: "The truth is, no one felt completely free to express ideas very divergent from Freud's basic concepts" (1956, p. 12).

Freud's Leadership

There is something of a tragedy in this outcome for Freud. As many who knew him agreed, he did not enjoy veneration and he was impatient with the dependency of his followers. Deutsch (1940), for example, commenting on the "atmosphere of absolute and infallible authority" created by his Viennese followers throughout the 1920s and 1930s, notes: "It was never any fault of Freud's that they cast him in this role and that they – so rumor has it – became mere 'yes men'. Quite the contrary; Freud had no love for 'yes men' ... He loved those who were critical, who were independent, who were of interest for their brilliance, who were original" (pp. 189–90). Similarly, Sachs (1945) has written movingly of knowing that he was not among those who had the capacity to stimulate this interest and intimacy with Freud.

Deutsch points to Freud's disappointment in losing his original and brilliant followers. Much has been made of a kind of paradox in Freud that accounted for this: his need to work things out on his own, in his own way, and at his own pace (see Jones, II, 1955, p. 428). Thus Freud could find himself at cross purposes with the men he was attracted to and sought out, stubbornly unable to appreciate the very source of stimulation he required.

On one level, of course, are the "oedipal" explanations that Freud and his followers themselves favored. Each disciple was a son, bound to be in competition with the father as well as the other sons for the approval and favors of the father. The correspondence of Freud and his followers is, in fact, peppered with confessions of rivalry and protestations that more analysis has cured the problem. No less significant was the jealousy and rivalry among the Viennese.

Freud's own version of this explanation for group conflict was worked out in "Totem and Taboo" (1913). It is possible to see in that an acknowledgment of the father's reciprocal role with respect to his rebellious sons, certainly the fear evoked in him by the extent and depth of the murderous oedipal feelings in the group of sons. He was once reported to have said he could not stand the "parricidal look" in the eyes of one of the younger members of the society (Alexander, 1940, p. 200). No doubt, we see here Freud's underlying justification for his seizing the reins of control and acting in so decisive, if not brutal a manner.

On a deeper level, the drama was between Freud and the group as a whole. The very fact that Freud felt forced into seizing control through a "palace revolution" represented a victory for the group and a defeat of Freud's wish for greater independence. The group that feared abandonment by him, that experienced directly the transfer of his enthusiasm elsewhere, that was betrayed by him, in fact, as he planned with Jung to minimize their interests – this group finally succeeded in getting him to bind himself indissolubly to them. Moreover, they succeeded in getting him to weed out of their ranks any possible threat that they themselves might pose to his future control. Passively, indirectly, they manipulated him into the role of president for life he had sought to avoid.

How did Freud let this happen? We have seen all along how he struggled to maintain control over the independent minded and even unruly group he had called into being. Clearly, he wanted to control the development of psychoanalysis.

Moreover, he had difficulty grasping the need of his followers to establish their independence from him. He was fiercely independent – counter-dependent, more likely – intolerant of the dependency of others and of their struggles for independence. Indeed, it is what blinded him in his relations with others and made him, in Jones's phrase (III, 1957), so poor a judge of men (a "Menschenkenner"; see also Grosskurth, 1991; Rosensweig, 1992). Thus, even in promoting the independent status of the Viennese Society, following the establishment of the IPA, I doubt he understood how complex and stormy the process was likely to be.

Roustang (1982) has argued, "Although he denied it, Freud was possessed by an uncontrollable need to have disciples and to surround himself with completely devoted followers" (p. 15). But this is too simple a view. Freud did want to control the development of psychoanalysis, and he was fiercely punitive and unforgiving but I believe he was right to disparage his leadership ability. Despite his profound intellectual leadership, he failed to understand what was required to manage the development of a professional society (Levinson, 1994) and he was able to be manipulated by the group into the role of "aging despot."

In Bion's (1969) term, Freud's "valency" – his predisposition for a role in the group – was for the role of fight leader. The efforts of the Viennese to cast Freud in the role of the dependency leader, the one who could cause them to feel nurtured and protected, encountered his hostility. In mid-life, he characterized himself to Fliess as "a conquistador by temperament, an adventurer" (Masson, 1985, p. 398). His boyhood idol was Hannibal, the conqueror of Rome (Freud, 1900, p. 197). Sachs (1945) called Freud a fighter: "untiring and unbending, hard and sharp like steel, a 'good hater'" (p. 117). He saw psychoanalysis as constantly besieged by enemies; Stefan Zweig noted "above all when he is at war, fighting alone against a multitude ... there develops [in him] the unqualified pugnacity of a nature ready to face overwhelming odds" (Zweig, 1932, p. 94). Sulloway (1979) has emphasized this aspect of Freud's heroic identity, and Ellenberger (1970) has pointed out the exaggerated degree to which Freud viewed himself as under attack.

As we saw, he successfully mobilized the Viennese behind his plan to place Jung at the head of the psychoanalytic movement, despite their intense opposition, with his desperate portrayal of the threat they all faced from a hostile world.

Given the intense rivalry that characterized Freud's earliest followers and, moreover, given his characteristic dislike of dependency in his followers, we can easily see how his valency for the role of fight leader allowed him to incite high levels of aggression and competition in the group and to channel those into attacks on the group's external enemies. He never tired – nor did the group – of referring to their "enemies," their "opponents," their "adversaries," and the group gained coherence and confidence from this sense of being engaged in an embattled struggle under his leadership. They were, as Freud wrote Abraham, "partisans" (Abraham & Freud, 1966, p. 19). But the appearance of external rivals – most particularly, of course, Jung and the Zurichers – altered this dynamic pattern. As we saw in the meeting at which Freud first announced the Salzburg Congress, the Viennese immediately began to seek out a scapegoat to blame for the threatened loss of their leader.

Two years later, Freud himself had become convinced that a danger, at least as great as that posed by external enemies, lurked within. I believe that this is precisely true: much as Freud disapproved of these divergent ideas, and much as he disliked the covert attempts to get him to endorse them, what truly alarmed him and galvanized him into action, was his fear of the enemy within.

This fear did not originate solely with Freud. It was an intrinsic belief within the embattled society that any internal weakness or failure could aid the external enemy. So that, throughout the fall of 1910, as the society faced a real external danger in the form of Jung, newly installed as president of the IPA, and a growing internal danger in the form of Freud's support of Jung against them, an unconscious plan emerged in the society to put forward Adler as a target. Paradoxically, Adler, who represented the society's intellectual and organizational independence, became seen as the major threat to its existence.

Freud's valency for fight then, which was so helpful in galvanizing his initial band of followers into action – providing a "sophisticated work group" in Bion's term, a work group in which the underlying basic assumption is supportive of the task – proved also to be an Achilles' heel. His aversion to dependency meant that his followers could only bond to him and securely experience his leadership when he was engaged in a fight – when he had an enemy. To hold on to him, they had to continue to provide an enemy.

"An intimate friend and a hated enemy have always been requirements of my emotional life," he wrote in *The Interpretation of Dreams* (Freud, 1900, p. 483). But only the enemies proved enduringly reliable.

Reflections

From an institutional perspective, there are two points about Freud's leadership that emerge from this account: one is about his legacy to psychoanalysis, the other is about leadership in general.

Adler's was but the first of the notorious "defections" in the history of psychoanalysis, and his founding of a rival school the first of the "schisms." Psychoanalysis has been bedeviled ever since by this tendency toward institutional splitting. I do not think that the responsibility for this can be placed on Freud's shoulders, just as I think it is clear from this narrative that he did not bring about Adler's expulsion alone. But Freud set his stamp upon the movement so that the dynamic processes that were at work in the case of Adler were encouraged to develop elsewhere. That is, in placing emphasis upon leadership based on fight and, more importantly, fearing leadership based upon dependency, Freud left little room for psychoanalysts to acknowledge their dependencies. Indeed, the implicit lesson of these early years in Vienna is that the only way Freud's followers could be able to feel dependent upon him was to convince him that they would be faithful soldiers under his flag.

This is Freud's legacy. I have argued elsewhere (Eisold, 1994; Chapter 4 in this volume) that psychoanalytic organizations are weak and vulnerable to schisms in part because the real allegiances of their members are to their analysts and the lineages of analysts that define particular schools of thought. Thus, as dependency upon one's analyst has traditionally been thought a sign of unresolved transference, the way to ensure one's place in the lineage, one's secure relationship with one's analyst and his school, has been to be willing to fight on his behalf. Moreover, in doing so, one is able to project into the rival school one's own displaced fear and hatred of the leader. This is precisely the story of Freud and the early Viennese. From this perspective, the threat to psychoanalysis, far from being the internal enemy that has to be identified and rooted out, is the unacknowledged dependencies of analysts themselves.

The larger point I wish to make is about leadership in general. Turquet (1978), in an important article on leadership building on Bion's work on "basic assumptions," pointed out that the leader will inevitably have projected into him all the group's anxiety and doubt: group members simultaneously attempt to rid themselves of their fears while inciting the leader to act on their behalf. Thus the leader must not only be able to tolerate anxiety and doubt himself, he must be able to not act in response to these incitements and pressures. The point I wish to make is that in holding onto his capacity to not act, the leader has to reflect on the meaning of his action for the group he leads.

We analysts are accustomed to probing our own unconscious motivations, exploring our countertransferences in order to shed light on the transferences of our patients. We know what it is like to not act in our consulting rooms, subject to the pressure of an individual, but tend to be far less aware of pressures emanating from the group. We are less likely to think of unconscious collusive forces permeating our relationship with colleagues. We have not been trained, by and large, to detect the unconscious at work in our institutional relationships. More particularly, we are not used to looking at how our leaders are creatures of those they lead. We avert our eyes from the unconscious collusive pact we establish with our leaders, who are allowed to feel venerated and strong precisely because they act as they are required to act. Or, as is now increasingly the case, we disparage the leaders who carry out the agendas we require but fail to protect us from the problems we face.

If there is a lesson to be drawn from this story it is that we need to learn about the unconscious at work in our group and institutional relations. Our leaders ignore this at their peril – and ours.

References

Abraham, H. C. & Freud, E. L., eds. (1966). *A Psycho-Analytic Dialogue: The Letters of Sigmund Freud and Karl Abraham, 1907–1926*. New York: Basic Books.

Alexander, F. (1940). Recollections of Bergasse 19. *Psychoanalytic Quarterly* 9(2), 195–204.

The Early Years of the Viennese Society 29

Anzieu, D. (1984). *The Group and the Unconscious*, trans. B. Kilborne. London: Routledge & Kegan Paul.

Binswanger, L. (1957). *Sigmund Freud: Reminiscences of a Friendship*. New York: Grune & Stratton.

Bion, W. (1969). *Experiences in Groups*. New York: Basic Books.

Brabant, E. et al. (eds.) (1993). *The Correspondence of Sigmund Freud and Sandor Ferenczi* (Vol. 1). Cambridge, MA: Belknap Press of Harvard University Press.

Deutsch, H. (1940). Freud and his pupils. *Psychoanalytic Quarterly* 9(1), 184–94.

Eisold, K. (1994). The intolerance of diversity in psychoanalytic institutes. *International Journal of Psychoanalysis* 75, 785–800.

Ellenberger, H. (1970). *The Discovery of the Unconscious*. New York: Basic Books.

Ferenczi, S. (1911/1955). On the organization of the psycho-analytic movement. In M. Balint (ed.), *Final Contributions to the Problems and Methods of Psychoanalysis* (pp. 299–307). New York: Basic Books.

Freud, S. (1900). *The Interpretation of Dreams*. In J. Strachey (ed. and trans.), *The Standard Edition of the Complete Psychological Works of Sigmund Freud* (Vols. 4–5). London: Hogarth Press.

Freud, S. (1913). Totem and taboo. In J. Strachey (ed. and trans.), *The Standard Edition of the Complete Psychological Works of Sigmund Freud* (Vol. 13, pp. 1–162). London: Hogarth Press.

Freud, S. (1914). On the history of the psychoanalytic movement. In J. Strachey (ed. and trans.), *The Standard Edition of the Complete Psychological Works of Sigmund Freud* (Vol. 14, pp. 3–66). London: Hogarth Press.

Freud, S. (1921). Group psychology and the analysis of the ego. In J. Strachey (ed. and trans.), *The Standard Edition of the Complete Psychological Works of Sigmund Freud* (Vol. 18, pp. 67–143). London: Hogarth Press.

Gay, P. (1988). *Freud: A Life for Our Time*. New York: W.W. Norton.

Graf, M. (1942). Reminiscences of Freud. *Psychoanalytic Quarterly* 11, 465–76.

Grinker, R. R. (1940). Reminiscences of a personal contact with Freud. *American Journal of Orthopsychiatry* 10, 850–4.

Grosskurth, P. (1991). *The Secret Ring*. Reading, MA: Addison-Wesley.

Jones, E. (1953, 1955, 1957). *The Life and Work of Sigmund Freud*, 3 vols. New York: Basic Books.

Jones, E. (1959). *Free Associations: Memories of a Psycho-Analyst*. New York: Basic Books.

Kanzer, M. (1971). Freud: the first psychoanalytic group leader. In H. I. Kaplan & B. J. Sadock (eds.), *Comprehensive Group Psychotherapy*. Baltimore: Williams & Wilkins.

30 Psychoanalytic History

Kernberg, O. F. (1980a). Regression in groups. In *Internal World and External Reality* (pp. 211–34). New York: Jason Aronson.

Kernberg, O. F. (1980b). Organizational regression. In *Internal World and External Reality* (pp. 235–52). New York: Jason Aronson.

Kernberg, O. F. (1980c). Regressive effects of pathology in leaders. In *Internal World and External Reality* (pp. 253–73). New York: Jason Aronson.

Kerr, J. (1993). *A Most Dangerous Method*. New York: Knopf.

Lapierre, L. (1991). Exploring the dynamics of leadership. In M. F. R. Kets de Vries (ed.), *Organizations on the Couch* (pp. 69–93). San Francisco: Jossey-Bass.

Levinson, H. (1994). The changing psychoanalytic organization and its influence on the ego ideal of psychoanalysis. *Psychoanalytic Psychology* 11(2), 233–49.

Masson, J. M. (1985). *The Complete Letters of Sigmund Freud to Wilhelm Fliess, 1887–1904*. Cambridge, MA: Harvard University Press.

McGuire, W. (1974). *The Freud/Jung Letters: The Correspondence between Sigmund Freud and C. G. Jung*. Cambridge, MA: Harvard University Press.

Menzies-Lyth, I. E. P. (1967). *A Case Study in the Functioning of Social Systems as a Defence against Anxiety*. Tavistock Pamphlet No. 3. London: Tavistock.

Newton, P. (1995). *Freud: From Youthful Dream to Mid-Life Crisis*. New York: Guilford.

Nunberg, H., & Federn, E. (1962). *Minutes of the Vienna Psychoanalytic Society,* Vol. 1: *1906–1908*. New York: International Universities Press.

Nunberg, H., & Federn, E. (1967). *Minutes of the Vienna Psychoanalytic Society,* Vol. 2: *1908–1910*. New York: International Universities Press.

Nunberg, H., & Federn, E. (1974). *Minutes of the Vienna Psychoanalytic Society,* Vol. 3: *1910–1911*. New York: International Universities Press.

Nunberg, H., & Federn, E. (1975). *Minutes of the Vienna Psychoanalytic Society,* Vol. 4: *1912–1915*. New York: International Universities Press.

Paskauskas, R. A. (1993). *The Complete Correspondence of Sigmund Freud and Ernest Jones, 1908–1939*. Cambridge, MA: Harvard University Press.

Puner, H. W. (1947). *Sigmund Freud: His Life and Mind*. New York: Howell, Soskin.

Rice, A. K. (1963). *The Enterprise and Its Environment*. London: Tavistock.

Roazen, P. (1969). *Brother Animal*. New York: Knopf.

Rosensweig, S. (1992). *Freud, Jung, and Hall the Kingmaker: The Historic Expedition to America (1909)*. St Louis: Rana House/Hogrefe & Huber.

Roustang, F. (1982). *Dire Mastery: Discipleship from Freud to Lacan*. Baltimore: Johns Hopkins University Press.

Rustin, M. (1985). The social organization of secrets: towards a sociology of psychoanalysis. *International Review of Psychoanalysis* 12(2), 143–60.

Sachs, H. (1945). *Freud: Master and Friend*. Cambridge, MA: Harvard University Press.

Shapiro, R. L. (1979). Psychoanalytic knowledge of group process, APA Panel reported by K. T. Calder. *Journal of the American Psychoanalytic Association* 27, 145–56.

Stekel, W. (1950). *The Autobiography of Wilhelm Stekel*. New York: Liveright.

Stepansky, P. E. (1983). *In Freud's Shadow: Adler in Context*. Hillsdale: Analytic Press.

Sterba, R. (1982). *Reminiscences of a Viennese Psychoanalyst*. Detroit: Wayne State University Press.

Strozier, C. D. (1985). Lincoln and the crisis of the 1850's: thoughts on the group itself. In C. D. Strozier and D. Offer (eds.), *The Leader: Psychohistorical Essays*. New York: Plenum Press.

Sulloway, F. J. (1979). *Freud, Biologist of the Mind*. New York: Basic Books.

Turquet, P. M. (1978). Leadership: the individual and the group. In G. S. Gibbard, J. J. Hartman, & R. D. Mann (eds.), *Analysis of Groups*. San Francisco: Jossey-Bass.

Weiss, E. (1970). *Sigmund Freud as a Consultant*. London: Intercontinental Medical Books.

Wittels, F. (1924). *Sigmund Freud: His Personality, His Teaching, and His School*. New York: Dodd, Mead & Co.

Wortis, J. (1940). Fragments of a Freudian analysis. *American Journal of Orthopsychiatry* 10(4), 843–9.

Zaleznik, A. (1989). *The Managerial Mystique*. New York: Harper & Row.

Zoner, M., & Offer, D. (1985). Leaders and the Arab-Israeli conflict: a psychoanalytic interpretation. In C. D. Strozier and D. Offer (eds.), *The Leader: Psychohistorical Essays*. New York: Plenum Press.

Zweig, S. (1932/1973). Portrait of Freud. In H. M. Ruitenbeck (ed.), *Freud as We Knew Him*. Detroit: Wayne State University Press.

Chapter Two

The Splitting of the New York Psychoanalytic Society and the Construction of Psychoanalytic Authority

[Originally published as The Splitting of the New York Psychoanalytic Society and the Construction of Psychoanalytic Authority, *The International Journal of Psychoanalysis*, vol. 79/5 (October 1998), pp. 871–85.]

American psychoanalysis began to split apart, literally, on April 29, 1941, when Karen Horney, Clara Thompson, and three colleagues stalked out of a meeting of the New York Psychoanalytic Society. Clara Thompson reported the five rebels sang the spiritual "Go Down, Moses" as they jubilantly walked down the street, expressing the deeply felt – if highly dramatized – interpretation that they were victims escaping an authoritarian power seeking to enslave them (Eckhardt, 1978). Those left behind, though no doubt glad to see the rebels go, were far from homogeneous or, even, in agreement. Expelling Horney did not resolve their conflicts, and they faced the possibility of further splits.

The walkout was the response to a vote that evening to disqualify Horney as an instructor and training analyst. For several years there had been simmering tensions in the society over Horney's "deviancy" from Freudian theory, especially since the publication two years before of her *New Ways in Psychoanalysis*. But she was by no means the only source of controversy in the institute. Sandor Rado was also outspoken and provocative in his divergences from Freud. Originally brought to New York from Berlin in 1932 to set up and run the training program of the New York Institute, he had become increasingly critical of orthodoxy in the institute and alienated from the younger generation of analysts who, having gotten their training abroad, in Vienna, Berlin, and London, had recently taken over the running of the institute from the first generation of founding members.

In 1939, Lawrence Kubie, then president of the society and a member of the new generation, wrote to Glover (who had been his analyst in England) that cliques threatened to destroy the society: "Each group is more or less hermetically sealed from the other, and you can imagine how much confusion, lopsided and inadequate training, and mutual distrust and hostility all of this generated" (in Hale, 1995, p. 141). He had in mind three cliques, I believe: the group that coalesced around Horney, outspokenly revisionist; the group around Rado, critical of orthodoxy and seeking ties with medical psychiatry; and the growing group of refugee analysts who had recently fled Hitler. There was, in addition, a small remnant of older members. Finally, there was the group of young professionals, led by Kubie, dedicated to establishing firm and strict standards of training, such as they had themselves experienced abroad.

Probably not seeing himself as a member of a clique, Kubie proposed the "solution" of imposing a stricter and more systematic educational program on candidates, stressing Freud. Many of the candidates were unhappy about this, having just petitioned for more flexible courses and additional teachers (Quinn, 1987, p. 330), and a number of the faculty also objected. None the less, the reforms were adopted, along with more control by the Training Committee over the choices of candidates.

The following year, 1940, saw Kubie's educational proposals attacked as insufficient to control the threat to Freud. Wittels, who had come to New York the same year as Rado, circulated an impassioned attack on Horney – to which Kubie responded in ringing words that sound false to us now but which, no doubt, he wanted to believe at the time: "I am basically opposed to any form of purge in a scientific organization. I feel completely with Voltaire in this matter, and would defend the right to teach of those with whom I disagree profoundly" (in Hale, 1995, p. 142).

But elections the following year shifted the balance of power; Wittels and others siding with him became the majority faction of the education committee, and on their recommendation the members of the society took – ambivalently – the decisive action of punishing Horney at that meeting of April 29. I say "ambivalently" because the vote was 24 for disqualifying, 7 against, with 29 abstentions (Eckardt, 1976). That is, virtually the majority stood on the sidelines.

Later the same year, Rado was stripped of his role as educational director, a role he had been brought to New York to fill ten years earlier. The following year, 1942, he and a group of colleagues including David Levy, Abram Kardiner, and Phyllis Greenacre founded the independent Association for Psychoanalytic and Psychosomatic Medicine. Noting "an atmosphere of bickering, slander, and gossip in which none of us felt that we could function profitably either to the Society or to ourselves" (Eckardt, 1976, pp. 153–4), they signaled their intention to withdraw though not resign from the New York Psychoanalytic. Most of them went on to found the Columbia Institute, negotiating for themselves a continuing membership in the American Psychoanalytic Association and, therefore, the IPA – a feat that was not managed by the others.

This is the briefest of summaries of these complex events. After Horney left the New York Psychoanalytic, she founded the American Association for the Advancement of Psychoanalysis together with the other dissidents who had left with her, including in this new organization Sullivan and Fromm. That organization subsequently split, forming two additional institutes: the William Alanson White Institute and an institute at the New York Medical College. (See Thompson, 1955; Crowley & Green, 1968.) In 1956, these institutes joined up with other dissidents, including Alexander and Grinker in Chicago, to form the American Academy of Psychoanalysis.

The Issue of Authority

What is the meaning of these political events? Psychoanalytic institutes are notoriously unstable and intolerant of divergent points of view, and organizational splits or schisms are common (Eisold, 1994; Thompson, 1995). In general, I believe this is due to the fact that psychoanalysts tend to be scornful of institutional life in general, given the fact that they practice alone, and that typically their allegiances are to their own analysts and supervisors and the schools they represent, not their institutes. Thus, the schismatic solution seems relatively attractive. But each schism is a response to a particular conflict at a particular moment in history: a vital interest is always at stake.

My argument is that the issue underlying this series of splits in New York was the nature of the professional authority of psychoanalysis;

The Construction of Psychoanalytic Authority 35

the conflicts were essentially about what form that authority would take. Authority – power that is legitimate, as Max Weber defined it – is essential to the functioning of any organization or social institution or practice. It is what makes any action, any decision, seem appropriate and acceptable to those who must abide by it. As Hannah Arendt (1961) observed, the resort to violence is the sign that authority has failed; on the other hand, authority supersedes the need for persuasion and argument. Authority induces willing obedience, compliance. But, obviously, it takes many forms and operates on different levels, particularly in the modern world where traditional forms of established authority have eroded: legal authority, moral authority, parental authority, technical authority – these are just some of the forms of authority that must be welded together to make any enterprise involving human cooperation viable.

Any organization needs to be able to construct and exercise for itself the authority required for its work. Psychoanalytic institutes, for example, need to authorize their faculty members, supervising analysts, and training committee members in their various roles so they can credibly and effectively work toward the goals of training. Candidates need to accept the authority of teachers and supervisors. Obviously, insufficient authority undermines the ability of those in positions of responsibility to act; they will not be listened to or followed. Excessive authority – or authoritarianism, that is, authority beyond what is required for the work of an organization – leads to inhibition and covert forms of rebellion. Eventually, as in the example before us, it can lead to open revolt.

The situation Kubie described in the New York Psychoanalytic of each group "hermetically sealed from the other" can be seen as a crisis of organizational authority. Under such circumstances, members give authority only to the cliques; legitimacy is withheld by each group from the institution as a whole. Kubie's "solution" was to impose a stricter Freudian curriculum, that is, to enforce the supremacy of one group over the whole. Ultimately, the "solution" was to drive out the dissenters altogether.

From the point of view of the dissenters, of course, this "solution" was authoritarian, an abuse of institutional authority because it distorted the essential work of the institute, work requiring different points of view and theoretical development. This is, by and large, I believe, the perspective of history: It is seen as regrettable, damaging

36 Psychoanalytic History

to the scientific reputation of psychoanalysis, attributable to particular personalities or the stresses of the time (Frosch, 1991; Richards, 1995). Yet, from the point of view of the young professionals, it must have seemed urgent and necessary.

The key issue, though, the issue that led to this institutional crisis, was not organizational authority, authority necessary for the functioning of the institute or society. It was the professional authority of the psychoanalyst, the authority possessed by individual practitioners as they interact with clients in their own consulting rooms. That is, clients need to recognize and accept the professional authority of those with whom they contract for a service. Analysands need to accept, up to a point, the authority of their analysts. As Kernberg (1996) put it recently: "There is no reason why the patient should give any credence, respect, or money to a psychoanalyst who has no specific professional authority" (p. 143). Without the professional authority of the analyst, why would he work through his resistances or explore his negative transferences or accept the deprivations of his positive ones? It is the leverage of the analyst.

But professional authority, precisely because it operates outside of formal organizations, is more amorphous, subject to the vagaries of public opinion, harder to establish and control. More than most forms of authority, it is mediated and influenced by individual consciousness. Professional authority, of course, derives much of its effectiveness from the institutions that set standards of training, develop criteria for competence, and nurture the bodies of knowledge the professional is expected to know. But the point is that the public develops its confidence in the identity and credentials of the professional when it believes in the substance of those standards. This is what matters to the analyst in his practice – and what mattered then, at the point when analysis was getting under way as a serious profession in this country. That is, I believe, what the fight was all about: Who was going to shape and establish the specific professional authority of psychoanalysis in this country?

The new generation of psychiatrists that came along in the 1930s, the young professionals that took over the institutions of psychoanalysis from their elders, and that drove out the "deviants," did so in an effort to establish the unimpeachable authority of psychoanalysis. They did so deliberately and, at times, brutally; they were motivated by ambition as well as, I believe, ideals. But they were also driven by anxieties and contradictions. As a result, as we shall see, the authority they constructed and wielded became oppressive and authoritarian. It was enormously successful, yet, as we are now in a position to see, ultimately, it collapsed.

To create the professional authority of psychoanalysis, they wove two strands together from two very different – and, in the end, two essentially incompatible – sources: On the one hand, they took the professional authority of medicine, based on experimental investigation and strict standards of training and certification; on the other, they took the charismatic authority of Freud as the founder and decisive thinker of the psychoanalytic movement.

The Professional Authority of Medicine

The professional authority of medicine had only recently been firmly established in this country; it was based on dramatic reforms that physicians themselves had brought about. Before these reforms, medical education had been erratic and lax in the extreme, largely in the hands of individual practitioners who ran "proprietary" schools, with few, if any, criteria for admission or graduation, and no standardized curriculum. The Flexner Report of 1910 brought widespread attention to this scandalous state of affairs and catalyzed the transformation of the system. In several decades at the start of this century, medical schools and teaching hospitals devoted to research became established, and the profession rose dramatically in social esteem and status (Ludmerer, 1983).

The critical point, for this discussion, was that the physicians themselves accomplished these reforms and in the process managed to maintain virtually complete control over their profession and the market for their services. They established rigorous methods of training, strict standards of accreditation, and in the process ran out of business the proprietary schools and unlicensed practitioners that had dominated medicine before them. Those increasingly came to be seen as "quacks" and "charlatans." As a result, instead of becoming the "victims of capitalism," as did many other self-employed artisans during this time, as Starr (1982) put it, physicians "became small capitalists themselves" (p. 25). The key to their success was the establishment of their professional authority, gained by policing themselves. With this professional authority they were able to establish and maintain for themselves an exceptional degree of professional autonomy, keeping at arm's length the dual threats of government intervention and institutional employment.

This is the source for the adamant stance against lay analysis that historically has characterized American psychoanalysis. In order to establish their claim to professional respectability and share in the rewards of medical practice, the psychiatrists who had introduced psychoanalysis into this country felt strongly that they had not only to establish rigorous, self-policing standards but also to drive out the entrepreneurs and ill-trained "quacks" who also laid claim to their field. If they failed to do this, they would lack the professional authority they felt they needed, not only with respect to patients but also, perhaps more importantly, in the eyes of their medical colleagues.

The ambitious young professionals – such analysts as Lewin, Zilboorg, and Blumgart, in addition to Kubie – having been exposed to the fervor of the institutes in Berlin, Vienna, and London, felt impatient with and contemptuous of their seniors in America. Inspired by their training, and identified with their European analysts, to be sure, they had a different vision of the course that psychoanalysis could take in this country. But they also believed their elders were sporadically and poorly trained. Moreover, they felt the senior members of the society did not appreciate the importance of this issue. This was not entirely a matter of ambition. As the second generation of American analysts, struggling to establish themselves in the midst of the depression and concerned as well to establish themselves in the eyes of their medical colleagues, they were also driven by fear. As Hendricks (1955), looking back on these early years, put it in his Presidential Address to the American Psychoanalytic Association in 1955: There was no way to "have disproved those numerous critics who ... sometimes thought of us as crackpots, or emotional converts, or merely victims of perverted imagination, in 1930" (p. 561). And this was not merely a subjective fear: the New York Society's application to the State to establish a clinic in the late 1920s was denied on the grounds that the society had no ties with a larger medical center, grounds that supported this fear (Millet, 1966).

In 1935, the young professionals forced the issue of professional standards. Paul Schilder – a psychiatrist and member of the Viennese Society, who had emigrated to New York in 1929, by all accounts a brilliant teacher and prolific author – was disqualified as a training analyst. The issue was that, despite his talents and, even, his association with Freud, he had not been analyzed and, thus, did not fit the established standards. At a stormy meeting of the institute, the younger members rejected the recommendation of a committee appointed by Brill that his training analyst role be retained. By a vote of 18 to 8, they stripped Schilder of his role, an act that led not only to his resignation but also to Brill's withdrawal from the presidency and from active involvement in the affairs of the institute for several years. From this point on, the new generation was in charge.

Ernest Jones referred to these generational battles in the New York Society as the "psychoanalytical civil war," running roughly from 1931 to 1938 (Hale, 1995, p. 103). Brill complained to Jones – his counterpart in the British Society – of the "petty, paranoid plotting of the younger generation." Kubie, in turn, complained to Glover of Freud's laxity in training and authorizing the older generation: "This has created a group of badly trained, and intellectually and emotionally inadequate people in the older group" (in Hale, 1995, p. 104).

During this period, in a parallel development, the American Psychoanalytic Association – initially an interest group of mainly psychiatrists based outside New York that had been founded at about the same time as the New York Society – was transformed into an umbrella organization for local societies. This too was part of a larger effort to standardize and professionalize psychoanalytic practice. The American had contained not only many of the "inadequate people" Kubie complained of to Glover, but also numbers of others whose commitment to psychoanalysis was limited, men such as William Alanson White and Sullivan. The reorganization forced them to become members of a local society, for most of them the Washington-Baltimore Society. More importantly, it set up a national supervisory organization with the power to control membership and training in local societies. In this way, the new generation of analysts sought to extend their control over psychoanalysis outside New York.

Despite their differences, both sides in the "psychoanalytic civil war" seemed firmly agreed on the need to establish the credibility of psychiatry and to link it with psychoanalysis. Indeed, all of the American psychiatrists interested in psychoanalysis were deeply committed to the strengthening of the professional authority of psychiatry. They were all likely to agree, as Menninger put it in his Presidential Address in 1942, "we are physicians first, psychiatrists second, and psychoanalysts third" (Menninger, 1942, p. 290). Altogether they formed a wall of agreement that baffled and infuriated Freud, who correctly noted that in America "psychoanalysis is nothing more than one of the handmaids of psychiatry" (Hale, 1995, p. 129).

The ambition of the young professionals was to take over psychiatry from within, to establish psychoanalysis as the discipline within the discipline of psychiatry. The opposing point of view – held by psychiatrists with a more flexible and critical interest in psychoanalysis – inclined to take from psychoanalysis what it had to offer, to absorb psychoanalysis into psychiatry and psychosomatic medicine.

Alexander, founder of the Chicago Institute, had such a view. He noted in his 1938 Presidential Address to the American – setting out his program more than describing the actual state of affairs – that American psychoanalysis, "instead of remaining an isolated discipline … has become more and more a part of medicine in so far as it is a therapy, and a part of social science in so far as it deals with human relationships" (Alexander, 1938, p. 300). He attacked those who resisted the importance of "a rigid scientific verification of psychoanalytic findings, the demand for experimental proofs, and questioning of certain theoretical deductions" (p. 303).

Rado also worked hard to establish links to psychiatry and medicine, modifying psychoanalytic concepts and methods in the process (Roazen & Swerdloff, 1995). Throughout the late 1930s he collaborated with Adolph Meyer, the "dean" of American psychiatry, on various projects; for him the separation of psychoanalytic institutes and medical schools "proved harmful to both sides" (Tomlinson, 1996, p. 969).

Also in this camp – though clearly more identified with psychiatry – were Sullivan and White. Director of St. Elizabeth's Hospital in Washington, co-founder and editor of *The Psychoanalytic Review*, White kept a wary distance from Freud, whom he once called the "Pope in Vienna" (Hale, 1971). He had little direct exposure to psychoanalysis apart from some hours with Rank on one of his New York visits. And Sullivan, who called his journal *Psychiatry*, may have had none. Having gotten his medical degree from what he referred to as a "diploma mill" (Perry, 1982) in Chicago, he made it a lifelong objective to build up psychiatry by encouraging research as well as improving psychiatric training in medical schools. Psychoanalysis for him was an important contributor to psychiatry; but not only was he far from being a disciple of Freud's, he sought vital connections with other disciplines in social science.

We are now in a position to see that the battle that erupted in the New York Society in 1941 between the cliques was, among other things, a battle within psychiatry itself. On one side was a network of links between Rado and Adolph Meyer, between Horney, Alexander, Sullivan, and White. No one person or group of persons led this faction. Indeed, Meyer and White were competitive with each other, Alexander and Horney could not get along with each other, and Rado and Horney disliked each other intensely (Paris, 1994); but nonetheless they were linked with the larger world of American academic psychiatry and they had in common a view of the importance of incorporating many of the specific findings of psychoanalysis into psychiatry. In this view, psychoanalysis was a practice that developed new clinical observations, new theories, and links with other fields of medicine and social science, a practice that would itself be modified under the impact of those linkages.

On the other side was the faction, initially led by Kubie and subsequently by Menninger, that sought to affirm the primacy of psychoanalysis, as shaped by Freud, seen as a coherent and integral whole, and had the ambition to make it the core discipline of psychiatry. As Knight put it in his 1953 Presidential Address to the American – when the victory of this faction appeared complete – membership [in the APA] is "equivalent to certification in a specialty within a specialty" (Knight, 1953, p. 213).

This battle within psychiatry was one of the key elements culminating in Horney and Rado being stripped of their training roles. The core group of young professionals won out with their vision of psychoanalysis dominant over psychiatry: not only was Freud preserved but also psychoanalysis as an integral, distinct, and hierarchical discipline. But what caused the conflict over the establishment of the institutional authority of psychoanalysis to lead to, in effect, an oppressive authoritarianism? After all, some of those who were in the other camp – such as Alexander – did manage to negotiate for themselves a continuing presence in mainstream psychoanalysis, as did Rado eventually. Why was coexistence not possible?

The Authority of Freud

The second external factor profoundly influencing the creation of psychoanalytic authority stemmed from both the influx of refugee analysts from Europe and the death of Freud. The refugee analysts, in the late 1930s, who brought with them not only well-established reputations but also the cachet of ties to Freud, formed an alliance with the young professionals. If the ambitious and young psychiatrists saw themselves as building a professional identity upon unshakable medical foundations, the refugees were seeking to re-establish a security they had lost through their enforced emigration and the death of Freud.

This was not a simple process; the Americans assimilated the refugees on distinctly American terms. At the 1938 Paris Congress of the International, the Americans rejected the authority of the International Training Commission to accredit any analyst in America (Knight, 1953), an issue that had intensified as European analysts – both lay and medical – fled their homelands and sought the International's protection. At about the same time, the American Psychoanalytic Association formed a committee under Kubie to aid refugee analysts, but the intent of that committee was equally to control the process of assimilation; its charge stated "the primary functions of the committee were to restrict and control immigration, to direct it to communities not already overcrowded, and to keep the teaching of analysis centered in the hands of our recognized teaching institutes" (Muhlleitner & Reichmayr, 1995, pp. 108–9).

There are a number of painful and sad stories that emerged out of this process, but on the whole it was, as Coser (1984) put it, "an amazing success story" (p. 42). The refugee analysts willingly fitted into the opportunities provided. The American young professionals, for their part, strengthened by the presence of their authoritative European elders in their conflicts with more heterodox psychiatrists, solidified their control over psychoanalytic institutions. Together they moved against the dissidents.

For the refugee analysts, of course, the crushing of dissidents was a familiar story (Eisold, 1997; Chapter 1 in this volume). Some of the earlier refugees who had come under happier circumstances and by their own volition – such analysts as Horney, Rado, Alexander – welcomed the freer atmosphere in America and thrived with the opportunities provided here (Tomlinson, 1996). Indeed, some of them were probably motivated by a certain rebelliousness. Those analysts who were forced to flee were on the whole more conservative than their predecessors; not only accepting of Freudian orthodoxy, they were also more likely to accept and desire the hierarchical authority structures they had left behind in Europe. I think it fair to say that they welcomed the attempts to impose such control and authority on their new institutions, making them more familiar and secure for their own beliefs (Kurzweil, 1989).

At the same time, they had to conform to the requirements of their American hosts. Most particularly, they had to acquiesce to the American position on lay analysis, a position that not only brought hardship to some of their own members but also brought them into direct conflict with Freud's well-known and frequently expressed position on the relationship between psychoanalysis and medicine.

There is, in fact, not much direct evidence of the thoughts and feelings evoked by this state of affairs; this is no surprise, given the precarious and bewildering position of the refugees. In one of his *Rundbriefe*, Fenichel decried the "progressive suppression of the non-physician analysts" and linked it to the "progressive degradation of psychoanalysis into a psychiatric method" (Fenichel, 1998). Fenichel was referring to the situation in California, which was particularly outrageous in its treatment of lay analysts, and he was exceptionally outspoken. But it is not difficult to extrapolate his remarks to other expatriates.

Freud had always been anti-American, and it was no secret that he distrusted those analysts who "defected" to America. This, no doubt, colored the refugee's view of those who had "defected" earlier, such as Rado and Horney. These early defectors, moreover, had clearly profited from their earlier adjustment and become, in the process, more divergent from Freud. Thus it was easy for refugees to turn against the earlier émigrés. At the same time, the refugees faced the ambivalent feelings of the American analysts toward their past accomplishments and close ties with "the Professor." They were mindful of the difficulty of being fully accepted. As Helene Deutsch wrote about her experience in Boston, which on the whole was extremely successful: "Of course, for a small circle I am Helene Deutsch with 20 years of fame behind me. But this brings only *distrust* and criticism" (Roazen, 1985, p. 285).

So there was every reason for the refugees to do their best to link up with their demanding and suspicious American benefactors and, in the process, turn against the "deviants." And it should be no surprise that it was Wittels who led the attack in New York, because not only had he been one of the first to leave Vienna for a more lucrative American practice but also was an early rebel himself, publishing an early unauthorized and unflattering biography of Freud (Wittels, 1995). Now, he disowned his own deviancy in standing up so vehemently for the authority of "the Professor."

In a somewhat parallel process, this is what the refugee analysts did: For the price of capitulating on the issue of lay analysis, they set themselves up to become the representatives of psychoanalytic tradition and the bearers of Freud's charisma. Coser (1984) notes that the refugee analysts came to be disproportionately seen as leaders and trainers of American psychoanalysts in ways that cannot be entirely explained by their superior achievements and insights. He concluded: "The present shape and stature of psychoanalysis were largely the result of the arrival of the refugee psychoanalysts ... the bearers and inheritors of the original tradition of the European founding fathers" (p. 54).

Through the refugees, psychoanalysis in America became blessed by Freud at last. And they, in turn, were able to add to the professional authority of medicine the charismatic authority of Freud. On these twin foundations, the professional authority of psychoanalysis became established in this country.

The Outcome

This authority enjoyed unprecedented success. Psychoanalysis did indeed virtually take over psychiatry, as the core discipline, the discipline within the discipline, and received virtually unqualified public acceptance. As Menninger (1948) put it in his history of psychiatry, modern psychiatry could be said to have begun at this point, having been given a solid basis in psychoanalysis and shown its usefulness in World War II.

But, as I suggested at the start, what was fused together in the creation of this professional authority were essentially different and – at this point – increasingly incompatible elements. Despite the appearance of fusion and despite the undeniable "success" it enjoyed, it never was as stable as it seemed.

The successful establishment of the professional authority of medicine earlier in this century was based on the principle of learning from experimental methods, through testing and observation (Ludmerer, 1983). Psychiatry could not continue to earn the respect of the other fields of medicine unless it hewed to this principle as well. That was the point of Alexander's 1938 Presidential Address, calling for "scientific verification" and "experimental proofs." But the increasing reliance on the charismatic authority of Freud and the neglect of empirical research and competing theories undermined this principle.

Convinced for the most part that psychoanalytic treatment itself was the only research that mattered, psychoanalysts for the most part neglected the kind of research that in modern American medicine had been integral to its successful reputation. In his history of psychiatry, Menninger (1948) claimed "psychoanalytic psychiatry" was "the only psychiatry that formulated theories of anatomy and of the physiology of the personality" (p. 50). But it did not show sustained or deep interest in testing those theories, nor did it commit itself to demonstrating its treatment outcomes. It did not keep up.

Even as early as 1952, a committee of the American Psychoanalytic Association reported, after four years of deliberation, that it was "impossible to find a definition of psychoanalysis that is acceptable to even a large group of members." This in itself is alarming for a discipline with scientific claims. But, then, it added: "a very strong resistance exists among the members ... to any investigation on the problem of evaluating results" (Oberndorf, 1953, p. 234).

It is true that there were pockets in the analytic community where research was supported, notably at such institutes as Columbia and Chicago where the influence of Rado and Alexander prevailed for a time. Moreover, the Menninger Foundation has provided sustained support for research on psychotherapy. But, on the whole, as the editors of a recent text on psychotherapy research observed: "for several decades the field was faltering in its research" (Miller et al., 1993, p. xx). As Simon (1992) summed it up, speaking as a psychoanalytic psychiatrist, "Our canons for use of evidence are sloppy and inconsistently applied, our commitment to serious empirical testing is weak … only a few research-minded analysts are willing to survey the overall results of analytic treatment. We are prone to the undue influence of charismatic and persuasive leaders" (p. 966).

Significantly, the only official role that was made available for lay analysts was that of "Research Analyst," signaling what became the peripheral value of both psychology and research. I believe that psychoanalytic psychiatry was forced into this position because it could not afford to probe deeply into the empirical foundations of its beliefs and practices. As Cooper put it recently: "Research is dangerous, and some of our more cherished theories and even our most hallowed techniques might be proved wrong" (1997, pp. 11–12). Arlow (1982) has observed that in the "postapostolic era in psychoanalytic history" (p. 18), psychoanalytic research is more important; it is also less threatening.

The alliance was threatened from the other side as well. Freud had always opposed the medicalization of psychoanalysis and had argued powerfully in "The Question of Lay Analysis" (Freud, 1926) that psychoanalysis was not only not reducible to a therapy but belonged in the hands of those with wider cultural knowledge. With the arrival of the refugees and their assimilation into American practice, the issue of lay analysis was resolved on the surface – but, of course, it remained alive in the minds of the Americans and the refugees. And it could not be put to rest so long as there were so many – and such prominently successful – lay analysts as Erikson, Fromm, Kris, Reik, Waelder, and so on. Moreover, it was clear that the authority of psychoanalysis abroad fully extended to such lay figures as Mrs. Klein and Miss Freud. And it was not uncommon for the wives of analysts to get training and set up practices outside the recognized institutes (Kurzweil, 1995). All these lay analysts did not fit under the narrow umbrella of "Research Analysts."

We are now in a position to grasp more fully the meaning of those events in 1941 with which we began. The driving out of Schilder in 1935 can be seen as a harsh but still rational act: The young professionals wanted to establish clearly the importance of professional standards and to ensure that the leadership of the New York Institute was responsive to this issue and their professional concerns. But the situation in 1941 was far more complex, the anxieties far greater, and the solutions less apparent. Much was at stake about the future both of psychoanalysis and psychiatry – and, of course, about the careers of the protagonists.

This might have continued as a fruitful and stimulating conflict, albeit laden with anxiety for both sides. But the arrival of the refugees injected a new dynamic into the struggle. The young professionals took them in and attempted to make them allies in their struggle with the older dissidents. In a sense, of course, they succeeded – but in another sense they failed, because the refugees never did fully ally with them. Rado's cynical commentary on this process is that "after they were established, the first man they pushed out was Kubie, because they wanted to be the leaders themselves" (Roazen, 1995, p. 124). The refugees gave in on the issue of lay analysis – indeed, they had no choice in the matter – but, in turn, they forced the issue of loyalty to Freud. There was to be no tolerance of deviant theories. And the Americans, who had been deviants from Freud on the issue of lay analysis themselves, who had, indeed, never been accepted by Freud in their adherence to psychiatry, were put to the test. They were forced to take a decisive, authoritarian stance. Like Wittels himself, they suppressed and atoned for their own deviance by projecting it all into the "deviants" Horney and Rado, and casting them out.

But it may be misleading to suggest that the refugees themselves forced the issue. I suspect they forced it in the sense that they stood there and embodied it at the point in history when Freud ceased to exist. Most likely, theirs were the abstentions in the vote that disqualified Horney. Formally – and, perhaps, consciously – they probably saw themselves not getting involved, much as they had tried to stay apart from the politics in Austria and Germany that eventually forced them from their homes. But, none the less, theirs was now the balance of power, and in "not acting" they exerted a decisive influence. Passively but powerfully, they observed the Americans declare themselves on the issue of their loyalty to Freud.

Clearly for the displaced refugees, the death of Freud was more of a loss. It is no wonder that their identification with him would solidify in their mourning. But for the others, I believe, the death of Freud also created a crisis of sorts: all that remained of him and still remains is what he had written and the disciples who carried his word. As Slater (1966) observed in general of the followers of an authority who withdraws direction and personal presence from his followers: "Frightened by the freedom and responsibility ... they begin to mold from early parental images a fantasy of an omniscient and omnipotent protector" (p. 22). That protector can be represented by a stone – or a book – or a band of apostles.

It is striking that the British Society went through a virtually identical crisis at this time (King & Steiner, 1991). A flood of refugee analysts entered with Freud, arousing comparable fears of unemployment and conflict between rival camps. As Balint (1948, 1954) pointed out, the idealizations of training analysts under these circumstances led to a process of splitting and the search for scapegoats. (See also Eisold, 1994.) After Freud died, there was a concerted attempt to identify Melanie Klein as a deviant who should be expelled. In the case of the British Society, the "controversial discussions" led to a compromise in which both factions, eventually, found the way to coexist. But the fact that the conflict in England at this time so closely paralleled the conflict in New York suggests not only the role of internal conflicts over competing schools of thought but, in addition, the importance of the loss of Freud, the founding father, and the defensive evocation of loyalty and conformity.

I believe we are looking here at several processes largely operating out of awareness: conflict between competing schools fomenting projective processes, the projection of deviancy into a single scapegoat, anxiety over the loss of charismatic authority, the creation of an authority rooted in contradiction. The presence of such anxiety and the conflicting and pathological defenses invoked against anxiety, which in turn creates more anxiety, explains the virulence of the authoritarian behavior we set out to explain. Complex and creative individuals, subject to such anxieties in organizations where they are immersed in preserving their identities and interests as members, become caught up in "social defenses" (Menzies, 1967) and behave irrationally. Complex and creative if difficult people become demonized, "ideals" protected at all costs. Organizations – especially those based on personal ties and individual loyalties – split apart.

The irrational and contradictory behavior persists because the underlying issue was not merely about the fate of one organization but, rather, the construction of the professional authority of psychoanalysis as a whole: the fate of the entire field comes to seem at stake. I suggested at the start of this paper, the successful pursuit of any organizational or professional activity requires, among other things, an authority that is adequate and appropriate to the task. But if that authority is deeply flawed, the work is compromised.

A deeply flawed authority is ultimately detected, of course. In operation, it compromises the ability of those working within the system; they are inhibited not only in addressing the challenges coming from outside but also in thinking effectively about their work. We have seen the signs of this difficulty embedded in the story of this success: theoretical conformity, a claim to omniscience (Sharaf & Levinson, 1964), the neglect of the scientific spirit of testing, bad faith and corruption in the attitude toward lay analysts. Flawed authority is a constant source of insecurity. It creates anxiety. It establishes limits to thinking.

Bion (1970) commented on this dilemma in some of his remarks on the relationship between the mystic and the group – and it is clear that he had Freud and American psychoanalysis specifically in mind. The mystic and the group, or the genius and the establishment, need each other: the mystic needs the group to receive and apply his revelations, the group needs the mystic to carry it beyond itself. At best this relationship is symbiotic; filled with suspicion and hostility, if also potential benevolence, it can be mutually enlivening. But it can become parasitic: "The parasitic group can be primarily concerned to destroy the mystic, or mystic ... ideas, but if it fails to do so it must 'establish' his or their truth" (Bion, 1970, p. 79). That is, it must make the ideas fixed, no longer susceptible to thought. They are put at the service of something else.

I think such phenomena are embedded in the "success story" of postwar American psychoanalysis. Preoccupied with technical competence and political control, the establishment of psychoanalysis enjoyed unforeseen successes – until, blow by blow, it lost departments of psychiatry, exclusive rights to insurance coverage, control over lay access to training, and, finally, the confidence of the public. It seemed powerless to think about what was happening. And this is to say nothing about the effect of this upon those who were split off, kept out of the mainstream.

Conclusion

Now, of course, what was put together has come apart: the professional authority of psychoanalysis is in tatters. Psychoanalysis has lost its preeminent standing in psychiatry, barely holding its own as one treatment modality among many. Many question whether it is scientific at all, belonging among the other medical procedures and practices supported by empirical research. Analysts themselves question what has come to be called "the medical model." Moreover, the reputation of Freud has suffered a shattering reversal. Not only has the public come to view him with suspicion, but analysts themselves have come to be dispersed among so many varied analytic schools that Freud no longer represents the authoritative center of psychoanalysis as he once did.

With hindsight we can see more clearly that there were complex problems embedded in the positions of every faction. It is still by no means clear how psychoanalysis links to other disciplines, hermeneutic, scientific, or healing. Research into treatment outcomes has been hampered by difficulties in establishing and implementing criteria (see Bachrach et al., 1991). Funding has been scarce. As Holt (1985) has pointed out, empirical research into the fundamental principles of "metapsychology" has been, at best, disappointing. Folding psychoanalysis into psychiatry might have diluted its development, restricting it even more fully to a treatment modality, as Freud feared. Nor is it at all apparent that psychoanalysis could have altogether escaped its current downturn in the eyes of the public had its leaders been less arrogant in their period of greatest hegemony.

The important point, I believe, is not that the "wrong" faction won out in this battle. Nor is it that the leadership of psychoanalysis was arrogant. It is not even that the professional authority of psychoanalysis was composed of contradictory and conflicting elements, debilitating as those internal contradictions were to the development of the field.

The problem was – and, I believe, still is – the splintering and fragmentation of the psychoanalytic community: split apart, psychoanalysts lost the capacity to talk across their differences. The normal processes of competition, of giving vent to passionate disagreements, of criticism, of challenges to questionable or merely divergent practices – all these were severely curtailed as each camp withdrew behind its own barriers. Obviously there was no need to contend with ideas no longer represented in one's own camp. Less obvious was the subtle inhibition of thoughts that might at times stray in the direction of the enemy.

On the level of individual psychopathology, splitting inhibits adaptation to reality. At the level of the group, it destroys community. In the early years of psychoanalysis, the imagery of war was frequently invoked against its internal as well as external enemies. Freud, a self-identified "conquistador" (Masson, 1985, p. 398), was a "good hater" (Sachs, 1944, p. 117). He demanded of his followers that they do battle with him against his enemies. It is questionable that that attitude was useful then (Eisold, 1997). There is no question about it now.

Psychoanalysis is far from dead – at least among psychoanalysts. Not only do we continue to be enlivened by our work and by discussions among ourselves about the nature of mind and experience, but also – as Freud insisted all along, and Sullivan too – psychoanalysis is much more than a therapy. The fact is that we are dealing with real, albeit elusive, phenomena: the pervasive and tenacious impact of irrational forces on human behavior. The mystic has not deserted the group. Those phenomena remain powerfully present, and there is no other discipline that begins to have the means to think about them. For better or worse, we are stuck with that work.

The problem we face, institutionally, is the reconstruction of our professional authority. That cannot be on the old basis – or, I think, on the old certainties. I suspect that in the world that is now coming into being, such certainties will have no place. Perhaps the professional authority of psychoanalysis can be based less on what we analysts claim to know, the bodies of knowledge we can claim to have acquired, than our competence in not knowing and not understanding, our willingness to look at and think about the irrational, frightening, and elusive aspects of human behavior.

52 Psychoanalytic History

But if we do that, we have to be willing to look at our own capacity for institutional irrationality and to work at rebuilding our community.

References

Alexander, F. (1938). Psychoanalysis comes of age. *Psychoanalytic Quarterly* 7, 299–306.

Arendt, H. (1961). *Between Past and Future*. New York: Viking.

Arlow, J. A. (1982). Psychoanalytic education: a psychoanalytic perspective. *Annual of Psychoanalysis* 10, 5–20.

Bachrach, H. M., Galatzer-Levy, R., Skolnikoff, A., and Waldron, Jr., S. (1991). On the efficacy of psychoanalysis. *Journal of the American Psychoanalytic Association* 39, 871–916.

Balint, M. (1948). On the psychoanalytic training system. *International Journal of Psychoanalysis* 29, 163–73.

Balint, M. (1954). Analytic training and training analysis. *International Journal of Psychoanalysis* 35, 157–62.

Bion, W. R. (1970). *Attention and Interpretation*. London: Tavistock Publications.

Cooper, A. M. (1997). Psychoanalytic education: past, present and future. Address to the Association for Psychoanalytic Medicine, November 4, 1997. New York.

Coser, L. (1984). *Refugee Scholars in America*. New Haven: Yale.

Crowley, R. M., & Green, M. R. (1968). *Revolution within Psychoanalysis: A History of the William Alanson White Institute*. New York: William Alanson White Institute.

Eckhardt, M. H. (1978). Organizational schisms in American psychoanalysis. In J. M. Quen & E. T. Carlson (eds.), *American Psychoanalysis: Origins and Development*. New York: Brunner/Mazel.

Eisold, K. (1994). The intolerance of diversity in psychoanalytic institutes. *International Journal of Psychoanalysis* 75, 785–800.

Eisold, K. (1997). Freud as leader: the early years of the Viennese Society. *International Journal of Psychoanalysis* 78, 87–104.

Fenichel, O. (1998). *119 Rundbriefe (1934–1945)*. Eds. E. Muhlleitner & J. Reichmayr. Basel/Frankfort: Stroemfeld Verlag.

Freud, S. (1926). The question of lay analysis. In J. Strachey (ed. and trans.), *The Standard Edition of the Complete Psychological Works of Sigmund Freud* (Vol. 20, pp. 177–258). London: Hogarth Press.

Frosch, J. (1991). The New York Psychoanalytic Civil War. *Journal of the American Psychoanalytic Association* 39(4), 1037–64.

Gitelson, F. H. (1983). Identity crises: splits or compromises – adaptive or maladaptive. In E. D. Joseph & D. Widlocher (eds.), *The Identity of the Psychoanalyst* (pp. 157–79). New York: International Universities Press.

Hale, N. G. (1971). *Freud and the Americans*. New York: Oxford University Press.

Hale, N. G. (1995). *The Rise and Crisis of Psychoanalysis in the United States*. New York: Oxford.

Hendricks, I. (1955). Presidential address. *Journal of the American Psychoanalytic Association* 3, 580–2.

Holt, R. R. (1985). The current status of psychoanalytic theory. *Psychoanalytic Psychology* 2(4), 289–316.

Kernberg, O. F. (1996). The analyst's authority in the psychoanalytic situation. *The Psychoanalytic Quarterly* 65(1), 137–57.

King, P., & Steiner, R. (1991). *The Freud–Klein Controversies, 1941–45*. London: Routledge.

Knight, R. P. (1953). Present status of organized psychoanalysis in the United States. *Journal of the American Psychoanalytic Association* 1, 197–221.

Kurzweil, E. (1989). *The Freudians: A Comparative Perspective*. New Haven: Yale University Press.

Kurzweil, E. (1995). USA. In P. Kutter (ed.), *Psychoanalysis International 2* (pp. 186–234). Stuttgart: Frommann-Holzboog.

Ludmerer, K. M. (1983). *Learning to Heal: The Development of American Medical Education*. New York: Basic Books.

Mahony, P. (1979). The budding international association of psychoanalysis and its discontents. *Psychoanalysis and Contemporary Thought* 2, 551–93.

Masson, J. M. (1985). *The Complete Letters of Sigmund Freud to Wilhelm Fliess, 1887–1904*. Cambridge, MA: Harvard University Press.

Menninger, K. (1942). Presidential address. *Psychoanalytic Quarterly* 11, 287–300.

Menninger, W. C. (1948). *Psychiatry: Its Evolution and Present Status*. Ithaca, NY: Cornell University Press.

Menzies, E. (1967). *The Functioning of Social Systems as Defense against Anxiety*. London: Tavistock Publications.

Miller, N. E, Luborsky, L., Barber, J. P., & Docherty, J. P. (eds.) (1993). *Psychodynamic Treatment Research*. New York: Basic Books.

Millett, J. A. P. (1962). Changing faces of psychoanalytic education. In L. Salzman & J. H. Masserman (eds.), *Modern Concepts of Psychoanalysis*. New York: Philosophical Library.

Millett, J. A. P. (1966). Psychoanalysis in the United States. In F. Alexander, S. Eisenstein, & M. Grotjahn (eds.), *Psychoanalytic Pioneers* (pp. 546–96). New York: Basic Books.

Muhlleitner, E., & Reichmayr, J. (1995). The exodus of psychoanalysts from Vienna. In F. Stadler & P. Weibel (eds.), *The Cultural Exodus from Austria* (pp. 98–121). Vienna: Springer Verlag.

Oberndorf, C. (1953). *A History of Psychoanalysis in America*. New York: Grune & Stratton.

Paris, B. J. (1994). *Karen Horney*. New Haven: Yale University Press.

Perry, H. S. (1982). *Psychiatrist of America: The Life of Harry Stack Sullivan*. Cambridge, MA: Harvard University Press.

Quen, J., & Carlson, E. E. (1978). *American Psychoanalysis: Origins and Development*. New York: Brunner/Mazel.

Quinn, S. (1987). *A Mind of Her Own: A Life of Karen Horney*. New York: Summit.

Richards, A. D. (1995). A.A. Brill: the politics of exclusion and the politics of pluralism. The 47th A.A. Brill Lecture, presented at the New York Psychoanalytic Society, November 28, 1995.

Roazen, P. (1985). *Helene Deutsch: A Psychoanalyst's Life*. Garden City: Doubleday.

Roazen, P., & Swerdloff, B. (1995). *Heresy: Sandor Rado and the Psychoanalytic Movement*. Northvale, NJ: Aronson.

Sachs, H. (1944). *Freud: Master and Friend*. Cambridge, MA: Harvard University Press.

Sharaf, M. R., & Levinson, D. J. (1964). The quest for omnipotence. *Psychiatry* 27, 135–49.

Simon, B. (1992). "Incest – see under Oedipus Complex": the history of an error in psychoanalysis. *Journal of the American Psychoanalytic Association* 40(4), 955–88.

Slater, P. E. (1966). *Microcosm: Structural, Psychological and Religious Evolution in Groups*. New York: John Wiley & Sons.

Starr, P. (1982). *The Social Transformation of American Medicine*. New York: Basic Books.

Thompson, C. (1955). The history of the William Alanson White Institute. Address to the Harry Stack Sullivan Society.

Thompson, N. L. (1995). Spaltungen in der psychoanalytischen Bewegung Nordamerikas. In Ludger M. Hermans (ed.), *Spaltungen in der Geschichte der Psychoanalyse*. Tubingen: diskord.

Tomlinson, C. (1996). Sandor Rado and Adolf Meyer: a nodal point in American psychiatry and psychoanalysis. *International Journal of Psychoanalysis* 77(5), 963–82.

Wittels, F. (1995). *Freud and the Child Woman: The Memoirs of Fritz Wittels*. New Haven: Yale University Press.

Chapter Three

Psychoanalysis and Psychotherapy

A Long and Troubled Relationship

[Originally published as Psychotherapy and Psychoanalysis: A Long and Troubled History, *The International Journal of Psychoanalysis*, vol. 86 (2005), pp. 1175–95.]

Recently, Wallerstein (2001) noted: "the complacent certainties about the distinct enough compartmentalizations of psychoanalysis and the psychoanalytic psychotherapies no longer exist. The borders between them are now blurred, and they shift constantly, depending on one's vantage point and one's theoretical predilections" (p. xvi). But while many would agree that psychoanalysis is at such a point, the fact is that the distinction was always blurred. Wallerstein's framing of the issue obscures the interesting fact that while, for most analysts in the past, there were indeed "complacent certainties" about the existence of such a distinction, there was never agreement on what it was, never clarity on where or how the line was to be drawn. As a result, we seem to be in an odd place for psychoanalysts: having resolved or transcended a conflict without understanding what it was about.

Typically, the debates and discussions centered on theoretical or technical issues. Gill (1984) usefully distinguished between formal or "extrinsic" factors, such as the use of the couch, the frequency of sessions, or the training of the analyst, and "intrinsic" factors, the analysis of transference, the use of free association, regression, etc. Arguing that the "intrinsic" factor of transference analysis was the key, however, he did not succeed in persuading most analysts that it was the defining characteristic of psychoanalysis or that it was irrelevant to psychotherapy. More recently, Kernberg (1999) has attempted to stake out definitive boundaries between "psychoanalysis," "psychoanalytic psychotherapy," and "supportive psychotherapy." But even he has had to acknowledge not only the formidable counter-arguments to his case but also the fact that the proliferation of psychoanalyses has brought us to the point where his proposed boundaries would necessarily exclude certain contemporary schools of thought.

As a result of what now appear to be insuperable difficulties with establishing clear and valid distinctions, many have backed off the topic, referring, like Wallerstein, to the plurality of "psychotherapies" and "psychoanalyses." This does not mean that there are not useful or even necessary distinctions to be made, but it does appear to acknowledge that past efforts for clarity have not led to clear or usable discriminations.

My argument in this paper is that the debates in the past have been contaminated by two covert, underlying issues. First, the debate about psychotherapy was muddied by the fact that, on an institutional level, psychoanalysis did become, as Freud feared, a "mere handmaiden of psychiatry." The fate he foresaw in "On the Question of Lay Analysis" has come to pass: "swallowed up by medicine," psychoanalysis will find its "last resting place in a textbook of psychiatry under the heading 'Methods of Treatment', alongside of procedures such as hypnotic suggestion, autosuggestion, and persuasion" (Freud, 1926, p. 248). Thus the attempt repeatedly to affirm and define the distinction – and the inability to succeed at it – reflects the fact that psychoanalysis became a form of psychotherapy, in fact, but continued to claim that it was distinctly privileged and different.

I am not speaking here of the "medicalization" of psychoanalysis, attempts to restrict psychoanalytic training and practice to medically trained psychiatrists. That issue, obviously a key focus of Freud's "On the Question of Lay Analysis," has been supplanted by the enormous expansion of psychotherapy in the mid-twentieth century, well beyond the boundaries of psychiatry. My point is that psychoanalysts today – whether they start out as psychiatrists, psychologists, social workers, ministers, nurses, or specialists from fields outside the traditional disciplines of mental health – see themselves as providing a psychotherapeutic service. They are "mental health practitioners," a term that did not exist in Freud's day, delineating a field that began to be defined in the 1930s but which robustly came into existence following World War II. In that sense, they are a part of medicine.

The original mission of psychiatry now extends to all forms of mental health service. Psychoanalysts seek reimbursement privileges and insurance coverage, along with other practitioners. Their training is about the treatment of patients, and their professional journals and meetings focus almost entirely on patient outcomes. As a "method of treatment" psychoanalysis may not be in competition with "hypnotic suggestion, autosuggestion, and persuasion," as Freud predicted, but today it is in competition with cognitive-behavioral therapy, psychopharmacological treatments, group therapy, etc. etc. My point here is not about the issue of "lay analysis," as it has been traditionally understood; it is about the immense expansion of psychotherapy, what Rieff (1966) referred to as "The Triumph of the Therapeutic" in our culture.

The second underlying issue in the debate stems from the closed and hierarchical nature of psychoanalytic institutions. Historically preoccupied with maintaining the purity of their doctrines and affirming allegiance to Freud, while searching out internal enemies, many mainstream psychoanalysts were averse to modifying their theories and practices in order to adapt to external pressures and demands. Thus, in the postwar era, any attempt to engage with "psychotherapy" was likely to be attacked as a form of psychoanalytic deviance.

In recent times, the issues have changed. As psychoanalysts, less driven by ideological debates, have fewer analysands in their practices, the matter has become more practical. A new hierarchy has evolved out of the old caste system, separating "psychoanalysts" and "psychotherapists," creating sometimes painful and poignant conflicts among groups within psychoanalysis but also between analytic generations. Moreover, the particular forms of dynamic psychotherapy spawned by psychoanalysis are now themselves under attack, weakened by the same social and economic forces that have weakened psychoanalysis. They are all the more vulnerable to attack as psychoanalytic institutions maintain their aloofness from psychotherapy.

Let me make it clear at the outset, however, that the argument in this paper is in no way meant to imply that psychoanalysis does not have a valuable and potentially important role to play or, even, that it would not be possible to arrive at a definition of what it is. The point is that we have been caught up in conflicts derived from our history that have

The Post-World War II Years

The *locus classicus* for the debate is Freud's address to the Budapest Society at the end of World War I. Foreseeing the day when the demand for psychoanalysis would greatly increase but also that, when it did, psychoanalysis would have to be modified to accommodate such numbers, he said: "We shall then be faced by the task of adapting our technique to the new condition ... It is very probable, too, that the large-scale application of our therapy will compel us to alloy the pure gold of analysis freely with the copper of direct suggestion" (Freud, 1919, p. 167).

It wasn't until after World War II that the opportunities – and the pressures – to develop the "alloy" of psychoanalysis that Freud foresaw arose with any significance. What seemed in 1918 a simple enough suggestion and a clear enough distinction then became the object of a virtually endless stream of speculation and debate.

Wallerstein has noted that the debate over psychotherapy appears to be primarily an American preoccupation – and for good reason. In America, psychiatry embraced psychoanalysis and psychoanalysis, in turn, conferred on psychiatry a monopoly on eligibility for training. Other countries exhibited similar tensions over the medicalization of psychoanalysis, but it was in America that the strongest alliance was forged. Thus two distinct camps emerged: those whose primary identity was psychoanalytic, determined to preserve the legacy of Freud, and those whose primary identity was psychiatric, determined to take from psychoanalysis whatever it could in the service of developing effective forms of psychotherapy (Hale, 1995; Eisold, 1998). There was superficial agreement between these camps on such issues as "lay analysis," that is, maintaining the medical monopoly, but the underlying tension repeatedly manifested itself around this issue of psychotherapy.

Interestingly, the pressure to modify or adapt psychoanalysis toward psychotherapeutic ends was spearheaded in America before World War II by several early émigré analysts such as Alexander, Rado, Horney, and Fromm-Reichman, who clearly enjoyed their independence from the orthodox constraints of the institutes in Vienna and

Berlin where they had trained. They forged alliances with American psychiatrists such as Adolf Meyer, William Alanson White, Harry Stack Sullivan, Dexter Bullard, and the Menninger brothers in order to develop new approaches to the treatment of mental disorders. On the other side of the conflict were the second generation of American analysts, who went to Europe precisely to get the orthodox training unavailable in America, psychiatrists such as Kubie, Hendricks, and Lewin. Later they formed a strong alliance with the second wave of more conservative émigré analysts, fleeing the Nazis, who sought to recreate in America the orthodox and authoritarian institutions they had lost. The tensions between these two camps led to a series of conflicts and schisms (Eisold, 1998; Chapter 2 in this volume) centering on the New York Institute during the war, as a result of which that institute gradually emerged as the center of a new orthodoxy in the form of ego psychology. The deviants went elsewhere. It was after the war, however, that the tensions erupted into prolonged open conflict, when the "condition" that Freud foresaw in 1918 finally came to pass.

In 1946, William Menninger, former chief psychiatrist of the U.S. Army and newly elected president of the American Psychoanalytic Association, proposed that membership be opened to interested physicians and social scientists and that training programs be established for psychiatrists in psychoanalytic applications of psychotherapy. He argued that the immense need for psychological help in the postwar population could only be met if some of the resources of psychoanalysis could be bent to this task. Meeting the need required shifting the stress from the "psychoanalyst per se" to the "psychoanalytically oriented psychiatrist" (Hale, 1995, p. 212). Menninger, with his impressive army experience as well as experience in his family's clinic, was concerned with the practical issue of meeting a social need. But the association, swayed by the opposition of Hendricks and Lewin, voted down his proposals, holding to a narrower and more exclusive vision of psychoanalysis as a separate discipline in its own right. Indeed, the American Psychoanalytic Association at that meeting voted to make membership requirements more stringent.

The same year, the association also approved Rado's application for a new institute affiliated with Columbia University's medical school, after having denied it several years earlier. The nucleus of this group, which had formed at the New York Institute at the time Rado was removed as director of training (at about the time Horney was stripped of her faculty role), looked for greater academic freedom and opportunities for research, which they believed could only be found in a medical school setting, apart from the growing orthodoxy and conservatism of institutes increasingly dominated by the new émigré analysts. This was something of a victory for the liberal psychiatrists. As David Levy put it on the tenth anniversary of the Columbia Institute: its founding was a "protest against authoritarianism in science" (Hale, 1995, p. 218).

Also in 1946, Alexander and French published *Psychoanalytic Psychotherapy*, the book that became infamous for proposing the "corrective emotional experience." The outpouring of discussion and debate this produced was clearly less about their specific clinical suggestion than it was about their commitment to psychotherapy and their willingness to consider modifications of standard technique that promised therapeutic gains. The concept of the corrective emotional experience bore the brunt of the attack, but as Stone (1951) put it in his review, the Alexander-French position undermined the very structure of psychoanalysis as "a specific and unique therapy with its distinctive and constant 'ensemble'" (p. 218).

Stone's fear was warranted. In their introductory comments, Alexander and French noted that they had started out attempting "to differentiate sharply between 'standard' psychoanalysis and more flexible methods of psychotherapy." But they concluded: "in every case the same psychodynamic principles are applied for the purposes of therapy ... In other words, we are working with the same theories and techniques, the same kit of tools ... We therefore regard all of the work set forth in this book as 'psychoanalytic'" (Alexander & French, 1946, p. vii). The chief point of the book was what they called "the principle of flexibility," whereby the psychotherapist sought "to fit the therapy to the patient."

The book was like a shot fired across the bow of the orthodox establishment, and it was immediately counter-attacked. Jones, Eissler, Knight, Gitelson, Hartmann, Greenacre, Zetzel, Loewenstein, Gill, and Rangell, among others, weighed into the battle in addition to Stone. As Wallerstein has commented: "The intensity of the debate stirred up by Alexander's concept of the corrective emotional experience and the related technical precepts he introduced attest ... to the depth of the fear that they threatened the very heart of the psychoanalytic enterprise" (1995, p. 55).

That this was not entirely an overreaction is attested to by a report filed by a component institute of the American Psychoanalytic Association in the midst of the debate: "There is unanimous opinion in our group that no sharp demarcation can be drawn ... They suggest that all treatment utilizing the basic psychoanalytic psychodynamic concepts in an uncovering insight type of psychotherapy should be considered psychoanalytic therapy" (cited in Rangell, 1954b, p. 736). While this was distinctly a minority point of view within the association as a whole, it was clear that Alexander was not alone in suggesting that the boundary between psychoanalysis and psychotherapy be dismantled.

Eissler's (1953) prescription of standard technique, introducing the notion of "parameters," was the establishment's more considered response to Alexander's "flexibility." The psychoanalytic establishment gradually coalesced around a firm affirmation of correct technique, much as the American Psychoanalytic Association responded to Menninger's proposals for looser membership boundaries by making them more rigid. The ideological battle was joined.

This is the context in which the debate in America over psychotherapy emerged. The voices of Alexander and others concerned with finding various effective and flexible forms of psychotherapy that addressed a wide array of mental disorders were pitted against the orthodox insistence on correct technique and faithfulness to the legacy of Freud. The American Psychoanalytic Association organized a number of panels on the topic at several consecutive meetings (Zetzel, 1953; English, 1953; Rangall, 1954a; Ludwig, 1954; Chassell, 1955), as did individual institutes (see Wallerstein, 1995, pp. 72–87). Alexander and his allies, of course, lost this battle; and, eventually, even the Columbia Institute gravitated toward the mainstream (Cooper, 1986).

The need for various flexible forms of psychotherapy, however, did not dissipate. Psychiatry could not take the position that non-analyzable patients were beyond help or that those who could not afford analysis did not deserve it. Its professional integrity required it to search out effective treatments. In particular, those psychiatrists connected with residential treatment centers or involved with training residents were under continual pressure to find treatments that worked. On the other hand, the orthodox psychoanalysts, concerned with maintaining the purity of their Freudian heritage, defended it against the deviations that seemed continually to threaten.

Thus the discussion came to have an inevitably tendentious and prescriptive cast. Occasionally, a discussant would note that psychotherapy was not necessarily inferior to psychoanalysis, but usually it was assumed that psychoanalysis was the "pure gold" as opposed to the "dross" or the "copper" of psychotherapy, as Freud's 1918 metaphor came continually to be misread. Generally it was taken for granted that psychoanalysis was the treatment of choice, but this could not be demonstrated with experimental data. Over thirty years ago, Arlow, noting the repeated warnings he had heard on the Board of Professional Standards of the American Psychoanalytic Association "not to adulterate the pure gold of psychoanalysis with the dross of psychotherapy," acerbically commented: "In the light of the fact that three or four panels on the program of this Association could not agree on how to distinguish between psychoanalysis and psychotherapy, one can only marvel and envy those who possess so certainly the definitive word on so difficult a topic" (quoted in Kirsner, 2001, p. 120).

The strain of the conflict permeated the massive study undertaken at Menningers, beginning in 1954 at the height of the debate, reported in Wallerstein's (1986) *Forty-Two Lives in Treatment*. The tension between the desire to affirm traditional psychoanalytic methods and distinctions, on the one hand, and the integrity of clinicians and researchers to adapt to the needs of patients and accurately report results, on the other, runs like a leitmotif through the book. At the end, Wallerstein conscientiously acknowledges the "lesser than expected success of psychoanalytic approaches" (p. 727), and notes: "supportive therapy ... deserves far more respectful specification in all its forms and variants than has usually been accorded in the psychodynamic literature" (p. 730).

The persistent underlying disadvantage of psychoanalysis in the debate has been that it has not been able consistently to define its aims in a way that differentiates it from the aims of psychotherapy. Continuously bedeviled by theoretical disputes, it could not arrive at agreement. As Rangell put it in 1954, speaking of the work of the Committee on Evaluation of Psychoanalytic Therapy set up under Menninger's presidency: "In the [five] years of its work since then, it was never able to pass the initial and vexatious point of trying to arrive at some modicum of agreement as to exactly what constitutes psychoanalysis, psychoanalytic psychotherapy, and ... transitional forms" (Rangell, 1954b, p. 734). The difficulty has not gone away. More recently Gabbard (2001) noted in a special issue of *The Psychoanalytic Quarterly* devoted to "The Goals of Clinical Psychoanalysis" that there was a disturbing lack of agreement among the contributors, adding: "we had better have some idea of which outcomes are unique to analysis if we are to retain credibility" (p. 188).

Psychotherapy clearly has the upper hand here, with its simple and unambiguous goal of relieving psychological distress. As Schlesinger is reported to have said: "the (external) question that challenges psychoanalytic psychotherapy is, 'Are we getting anywhere?' rather than the (internal) question posed to psychoanalysis, 'Are we getting it right?'" (Wallerstein, 1995, p. 147). Almost certainly he did not mean this as a criticism of psychoanalysis. But his statement does imply that psychoanalysis has been constrained by the rules and prescriptions derived from its theoretical base.

The repetitive and predictable quality of the discussions and debates on this topic over the years suggests strongly that we are in the presence of a "social defense" (Jacques, 1955; Menzies, 1967), an unconscious, collectively elaborated effort to keep anxiety at bay. Persistently and rigidly, the community of mainstream psychoanalysts split the two entities apart, maintaining "complacent certainties" about a distinction that could not adequately be justified. As Wallerstein suggested, beneath this debate is the fear that psychoanalysis ultimately cannot sustain its privileged differentiation from psychiatry or, in today's world, the larger industry of mental health. One by one, most of those who took up the issue in the past have modified their stance, become more conciliatory, or simply retreated into silence. What Freud feared has come to pass.

Perhaps, now, the only prescription that it is possible to enforce is the rule of frequency, three, four, or five times a week. There is virtually no research legitimizing the rules of frequency, and few serious thinkers can be comfortable taking refuge behind the barrier of such an arbitrary seeming regulation. Sensing this, perhaps, our organizations are having difficulty compromising on this point.

The Current Scene

In the postwar years, when the American Psychoanalytic Association rejected Menninger's call to train psychiatrists in psychotherapy, the demand for psychoanalysis was rising. The elitist alternative was a viable option for the profession. But today, most candidates cannot look forward to careers as analysts, that is, with practices of patients who come three, four, or five times weekly, and that has profoundly affected the course of the debate.

Hard facts about the decline of psychoanalytic treatments are difficult to come by, but the trend is unmistakable. Informal surveys suggest that most analysts today have between one and two patients in psychoanalysis; Newell Fischer, former President of the American Psychoanalytic Association, estimates that between 40 and 50 percent of analysts in the association have no analytic cases at all (2004, personal communication). According to a task force established by the International Psychoanalytic Association, candidates no longer seek training in the numbers or with the competitive avidity of the past (RHDC, 1995); in 2001, 65 candidates entered training in the institutes of the American Psychoanalytic Association, down from an average of 116 the previous three years (Fischer, 2002a), and way down from previous years. Professional organizations face aging members and fewer applicants (Fischer, 2002a).

Today, departments of psychiatry in medical schools turn out few psychiatrists interested in pursuing the arduous additional training that psychoanalytic careers require. Professorships and department chairs, once almost uniformly filled by psychoanalysts at the most prestigious medical schools, are now more often occupied by its critics. In psychology, an increasingly small percentage of graduate programs teach psychoanalytic theories to aspiring psychologists, and few graduate students identify themselves as having a psychoanalytic orientation (Norcross, Karg, & Prochaska, 1997). As Bornstein recently put it: "Psychoanalysis is now on the fringe of scientific psychology, accepted by few and ignored by many" (2001, p. 5).

Many psychotherapists, meanwhile, more securely established in our culture, increasingly disparage psychoanalysis. A recent marketing survey initiated by the American Psychoanalytic Association found that groups composed of mental health professionals – psychiatrists, psychologists, and social workers – associated "psychoanalysis" to words like "rigid," "restrictive," "time-consuming," "expensive." Psychoanalysts were seen as "passive," "intellectualized," "uninvolved." Other associations to psychoanalysis were "cult-like," "secretive," "authoritarian," "esoteric." But the most disturbing feature of these reports was that no one was inclined to recommend it (Zacharias, 2002; Fischer, 2002b).

But though the numbers of candidates are decreasing, many still do come for training, partly because psychoanalytic training continues to be immensely useful to a dynamically oriented therapist, partly because of the continuing prestige of psychoanalysis in some quarters of the mental health industry, and partly because of the lure of the old careers, now curtailed but not entirely gone by any means. Moreover, besides these practical motivations, psychoanalysis retains an intellectual excitement and a spirit of discovery that it is lacking in more contemporary "cook book" approaches to psychotherapy. Creative minds are drawn to the opportunities it provides for complex, layered, and challenging thinking.

But psychoanalytic institutions, by and large, have not been set up to adapt and change. On the contrary, they are largely closed systems, focused inwardly on maintaining standards, conveying established theories and practices, and thus duplicating themselves. In a period of expansion, they are able to become more exclusive. The hierarchy that ensures control has an easier time recruiting enthusiastic acolytes, maintaining conformity, and guaranteeing its own power. These tendencies in the psychoanalytic training system have been repeatedly commented upon over the years, to little effect (see, for example, Balint, 1948, 1954; Rickman, 1951; Bibring, 1954; Thompson, 1958; Greenacre, 1966; Arlow, 1972; Orgel, 1978, 1990; Kernberg, 1986, 1996).

In the past, the idealization and awe, if not fear, inspired in candidates by their training and supervising analysts pervaded the governing structures of our institutes as well as social relations around them. Decisions about promotions were often made secretly and without explicit criteria. The senior members of institutes were invested with an aura of generalized competence and wisdom and entrusted with ethical, administrative, and financial responsibilities, often beyond their specific competencies as analysts. The other side of this idealization and presumption of wisdom, psychoanalysts know only too well, is covert hostility and contempt. These tensions have contributed significantly to the rigidity of institutes and their susceptibility to schism (Eisold, 1994; Chapter 4 in this volume), as is the case in any authoritarian system. Nonetheless, training institutes have been able to function because, until recently, there has been enough work for everyone. Those who did not make it to the top still enjoyed significant prestige as well as access to substantial analytic practices.

In the emerging new hierarchy, however, fewer and fewer actually practice long-term psychoanalysis characterized by frequent sessions. Those managing the training system can hope to analyze candidates in training; the rest will be practicing primarily psychotherapy. Thus the continuing debate about psychotherapy is now about the actual careers that are available to the vast majority of current candidates, the more and less privileged forms of work they can hope for. But everyone is affected by the tensions and strains of these changes: the candidates, the senior faculty, and the administration of institutes and professional associations.

Perhaps the most remarkable fact in the face of this situation is how infrequently it is acknowledged and what little effort is made to adapt the training of candidates to this changing reality. There is little attention paid in training to the problems of shorter or less frequent treatments or adapting standard analytic concepts or techniques to the conditions under which graduates will actually work.

Some institutes have taken the step of setting up separate psychotherapy training programs. This has the advantage of recruiting from a wider pool, appealing to those potential applicants seeking more training but currently ineligible for it or unwilling to make the commitment to full analytic training while sidestepping the objections of current candidates and recent graduates to having their own training "diluted" or "compromised." These programs are often being justified on the additional grounds that they may attract students who will want to go on for full analytic training. But it remains to be seen if the institutes taking this step will succeed in convincing applicants that their psychotherapy programs are serious good-faith efforts, on a par with their analytic programs, or if the institutes themselves will be able to keep up the necessary level of commitment to both kinds of programs for them to succeed without generating excessive internal tension and conflict.

Even if this strategy works, it still leaves analytic candidates without help in preparing for their psychotherapeutic careers. In a recent chapter on once weekly psychotherapy, Coles speculates that "there may be therapists, like myself, whose thinking has been muddled by ignorance and prejudice," believing "that more intensive work was more effective … and therefore to become a respected therapist I had to show that I was working with most patients at least three times a week" (2001, pp. 50–1). Noting a number of differences stemming from frequency that she has become aware of over the years of her practice, she has argued cogently: "it is not enough to assume that once-a-week work can be done if one has lain on the couch for four or five times a week. It demeans the once-a-week patient and diminishes the therapist" (p. 61).

On the other hand, candidates themselves are often conservative on this issue, if not silent, fearing the dilution of their training or the lessening of their status. Supplementing psychoanalytic training with attention to psychotherapy can seem to undermine the historic promise of psychoanalytic careers. Similarly, the temptation institutes face of opening training to candidates of lesser status in the mental health professions threatens current candidates with the loss of the status they have worked hard to win.

A second set of problems affects senior faculty. Institutes, once pathways to prestigious and lucrative careers, have less to offer those upon whose labor they rely for teaching and management. Increasingly, senior faculty shy away from assuming responsibility and some even avoid the tasks of analyzing and supervising candidates because of the lower fees they are often required to charge. Far more troubling, under these conditions, it is becoming more and more difficult to induce senior members to take on the increasingly onerous burdens of leadership (Dick Fox, personal communication, 2004).

From the perspective of the younger generation, the seniors are vulnerable to the charge of having failed in their guardianship of the profession, a charge that sometimes takes the form of a grudging recognition of their less vulnerable position. The senior analysts for their part often note that candidates are "not what they used to be." Moreover, training and supervising analysts are reluctant to change the system by adapting to the social and demographic changes that are occurring because that would lay them open to the charge of further undermining the profession of which they are guardians. It is not difficult to see how this situation contributes to a pervasive sense of demoralization as each side, refraining from blaming the other but stalemated in talking about the limited options they face, can feel increasingly disengaged.

As a result, fewer graduates appear to seek the forms of higher certification that professional organizations offer, and some institutes are beginning to question the value of continuing to implement them. In addition, there is a leakage of membership from our graduate societies and professional organizations. Our institutional leaders, often preoccupied with the effort of putting out local fires, which frequently derive from these underlying tensions, as well as the immediate survival issues of recruitment and fund raising, are also hampered by a lack of experience in managing such complex, tension-ridden enterprises. In the days when institutes could simply continue on in traditional ways, the minimal skills required to manage them were relatively easy to absorb. But the problems facing institutes and professional associations today require a sophistication about groups and systems that traditional psychoanalytic training does not provide.

One positive outcome of this situation is that, increasingly, institutes have sought consultation to cope with their difficulties, bringing in outsiders with more knowledge about management as well as greater detachment from the specific issues affecting particular institutes (see Maccoby, 2004). Paralleling the role of the analyst with an analysand, consultants can not only offer insights and observations to clarify disputed issues, but also help to create a reflective space allowing institutes to step back from their own internal conflicts.

Meanwhile, there are serious issues about psychotherapy in need of clarification. The impossibility of establishing a clear and firm boundary between psychoanalysis and psychotherapy does not mean that there are no differences in the effects of various techniques and strategies, or variations to consider with particular patients or under different circumstances. Clearly, different frequencies of treatment have different effects, on the therapist as well as on the patient, and different mental disorders may ideally benefit from differences in intensity. The use of the couch has received only impressionistic commentary, while the question of strict adherence to the analytic frame, though arousing much discussion and controversy, needs far more systematic study than it has received. It has been discussed to be sure, and certainly many practitioners have learned a great deal about how to vary these factors in their work, but a climate of ideological conflict has made it difficult to approach these issues in a dispassionate manner.

This goes for the "intrinsic" issues as well: the focus on transference, regression, free association, abstinence, and so forth. So many traditional concepts are so linked to specific theories that they are difficult to operationalize; indeed, it has seemed at times that, as theoretical winds shift, certain clinical phenomena disappear from view. Clearly, it would be useful to try to delineate such concepts more sharply and to study when and where they are useful. Indeed, it might even be possible to understand them better if they could be discussed free from the preoccupation of which technique belongs to which modality.

The Situation Elsewhere

This discussion has focused on the situation in the United States, but the relevance of these issues is worldwide. Different political, cultural, and historical situations have produced wide variations in the institutional life of psychoanalysis, and yet these issues have affected our institutes and professional organizations to some degree everywhere.

As psychiatrist-psychoanalysts throughout the world brought psychoanalysis into their psychotherapeutic practices, they often felt the strain between their psychoanalytic identities, based on the rules and the codes of their psychoanalytic professional associations, and their medical identities, based on their ties to their medical associations, their patients, and the various organizations representing patients. Moreover, hospitals and clinics, insurance companies, and government agencies, when involved, tend to insist on treatments that are demonstrably effective, that relieve suffering, regardless of how pure or venerable the methods used in achieving that goal may be. Psychoanalysts and psychotherapists not medically trained will feel this differently, but the underlying tension is still there so long as psychoanalysis and psychotherapy are viewed as medical procedures, aimed at treating mental illness.

In Germany, for example, where psychoanalysis has enjoyed an unprecedented degree of official recognition since 1967, when coverage for psychoanalysis was first included in health insurance plans, state control over the provision of psychotherapy benefits has gradually led to an erosion of the status and security of psychoanalysis as an autonomous profession. At first, other forms of psychotherapy, such as behavioral treatments, were included in the plans. Then, in 1991, undermining a long-standing compromise, patients were restricted in applying their benefits to four-times-weekly treatments, because the benefits of such frequency lacked empirical evidence. Danckwardt and Gattig (1998) noted: "health care systems regulated by the state tend to stabilize and ossify in rigid systems of regulation. Ideological distortions have again and again imposed an additional burden on the necessary debate between the parties." Bell (2001) concluded, more harshly, that today: "the standard psychoanalytic procedure is not possible in the health service context. Only psychoanalytic psychotherapy is possible" (p. 14).

This situation has exacerbated long-simmering tensions between the DPV (Deutsche Psychoanalytische Vereinigung), which is recognized by the IPA, and therefore obliged to hold to its four-times-weekly standard, and the DPG (Deutsche Psychoanalytische Gesellschaft), not recognized by the IPA, and which has held to a lesser frequency, more in line with the new regulations (Cremerius, 1999). But, perhaps more important, according to Cremerius: additional new "quasi-state training regulations define the training institute's curricula – including those of the DPV. The DPV institutes have to offer the following contents in training, though the IPA states they are 'foreign to analysis' ... the psychology of learning, group and family psycho-dynamics, theory and methods for short courses of therapy, psychotherapy, behavioral therapy, group psychotherapy and Balint groups, as well as psychological testing" (1999, p. 26).

Psychoanalytic training institutes have the option of rejecting such regulations, of course, and operating outside the established health care system. But that puts them at a disadvantage with patients who have come to expect or who may need to use their insurance benefits, and it increasingly puts their graduates at risk of lacking the competitive advantage of training in the range of psychotherapeutic modalities that other practitioners will have. The longer-range risk is that those providing treatments lacking evidence of efficacy will lose their state licenses. Kutter put it mildly when he wrote: "it was overlooked that the psychotherapy agreements gave the medical authorities influence on the psychoanalytical process; for example on its frequency and duration" (1992, p. 121). Korner's view is more dire: "To the extent that we can foresee the future today, incorporation into the German Act on Psychotherapy and the regulations for specialist doctors will lead to the profession of the psychoanalyst disappearing as a professional title" (1999, p. 101).

There are other effects of this primary orientation to health care in Germany. Kurzweil (1989) noted that, "therapy appears to have gained momentum at the expense of research" (p. 215). More recently, Kachele and Richter (1999) have agreed: "the development of psychoanalysis has been largely hampered by the situation in the psychoanalytic institutes," which have failed "to maintain the inseparable bond between therapy and research" (p. 59). Here as elsewhere, the pressure of clinical service tends to absorb resources.

Within institutes, the political and social orientation of psychoanalysis has been neglected as well, a situation that has elicited more comment and controversy in Germany perhaps than elsewhere, given the fact that memories of collaboration and the Holocaust are so pervasive and, indeed, so implicated in the institutional revival of psychoanalysis in the postwar era (see Goggin & Goggin, 2001). "The 'social critics' would like to apply the lever of psychoanalysis to society, whereas the 'therapists' see the challenge of their work primarily in the analysis of the psyche of the individual" (Kutter, 1992, p. 124). But in this divide, the therapists clearly have the upper hand. As a result of this trend, no doubt, the German membership in the IPA has grown to the point where it is second only to that of the United States. Research and social applications, on the other hand, have been conducted largely outside psychoanalytic institutes.

The official recognition of psychoanalysis in Germany in 1967 was a major achievement, a milestone of acceptance. But it does seem, in retrospect, that this began a process that contributes to the present beleaguered stance of psychoanalysis as a separate discipline. From the medical point of view, no doubt, psychotherapy has been enriched by its connection with psychoanalysis, and many if not most clinical psychoanalysts have profited from their roles as psychotherapists under the health care system. Moreover, it is at least arguable that the population has benefited from the diversification of mental health services that have become available.

But traditional psychoanalysis is on the defensive. The German experience illustrates that if psychoanalysis is primarily a treatment for disorders of mental health – in Freud's terms, a "handmaiden of psychiatry" – it will inevitably be subject to the expectations, standards, and controls that increasingly govern medicine. Kurzweil has put it somewhat more ominously, no doubt mindful of the loss of the critical spirit that can also be a feature of this ambiguous success: "the reimbursement policies mandated by the German government have been functioning as a benign big brother" (1989, p. 313).

In England, the links between psychoanalysis and psychiatry have not proven so decisive. Though Jones worked hard to retain psychoanalysis as a medical specialty in the 1920s and 1930s, opposing Freud's position on lay analysis as much as his loyalty allowed, in the post-World War II era that issue subsided. The British Psychoanalytical Society did not seek to play a role as a provider of mental health services to meet an expanding need. As in the American mainstream, it maintained a distinctly elitist position. Indeed, throughout the wartime "controversial discussions," both sides insisted on the disinterested "scientific" nature of psychoanalysis, its value as a method in the search for truth rather than as a treatment for neuroses (King & Steiner, 1991).

The role of applying psychoanalysis to a larger social need largely fell to the Tavistock Institute, viewed by Jones and Glover as the "poor relation" of the British Society (Rayner, 1991, p. 267). Many psychiatrist-analysts, returning from their wartime experience, found there an institution eager to apply their new ideas to the burgeoning social need for psychotherapy, group and marital psychotherapy, as well as other applications of psychodynamic thinking. The Tavistock Institute joined the National Health Service; the British Society did not. There the divide was institutionalized, though increasingly analysts could move back and forth between the two institutions (see King & Holder, 1992).

Other institutions responded to the need to provide various forms of psychotherapy and relevant training programs: the Cassel Hospital, the Portman Clinic, the British Association of Psychotherapists (founded in 1951), the London Centre for Psychotherapy, the Lincoln Institute, and others. The British Psychoanalytical Society was thus freed from pressure to modify its position outside the NHS and respond to this social need; it could maintain its single-minded commitment to classical psychoanalysis. Many of the newer programs and services sought out its graduates to staff its programs and to supervise its trainees. Some of them, in fact, require that their trainees be supervised only by "psychoanalysts," meaning graduates of the British Society, as no one else in the UK is entitled to call him or herself a "psychoanalyst."

Thus a society-wide caste system has emerged in Great Britain with many obvious as well as subtle effects. Among the more obvious consequences of this system is that training to become a "psychoanalyst" is simply unavailable outside London. Those in Scotland, for example, who train at the Scottish Institute for Human Relations have no choice but to accept the lesser designation of "psychotherapist." Experienced and competent as they may be, their lack of access to properly trained "psychoanalysts" and analytic supervisors ensures their lesser status. Moreover, those who train at the various psychotherapy courses available in London requiring supervision by "psychoanalysts" could not until recently aspire to become supervisors at their own institutions; those positions most often are still occupied by outsiders, a form of professional colonialism that appears to have effects on graduates, who tend to feel second class.

Another effect: the British Society, as a result of its status, has little incentive to modify its programs or procedures. Thus it can hold to the "strictest" five-times-weekly standards, despite the difficulty it experiences in finding cases for candidates; and it can be equally strict in its demands upon and responses to candidates, though the pool of applicants is diminishing. While high standards do have some marketing appeal, it remains to be seen if it will provide immunity from the worldwide decline in the numbers of psychoanalytic candidates, patients, and training cases (see RHDC, 1995).

One of the more subtle effects of this system is a pervasive sense of inadequacy among those who have the "lesser" trainings. Coles (2001), for example, cited above, was speaking of her experience as a graduate of the Lincoln Institute in London. Though she wrote of being "muddled by ignorance and prejudice," appearing to blame herself for her confusion and sense of inadequacy, it is clear she is a product of the system that trained her. The idea that to "become a respected therapist" she had to show that she "was working with most patients at least three times a week" clearly derived from the caste system she was embedded in.

It may well be that, in England, the strength of the social class system makes such distinctions easier to accept. Working under foreign masters, subject to external rules, tends to make one a harsh judge of oneself and others, if not, alternatively, rebellious. There are a number of other training programs in the UK spread throughout the country, however, developed by a Joint Committee of Higher Psychiatric Training, programs that have a strong if not exclusive psychoanalytic influence. Since, as Pines (1999) has observed, "very few analysts could be persuaded to leave London to work in the provinces" (pp. 19–20), such programs may be freer from self-deprecating tendencies.

Identifying with the aggressor is by no means a purely English trait. Outside the UK, those who have had psychotherapy training apart from the training systems of psychoanalysis may not suffer as intensely from a sense of inferiority. They may feel that psychoanalytic training is valuable and useful, perhaps even superior, but if they have not been identified with the "dross" of psychotherapy, they need not judge themselves for not being better than they are.

Meanwhile, in England, increasing government involvement in the provision of psychotherapeutic services appears to be intensifying this divide. According to Pines: "Psychotherapists are now having to audit their work and attempt to show they are efficient in their administration and efficacious in their work." According to Pines, "The Tavistock Clinic is leading the way in setting up comprehensive audit programmes within all its departments" (1999, p. 24). Such audits will not only increasingly satisfy the government and consumers but can also help therapists assess the benefits of their work. Psychoanalysis, so far, stands apart from this development, though recent efforts by the government to regulate the use of the term "psychoanalyst" may force greater involvement (Casement, 2004).

In retrospect, comparing developments in Germany and the UK suggests that neither pathway solves the problem of psychotherapy for psychoanalysis. Becoming part of the health system, as in Germany, leads to increasing governmental regulation and interference, compromising the ability of the psychoanalytic profession to set its own standards. On the other hand, maintaining a more elite apartness, as in the UK, does not prevent the increasing marginalization of psychoanalysis, while it also produces its own pervasive discontents. These results are far from conclusive, but they suggest that there is no easy escape from the dilemmas of the uneasy relationship between psychoanalysis and psychotherapy.

The Future of Dynamic Psychotherapy

For psychoanalysis, psychotherapy has come to appear as the powerful threat that could absorb and annihilate its distinctive features. But even if psychoanalysis could disentangle itself from the professional project that has embedded it in the specific concerns of mental health, psychotherapy will continue to turn to it for insight and guidance. Conversely, psychoanalysis will need psychotherapy, for sure, as it will be hard to imagine it without patients and without treatments for mental disorders.

For that reason alone, psychoanalysts will inevitably become more alarmed over the precarious future of dynamic psychotherapy. There are many reasons for this threat: An increasingly competitive culture that places a premium on immediate results, the development of other, simpler approaches, and a spiraling crisis in health care cost that have brought about the draconian remedies of managed care.

These profound pressures have already moved dynamic psychiatry to a crisis point. As Luhrmann, a medical anthropologist, has observed in her recent study of psychiatry in the United States: "Faced with the fear that psychiatric care would not be reimbursed, many psychiatrists, psychiatric lobbies, and patient lobbies ... have argued that psychiatric illness is a medical disease like any other and deserves equal coverage or 'parity.'" But, she adds, "as the debate continues, it encourages psychiatrists and nonpsychiatrists to simplify the murky complexity of psychiatric illness into a disease caused by simple biological dysfunction and best treated by simple pharmacological interventions" (Luhrmann, 2000, p. 250).

This trend is more advanced in treatments for the more seriously disturbed. Speaking of hospital residents in psychiatry, Luhrmann notes, "the more time they spend on the phone with insurance agents negotiating for a six-day admission to be extended to a nine-day because a patient is still suicidal, the more admissions interviews they need to do, the more discharge summaries they need to type, the less the ways of thought and experience of psychodynamic psychiatry fit it, the less they seem relevant or even real, and the more psychiatrists are willing to fall back on the ideological position that the cause and treatment of mental illness is biological and psychopharmacological." As Luhrmann summarizes: "it is not just managed care but managed care in the context of ideological tension that is turning psychodynamic psychiatry into a ghost" (2000, p. 238).

These developments help to account for the decline in psychodynamically oriented residency programs as well as the recent struggles and relocation of the Menninger Clinic and the closing of Chestnut Lodge. This is all the more unfortunate as it is just at this moment that a new vision of an integrated psychiatric treatment is emerging. As Gabbard has put it: "There is irony in the polarization of psychiatry into a biological and psychodynamic approach because we now stand on the threshold of embracing a sophisticated understanding of the interaction between the brain and the environment that can lead to truly integrative treatment strategies" (2000, p. 16).

Training in psychology is undergoing a similar decline of interest in psychoanalytic and psychodynamic ways of thinking. As Bornstein (2001) recently noted: "Treatment approaches that do not conform to today's emphasis on biochemical and time-limited cognitive-behavioral interventions are no longer valued in most graduate training programs" (p. 16). In 2000, only 4 percent of APA-approved graduate programs emphasized psychoanalysis, reflecting a steady decline, while 21 percent were behavioral, and 76 percent cognitive-behavioral (APA, 2000).

More immediately, most practitioners in the United States notice that in their private practices managed care has put increasing obstacles in the way of patient benefits, encouraging psychopharmacological interventions and behavioral treatments, subtly inducing doubt in patients about the value of the long-term talking treatments no longer underwritten. Many of us may not realize how widespread this trend is – or how dangerous to the future of psychodynamic treatments. The downward trend in reimbursements means, as well, that increasingly those less well trained are moving into psychotherapeutic roles, a trend exacerbated by the increasing tendency of analysts to refuse to participate in managed care. An interesting recent development is toward the licensing of "psychoanalysts" in the U.S., a category aimed to cover "lay analysts," those who are not already licensed providers of mental health services such as psychiatrists, psychologists, and social workers. It is too early to know how this trend will play out, and it is likely to be somewhat different in each state; but there is the danger – and the irony – that newly licensed "psychoanalysts" could be held to a lesser standard (see Appel, 2004).

In the long run, it seems implausible to think that dynamic psycho-therapy, including psychoanalysis, will be extinguished. Certainly in the large cities, where it has been well established, the profession, battered as it is, carries a great deal of internal conviction, a conviction shared by large numbers of patients who have directly experienced the help it can provide. The accumulated weight of anecdotal evidence is formidable.

But the kinds of statistical evidence that carries weight in hospitals and academic settings, that impresses insurance companies and government agencies, are still sadly lacking. There is some evidence of our effectiveness, to be sure, but a strong case for the positive outcomes for our brands of dynamic psychotherapy cannot now be made. As Cooper warned some years ago: "Even if we do not feel impelled by our scientific and theoretical curiosity, we might respond to the demands of a society that will not forever allow us to practice clinical psychoanalysis without evidence of its efficacy" (1984, p. 259).

It seems unlikely that the learning that has grown out of the clinical experience of psychoanalysts over the years could disappear entirely, but it may be that psychoanalysis as a distinct profession will become increasingly marginal. What it has discovered to be of enduring value might well survive, absorbed into the practice of psychotherapy; the rest could fade away. But it would be ironic if our response to the "condition" Freud foresaw at the end of World War I leads us into further internal strife and immobility.

The opportunity to develop and test the alloys of psychoanalysis may slip away.

References

Alexander, F. A., & French, T. M. (1946). *Psychoanalytic Therapy, Principles and Applications*. New York: Ronald Press.
American Psychological Association (2000). *Graduate Study in Psychology*. Washington, DC: APA.

78 Psychoanalytic History

Appel, P. (2004). The New York State psychoanalytic license: an historical perspective. In A. Casement (ed.), *Who Owns Psychoanalysis* (pp. 105–22). London: Karnac.

Arlow, J. A. (1972). Some dilemmas in psychoanalytic education. *Journal of the American Psychoanalytic Association* 20, 556–66.

Balint, M. (1948). On the psychoanalytic training system. *International Journal of Psychoanalysis* 29, 163–73.

Balint, M. (1954). Analytic training and training analysis. *International Journal of Psychoanalysis* 35, 157–62.

Bell, K. (2001). Psychoanalytic psychotherapy – legitimate or illegitimate offspring of psychoanalysis? In S. Frisch (ed.), *Psychoanalysis and Psychotherapy* (pp. 1–18). London: Karnac.

Bibring, G. (1954). The training analysis and its place in psychoanalytic training. *International Journal of Psychoanalysis* 35, 169–73.

Bornstein, R. F. (2001). The impending death of psychoanalysis. *Psychoanalytic Psychology* 18, 3–20.

Casement, A. (2004). The British Medical Association: report of the Psycho-Analysis Committee, 1929. In A. Casment (ed.), *Who Owns Psychoanalysis* (pp. 105–22). London: Karnac.

Chassell, J. O. (1955). Panel reporter, Psychoanalysis and Psychotherapy. *Journal of the American Psychoanalytic Association* 3, 528–33.

Coles, P. (2001). Some reflections on once-a-week psychotherapy. In S. Frisch (ed.), *Psychoanalysis and Psychotherapy* (pp. 49–61). London: Karnac.

Cooper, A. M. (1984). Psychoanalysis at one hundred: beginnings of maturity. *Journal of the American Psychoanalytic Association* 32, 245–68.

Cooper, A. (1986). Some limitations on therapeutic effectiveness: the "burn-out syndrome" in psychoanalysis. *Psychoanalytic Quarterly* 55, 576–98.

Cremerius, J. (1999). The future of psychoanalysis. In J. Cremerius (ed.), *The Future of Psychoanalysis* (pp. 3–38). London: Open Gate Press.

Danckworth, J., & Gattig, E. (1998). Opinion: psychoanalysis and the health insurances in Germany. *International Psychoanalysis* 7(2).

Eisold, K. (1994). The intolerance of diversity in psychoanalytic institutes. *International Journal of Psychoanalysis* 75, 785–800.

Eisold, K. (1998). The splitting of the New York Psychoanalytic and the construction of psychoanalytic authority. *International Journal of Psychoanalysis* 79, 871–85.

Eissler, K. (1953). The effect of the structure of the ego on psychoanalytic technique. *Journal of the American Psychoanalytic Association* 1, 104–43.

English, O. S. (1953). Panel reporter, The essentials of psychotherapy as viewed by the psychoanalyst. *Journal of the American Psychoanalytic Association* 1, 550–61.

Fischer, N. (2002a). The numbers tell the story. *The American Psychoanalyst* 36(4), 3, 8.

Fischer, N. (2002b). We have a date. *The American Psychoanalyst* 36(3), 3.

Freud, S. (1919). Lines of advances in psycho-analytic therapy. In J. Strachey (ed. and trans.), *The Standard Edition of the Complete Psychological Works of Sigmund Freud* (Vol. 17, pp. 159–68). London: Hogarth Press.

Freud, S. (1926). The question of lay analysis. In J. Strachey (ed. and trans.), *The Standard Edition of the Complete Psychological Works of Sigmund Freud* (Vol. 20, pp. 177–258). London: Hogarth Press.

Gabbard, G. O. (2000). *Psychodynamic Psychiatry in Clinical Practice.* Washington, DC: American Psychiatric Press.

Gabbard, G. (2001). Overview and commentary. *Psychoanalytic Quarterly* 70, 287–96.

Gill, M. (1984). Psychoanalysis and psychotherapy: a revision. *International Review of Psychoanalysis* 11, 161–79.

Goggin, J. E., & Goggin, E. B. (2001). *The Death of a "Jewish Science."* West Lafayette, ID: Purdue.

Greenacre, P. (1966). Problems of training analysis. *Psychoanalytic Quarterly* 35, 540–67.

Hale, N. G. Jr. (1995). *The Rise and Crisis of Psychoanalysis in the United States.* New York: Oxford University Press.

Jaques, E. (1955). Social systems as defense against persecutory and depressive anxiety. In M. Klein, P. Heimann, & R. Money-Kyrle (eds.), *New Directions in Psycho-analysis* (pp. 478–98). London: Tavistock Publications.

Kachele, H., & Richter, R. (1999). Germany and Austria. In S. de Schill & S. Lebovici (eds.), *The Challenge to Psychoanalysis and Psychotherapy* (pp. 48–63). London: Jessica Kingsley.

Kernberg, O. F. (1986). Institutional problems of psychoanalytic education. *Journal of the American Psychoanalytic Association* 34, 799–834.

Kernberg, O. F. (1996). Thirty methods to destroy the creativity of psycho-analytic candidates. *International Journal of Psychoanalysis* 77, 1031–40.

Kernberg, O. F. (1999). Psychoanalysis, psychoanalytic psychotherapy and supportive psychotherapy: contemporary controversies. *International Journal of Psychoanalysis* 80, 1075–91.

King, P., & Holder, A. (1992). "Great Britain." In *Psychoanalysis International*, Vol. 1 (pp. 150–72). Frankfurt: Frommann-Holzborg.

King, P., & Steiner, R. (eds.) (1991). *The Freud–Klein Controversies.* London: Routledge.

Kirsner, D. (2001). Off the radar screen. In S. Frisch (ed.), *Psychoanalysis and Psychotherapy* (pp. 111–21). London: Karnac.

Korner, J. (1999). The professionalization of the profession of psychoanalyst. In J. Cremerius (ed.), *The Future of Psychoanalysis* (pp. 87–101). London: Open Gate Press.

Kurzweil, E. (1989). *The Freudians: A Comparative Perspective.* New Haven: Yale University Press.

Kutter, P. (1992). "Germany." In *Psychoanalysis International*, Vol. 1 (pp. 114–36). Frankfurt: Frommann-Holzborg.

Ludwig, A. O. (1954). Panel reporter, Psychoanalysis and psychotherapy: dynamic criteria for treatment choice. *Journal of the American Psychoanalytic Association* 2, 346–50.

Luhrmann, T. M. (2000). *Of Two Minds: An Anthropologist Looks at American Psychiatry.* New York: Vintage Books.

Maccoby, M. (2004). Achieving good governance for psychoanalytic societies. *The American Psychoanalyst* 38(1), 9, 13.

Menzies, E. (1967). *The Functioning of Social Systems as Defense against Anxiety.* London: Tavistock Publications.

Norcross, J. C., Karg, R. S. et al. (1997). Clinical psychologists in the 1990s. *The Clinical Psychologist* 50, 4–9.

Orgel, S. (1978). Report from the seventh pre-Congress conference on training. *International Journal of Psychoanalysis* 59, 511–15.

Orgel, S. (1990). The future of psychoanalysis. *Psychoanalytic Quarterly* 59, 1–20.

Pines, M. (1999). Great Britain. In S. de Schill and S. Lebovici (eds.), *The Challenge to Psychoanalysis and Psychotherapy* (pp. 15–27). London: Jessica Kingsley.

Rangell, L. (1954a). Panel reporter, Psychoanalysis and dynamic psychotherapy – similarities and differences. *Journal of the American Psychoanalytic Association* 2, 152–66.

Rangell, L. (1954b). Similarities and differences between psychoanalysis and dynamic psychotherapy. *Journal of the American Psychoanalytic Association* 2, 734–44.

Rayner, E. (1991). *The Independent Mind in British Psychoanalysis.* New York: Jason Aronson.

Rieff, P. (1966). *The Triumph of the Therapeutic.* New York: Harper & Row.

RHDC (1995). Report from the House of Delegates Committee on "The Actual Crisis of Psychoanalysis: Challenges and Perspectives." An internal document, the International Psychoanalytic Association.

Rickman, J. (1951). Reflections on the function and organization of a psychoanalytical society. *International Journal of Psychoanalysis* 32, 218–37.

Stone, L. (1951). Psychoanalysis and brief psychotherapy. *Psychoanalytic Quarterly* 20, 215–36.

Thompson, C. (1958). A study of the emotional climate of psychoanalytic institutes. *Psychiatry* 21, 45–51.

Wallerstein, R. S. (1986). *Forty-Two Lives in Treatment*. New York: Guilford Press.

Wallerstein, R. S. (1995). *The Talking Cures: The Psychoanalyses and the Psychotherapies*. New Haven: Yale University Press.

Wallerstein, R. S. (2001). Foreword. In S. Frisch (ed.), *Psychoanalysis and Psychotherapy: The Controversies and the Future* (pp. xiii–xix). London: Karnac.

Zacharias, B. L. (2002). *Strategic Marketing Initiative*. Chicago: American Psychoanalytic Association.

Zetzel, E. R. (1953). Panel reporter, The traditional psychoanalytic technique and its variations. *Journal of the American Psychoanalytic Association* 1, 526–37.

Part Two

Organizational Analysis

Chapter Four

The Intolerance of Diversity in Psychoanalytic Institutes

[Originally published as The Intolerance of Diversity in Psychoanalytic Institutes, *The International Journal of Psychoanalysis*, vol. 75/4 (August 1994), pp. 785–800.]

In an account of her experience surveying different training methods in European institutes, Ann-Marie Sandler (1990) noted her shock at discovering her own prejudices: "I found myself wanting to deride those methods which were different from those I was accustomed to, and it took some time to overcome my culture shock and to accept, at an emotional level, the reality that there were outstanding analysts who have followed a different training route" (p. 49). She was led to this confrontation with herself by the task she had undertaken, to survey different approaches to training, and by the sponsor of the task, the IPA; as a member of the British Psychoanalytical Society, she might have been expected to provoke some skepticism had she found the British system of training the only fully adequate one. Most analysts, however, find little reason to confront their prejudices. The historical corollary of this intolerance is the remarkable history of schisms in psychoanalytic institutes, testifying to the difficulty of containing, much less accepting, theoretical differences within existing organizations.

It might be worthwhile at the start to remind ourselves of the extent of this schismatic tendency in the institutional history of psycho-analysis – quite apart from the more familiar history of personal "defections," the stories of Freud's ruptures with Adler, Stekel, Jung, Rank, and Ferenczi. In the 1940s in New York, two groups split off from the New York Psychoanalytic Society (see Frosch, 1990; Eckhardt, 1978). One group calling itself the Association for the Advancement of Psychoanalysis suffered two schisms in turn; one group defected to form the William Alanson White Institute and a second to form the Comprehensive Course in Psychoanalysis at the New York Medical College. The second group splitting off from the New York Psychoanalytic Society formed the Columbia Institute. At virtually the same time, the British Psychoanalytical Society narrowly averted a split by agreeing to form into virtually autonomous Kleinian and Freudian subgroups; subsequently a third or "Middle Group" separated out. In European institutes, schisms have occurred in Germany, Austria, France, Sweden, and Norway (Eckhardt, 1978). In France, the controversies surrounding Lacan produced at least four surviving institutes: the Freudian School, the Fourth Group, the Paris Institute, and the French Psychoanalytic Association (Turkle, 1978). Gitelson (1983), in addition, notes schisms that have occurred in Spain, Brazil, Mexico, Argentina, and Venezuela, as well as, in this country, in Washington/Baltimore, Philadelphia, Boston, Cleveland, and Los Angeles. Arlow (1972) refers to half a dozen splits in the American Psychoanalytic Association, as many narrowly averted splits, and adds to the census of splits in the International Psychoanalytic Association, Columbia and Australia.

Alongside the sketchy data about such splits, there is very little public description of them. A notable recent exception has been the publication of the documents surrounding the "controversial discussions" in the British Psychoanalytical Society (King & Steiner, 1991). In a rare officially published glimpse behind the scenes, Fleming (1976, p. 911) wrote of the conflict that irrupted in the Los Angeles Institute, describing "the unrelenting hostility and distrust among various groups and individuals, whatever their theoretical orientation" and adding, with some bewilderment: "There was no single discernible basis for the presence of so much bad feeling." Henry Murray, of the Boston Psychoanalytic Institute, is reported to have commented on "an atmosphere too charged with humorless hostility ... an assemblage of cultists, rigid in thought, armored against new ideas, and (in the case of 2 or 3) ruthlessly rivalrous for power" (Fine, 1979, p. 137).

Nor are schisms within institutes the only symptoms of this tendency: The International Psychoanalytic Association arrived at a standoff with the American Psychoanalytic Association in 1938 over the issue of lay analysis (Oberndorf, 1953). The Academy of Psychoanalysis was formed in opposition to the American Psychoanalytic Association (Millett, 1962). Division 39 of the American Psychological Association is torn by conflict between Sections I and V (Meisels, 1990).

This does not take into account the more hidden history of factionalism and intellectual intimidation that besets institutional life. The official histories tend to be self-congratulatory and blandly free of reference to ingrained conflict (see, for example, Pollock, 1978; Morris, 1992). But there are repeated references in the literature on training to the problems of excessive orthodoxy, idealization, and intimidation, at least in the lives of candidates (see Balint, 1948, 1954; Bibring, 1954; Thompson, 1958; Greenacre, 1966; Widlocher, 1978; Orgel, 1978, 1990; Hinshelwood, 1985; Kernberg, 1986; Steltzer, 1986; King & Steiner, 1991) – references that echo all too readily with one's personal experience of the field. And there are frequent references, as well, to "heretical" leaders (see, for example, Frattaroli, 1992).

Why is this so? Typically, such conflicts are attributed to ambitious or narcissistic personalities. But while the role of such personalities is no doubt significant, such an explanation fails to account for the power they are able to mobilize among the members of analytic institutes and for the ubiquity of the problem. A more sophisticated version of such an explanation argues that such schisms are part of the analytic tradition, originating in Freud's anxiety over his succession (Roustang, 1982; Levinson, 1990). But I believe that the dynamic answers to this question have to be sought in an understanding of the anxieties aroused by the ongoing collective professional activities of psychoanalysts. That is, whatever Freud's ambitions and motivations may have been, and however much he may have put his stamp upon the psychoanalytic movement, the study of his particular conflicts cannot adequately account for why ongoing institutions, 50 years after his death, are still beset by rancorous and destructive conflicts about fundamental "beliefs." I do not believe Freud's contribution to the problem is irrelevant, by any means, as I will try to show; but it has to be situated in the context of ongoing institutional life.

As Jaques (1955) and Menzies (1967) have pointed out, building on the pioneering work of Bion on groups (1959), organizations not only provide opportunities to work collectively, they also provide "social defenses," ways in which the anxieties of members are collusively and imperceptibly addressed. My argument in this paper is that intolerance of diverse points of view in psychoanalytic institutes – an intolerance that ranges from automatic dismissal of differences on the one hand to schismatic annihilation on the other – is a social defense. If we look at the anxieties aroused by the nature of the work psychoanalysts are engaged in and by the work relations they enter into, we can begin to tease apart the beliefs and behaviors that are task-related from those that are more purely defensive and end up undermining task performance.

I do not think there can be much disagreement about the dysfunctional nature of this intolerance for intellectual differences in analytic institutes: it strikes at the heart of whatever claims analysts may make for being scientific observers of human behavior or serious clinical practitioners. It is a defense, then, but against what anxieties?

There are three sets of answers to this question, I believe, three areas of conflict that feed into and mutually reinforce this social defense of intolerance. One has to do with the nature of analytic work: the anxieties analysts encounter in the course of their work that lead them to feel the need to know with certainty what they believe. A second has to with the particular nature of the analytic organization and community: because, by and large, analysts work outside and quasi-independently of the organizations to which they belong, yet within strong systems of lineage, their membership in those organizations arouses particular ambiguities and anxieties. The third area of conflict has to do with what we could call the culture of psychoanalysis, deeply ingrained attitudes and assumptions about the value and meaning of psychoanalysis and its relationship to the world. Each of these areas of conflict is in itself complex and contains multiple aspects. Moreover, they intersect with and reinforce each other. Taken together, I believe, they account for the profound persistence of this disabling symptom.

The Nature of the Work

Psychoanalysts practice alone, without the assistance or corroboration of colleagues. To be sure, they engage continually in relationships with their patients, but in those relationships they have the unique responsibility to maintain the professional boundaries of the relationship, often in the face of pressure from patients, and to represent the task

The Intolerance of Diversity in Institutes   89

of inquiry and understanding. Participants as they are, they are also always observers and managers.

In addition, analysts are subject to continual assaults on their emotional lives, assaults which they must learn to remain open to experiencing and understanding because the instruments with which they work are parts of themselves: their empathy, their countertransference, their understanding (Buechler, 1992). They cannot reduce their patients to symptomatic signs or diseased organs. Their work recalls to them how much is at stake in the lives of their patients. Nor can they work with the expectation of gratitude. As Anna Freud (1966) put it, the personality of the analyst is continually at risk.

Moreover, the phenomena they engage are complex and obscure. Perhaps more than any other professional, psychoanalysts must cultivate an exceptional degree of tolerance for ambiguity. Unable to rest content with their diagnoses, they must continually be willing to notice the fleeting evidence of what both they and their patients are wishing to elude. Nor can they be certain when their work has been successful, even when they feel gratified. It is little wonder that analysts as a professional group are prone to depression (Dreyfus, 1978) or "burnout" (Cooper, 1986).

Under those conditions of isolation, uncertainty, and stress, analysts turn to their theories. As Friedman (1988) has sympathetically and cogently demonstrated: "stress and theory go hand in hand ... There are many ways that a therapist can be thrown off balance, and every time that happens, some aspect of theory will be important to him" (pp. 89–90). Moreover, in the isolation of the consulting room, particular theories or beliefs provide lifelines, so to speak, back to the psychoanalysts' own analysts, supervisors, and teachers, linking him to a community of like-minded practitioners.

That link through his theory to the community that trained and supervised him helps to reinforce and sustain the analyst in his isolated and anxiety-ridden work. Every theory he turns to – either because it feels reliable and true or because it seems indispensable or required – came from his experience with a supervisor, teacher, or analyst. It is what he has internalized from his training. Thus the analyst's theory serves a dual purpose: it is an indispensable set of tools that helps him to maintain his balance in his work, as Friedman points out, and it is also an aspect of his analytic identity. The point here is that the balancing act Friedman (1988) so respectfully and appreciatively describes is profoundly affected by the flexibility and openness of the analyst's identity, and that in turn affects and is affected by the larger community with which the analyst finds his professional identification.

Schafer (1979) has spoken warmly of this aspect of analytic life, of the value of the "many ties to people who have been central to [our] training ... All these people and experiences exert a kind of imprinting effect ... constituted of feelings of gratitude, loyalty, identification, gratification, and idealization" (p. 350). While such comments are not at all uncommon in the ongoing activities of institutes, at anniversary celebrations, promotion and book parties, festschrifts and graduation ceremonies (the occasion that prompted Schafer's comments), they are rarely found in print. Far more frequently these same feelings are identified in the literature on training as dangerous signs of incomplete analysis, especially dangerous in the training analysis. Idealizing is usually seen as a defense against hostility, loyalty as an aspect of resistance or factionalism, gratification as a form of bribery, etc. At the extreme such unanalyzed feelings can lead to a sense of inauthenticity or, even, fraudulence.

This is not a mere matter of hypocrisy. On the one hand analysts, like others, value the support and encouragement they receive from their teachers and trainers (when they don't feel criticized or persecuted), feel gratitude and loyalty (when they are not resentful or competitive), and are often willing to forgive the shortcomings of their elders (when not scornful) – if they do not elevate them into virtues. On the other hand, they know the dangers. "It took me a good 10 years of full-time psychoanalytic practice to feel myself a psychoanalyst and to be able to accept patients without some degree of anxiety and guilt," wrote Klauber (1983), "and I know I am not alone in this." The new analyst, he added, "turns to his identification with his analyst and, beyond him, with Freud. Or rather to the analyst who functions partly by means of a creative identification, and partly as an introject, so that he may find himself on occasion repeating irrelevant interpretations to his patients 20 years later. For many years the younger psychoanalyst functions – or at any rate I functioned – in part with an analytical false self ... with an analytical false self struggling with a dying language" (p. 46).

Though many analysts might wish to shrug off such a statement by attributing Klauber's "problem" to a poor training analysis, his candor speaks to a real problem in the process by which an analyst's identity is formed and sustained: identifications with analysts and supervisors, introjections, feelings of loyalty and gratitude, idealizations – all help to sustain the analyst in the anxiety of his lonely work. They are defensive, to be sure, but they are also part of who he is and what he needs to remind himself he believes as he works. Only gradually is an analytic identity formed that feels comfortable and true (King, 1983; Buechler, 1988).

This duality defines a contradiction imbedded in the use of psychoanalytic theory: on the one hand, it serves the purpose of guiding the analyst's relationship with his patient, helping him to maintain his balance; on the other, it serves to sustain his relationship with his colleagues through the medium of his analytic identity. And that identity, in turn, as Ellenberger (1970) has pointed out, is linked to a "school" in the sense of the ancient Greco-Roman philosophical schools. Analysts are Freudian or Kleinian or Sullivanian, etc. in much the same way that ancient philosophers were Epicurean or Stoic or Pythagorian. Internalizing their training as part of their identities, their very mode of thinking is a reflection of their distinctive points of view as members of particular schools.

Such schools cut across the boundaries of most institutes, however, and result in subgroupings or factions to which members turn to find support or confirmation of their analytic identities. Moreover, other differences in orientation and technique, less identifiable to the outside world as an analytic school, develop within institutes; indeed, such development often usefully facilitates differentiation and stimulates dialogue. But as King (1983, p. 189) has pointed out, the risk is ever present that analysts may find a "pseudoidentity" via such subgroups: "If they are unable to feel 'I am a psychoanalyst who has done this on my own' at least they can say 'I am an analyst who belongs to this group.'" (See also Bollas, 1993.) And to the extent that analytic identities are vulnerable – either because of internal crises, external threats, or because they have never been firmly established – the potential exists for factions to form that become increasingly rigid, intolerant of compromise, and dependant upon having the negative attributes that define their difference located in another faction.

This is a situation that is inevitable, I believe, when identity is so closely linked to work and so much at risk because of the nature of the work. One finds similar dynamics – and often comparable virulence – in academic life. But for analysts this situation is particularly troubling because it threatens to expose a contradiction at the heart of their work and their identity: it potentially undermines the confidence they have in the impartiality and "objectivity" of their response to their patients. Reviewing the "controversial discussions" in the British Psychoanalytical Society during 1941–3 (King & Steiner, 1991, *passim*), for example, one is struck by how the participants on all sides stressed repeatedly the "scientific" nature of the issues and their professional role as "scientists." The use of "science" by them in support of their professional identities reflects the positivistic bias of the time, of course, as well as their allegiance to Freud. But the important point, I believe, is that they did not want to think of themselves as limited in their response to the clinical data by political issues.

What is really threatening to the professional identities of analysts is not that they are not scientists but that their analytic beliefs may prevent them from being fully responsive to the material presented by their patients. The issue is comparable to the one posed by countertransference: an unexamined bias on the part of the analyst that distorts and limits his capacity to respond fully to his patient. Analysts may joke about how the patients of Freudians turn out to have Freudian problems or Jungian analysts produce Jungian patients, and so on. But it is not a joke for the analyst who is struggling to grasp and make sense of deeply disturbing and painful clinical material to think that his allegiance to the analytic concepts of his particular school limits his awareness of his patient. Nor is it a joke to the analyst who tries to explain his work to the larger world.

We can see now more clearly how much is at stake for the analyst in believing his theories are fully adequate and true to the clinical data and, therefore, why he might well want to join in the social defense offered by his "school" or his faction of identifying competing theories as misleading or inadequate, and in doing so not even being able to grant them the status of reasonable alternatives. To the extent that he sustains the belief that the theories he and his particular colleagues are using in their work are more "true" or less "false" than those guiding others – more powerful, less defective or dangerously misleading, more recognized, less suspect, etc. – he has less cause for the always threatening anxieties of self-doubt, incompetence, and failure.

Each analyst's reliance upon and contribution to the social defense of intolerance varies in response to a variety of factors, such as his own insecurity or his loyalty to his analytic fathers. I doubt that without the other factors we have yet to explore that sustain the defense it would exist as powerfully as it does. But the defense is securely present and readily available to help stabilize him in his lonely and difficult work.

The Nature of Membership

A second set of answers has to do with the analyst's need to secure a place in the network of his colleagues. Some of this is obvious. For opportunities to supervise and teach, for referrals, for continuing professional self-esteem as well as financial security, analysts are dependent upon maintaining their standing in their professional communities. Public deviance from established practices and beliefs is risky. During training, obviously, candidates are closely scrutinized and evaluated; after becoming full-fledged analysts, this scrutiny becomes more subtle but no less important as selections are made to key teaching, supervisory, and administrative roles.

These are crucial factors in the life of any professional community, and it is easy to see how the existence of factions influencing such decisions and altering the balance of power will arouse the most powerful anxieties and stimulate the most extreme defenses. In examining the history of the split in the British Psychoanalytical Society, for example, it seems clear that the immediate stimulus for the crisis was the retirement of Ernest Jones from the presidency after years in which he had carefully balanced opposing factions; his successor, Glover, who was a virulent anti-Kleinian, threatened the existing pattern of assignments of candidates to training and supervising analysts, referrals, and promotions (King, 1991).

But in order to understand how such issues of power can become particularly explosive in analytic institutes, we need to explore what are, in effect, structural weaknesses peculiar to such organizations, weaknesses that derive, I believe, from the kind and quality of belonging that members experience.

To begin with, there is a well-known and much-discussed contradiction embedded in the very notion of analytic training as it is currently understood. From the 1920s, the training analysis has been viewed as the core requisite for analytic candidates (Balint, 1948) – and for very good reason. The discovery of transference and with it, of course, countertransference imposed an inescapable demand for training. But then the training analysis takes on a dual function. On the one hand, of course, it is simply an analysis. On the other hand, it is the analyst's passport to acceptance and certification, his means of proving himself ready and adequate to the task of analyzing others.

Until recently, it was accepted practice for training analysts to report to training committees on the progress of their analysands in training, despite a widespread uneasy sense that the practice compromised the analysis (Lifschutz, 1976; Wallerstein, 1978). Even in institutes that officially proscribe such communication, in an attempt to protect the integrity of the candidate's analysis, it has been demonstrated that compromising communication takes place through unofficial channels (Dulchin, 1982a, 1982b). It is a commonplace in the history of psychoanalysis to read reports of analysts who are told that their differences and disagreements with colleagues are signs they require further analysis. The point here is that analysts are always vulnerable in the eyes of their colleagues to the most intimate *ad hominum* arguments. Even their own analyses, in a sense, are not available to them as free explorations of their own dynamic conflicts.

Interestingly Freud (1921) himself adumbrated the potential of this issue in his discussion of group psychology. Arguing that groups are held together primarily by two factors in addition to libidinal bonds – a common object or leader who replaces the ego ideal of individual members and the identification of members with each other, an identification originating in their common allegiance to the leader – he stressed the essentially conservative and conforming nature of group life. Individual psychoanalysis in fostering a developmental process of differentiating ego and ego ideal as well as ego and object would work to dissolve such bonds. Establishing and sustaining a group, on the other hand, would require creating and reinforcing such bonds.

Glover (1943), in the midst of the "controversial discussions" of the British Psychoanalytical Society, pointed out that the candidate in training "has little opportunity of emancipating himself from the transference situation ... The analysis may stop but the Candidate remains in an extended or displaced analytic situation." For him, this was a sign that the training system had broken down. Balint (1948), surviving those same discussions, described his experience of candidates' "submissiveness to dogmatic and authoritative treatment without much protest and too respectful behavior" (p. 167). He attributed this to the tendency of candidates to introject their analysts into their super-egos with a consequent weakening of the ego – the group process Freud (1921) had described – a tendency that he saw fostered by the training system.

Thompson (1958), speaking of her experience at the White Institute and using a different theoretical orientation, makes virtually the same point about the effect of the ongoing "incestuous" power relationships between candidates and their analysts: "More than any other analytic patient, the candidate is faced with realistic difficulty in resolving his infantile dependency" (p. 49). Arlow (1972, p. 561) noted that "psychoanalytic training often comes to be experienced as a prolonged initiation rite." He added that anxiety propels the candidate into identifying with the aggressor; he "remodels" himself in the image of his community's ideal (p. 562). More recently, Kernberg (1986) pointed to the containment of the transferential "radioactivity" that is a by-product of analytic training: the multifaceted or "incestuous" nature of relationships in training institutes promotes a splitting process. Candidates and graduates preserve the idealization of their own analysts by joining the social defense of projecting deviance and "error" elsewhere into other institutes or schools. Thus they maintain not only a sense of personal security but also sustain their common belief in the privileged position of their own group.

Lacan took this point to its ultimate conclusion (Turkle, 1978): "What does it mean to have an organization of psychoanalysts and the certificate it confers – if not to indicate to whom one can go to find someone who will play the role of this subject who is presumed to know?" For him the training implications that followed from this required the "self-authorization" of the analyst. In essence, he argued, each analyst had to determine for himself – as Freud did – if and when he was to become an analyst at all.

Lacan's uncompromising logic does help us to see in its clearest form the contradictions that lie at the heart of analytic training: What is the purpose of the training analysis, therapy, or certification? And what is the reason for analytic authority, empowerment, or control? All of those cited above who have wrestled with these contradictions – Balint,

Glover, Thompson, Arlow, Kernberg – in one way or another have attempted to suggest ways of ameliorating the tensions this gives rise to.

The issue is, on the one hand, about the integrity of the analysis: is it for the candidate's personal benefit, or is it his ticket of admission into the profession? The deeper side of this issue is about the link between the candidate and his analyst: how fully is the candidate tied to his analyst? Is the potential for idealization and gratitude inherent in this relationship subversive of the analysis? Does it, in other words, tend to insure the dominance and control of the old guard at the expense of the analytic freedom of the candidates? This is the point that has been most frequently stressed in the literature. But there is another side to this that – to my knowledge – has never been noted: the threat posed to the institute by the intensity of the idealized relationships between the pairs of analysts and candidates. Can an organization that is composed essentially of intense pairing relationships not feel threatened by those pairs?

Bion (1959) made an observation about the particular significance of the pair in psychoanalysis that suggests how intractable the problem is for psychoanalysis. Noting that the emphasis upon sexuality in psychoanalysis corresponds to the "basic assumption" of pairing and the projection onto the pair of the group's sexual fantasies, he observed: "the individual cannot help being a member of a group even if his membership of it consists in behaving in such a way as to give reality to the idea that he does not belong to a group at all. In this respect the psychoanalytical situation is not 'individual psychology' but 'pair'" (p. 131).

Psychoanalysis, of course, is based upon the pair, and psychoanalytic training in its most prominent features takes place in pairs: the pair of the candidate and his analyst, the pairs of the candidate and his individual supervisors, and the pairs of the candidate with his control or training cases. To be sure, there are classes and meetings of the training committees, etc. But I think there is little doubt in the minds of most psychoanalysts that psychoanalysis is fundamentally about the encounter that takes place between two people. If we add to this the fact that in the overwhelming number of instances those encounters take place in the private consulting rooms of analysts and supervisors, not in the physical space of institutes, and that the financial arrangements for analysis and supervision are negotiated by the pair, though there may be institutional rules governing fees in some cases, we have a situation where it is all too easy to deny that the enterprise of psychoanalysis is a collective or group enterprise. Indeed, most institutes are part-time affairs, seldom paying their key officials anything close to a living wage.

The institutional consequences of the fact that psychoanalysts for the most part do not consider themselves located within their institutions when they conduct their most essential work are, I think, profound. The institution tends to become, in the minds of its members, sets of particular relationships and affiliations, not an enterprise in itself. Add to this the stress on lineage in psychoanalytic training, not merely the link to one's own analyst but to one's analyst's analyst, etc., a linking that can transcend institutional boundaries, we can begin to see how the lack of firm institutional boundaries around work can lead to ambiguity and institutional conflict. Latent conflicts, negative transferences, potential perceptions undermining idealizations or narcissistic distortions – all the psychological "radioactivity," in Kernberg's term, affecting the multiple pairing relationships of psychoanalysis – find fertile ground outside the pairs, within the loosely containing institution, and, even better, within other institutions yet more remote.

The effect upon institutes of these powerful centrifugal forces, paradoxically, I believe, has been the creation of massively "over-bounded" (Alderfer, 2011) organizational systems, systems with excessively impermeable boundaries, rigid hierarchies, and inflexible role and task assignments. Institutes show all the typical signs of such "overbounded" systems; they have strict and restrictive admissions criteria; they typically exhibit rigid hierarchical structures leading to tightly controlled decision-making processes; they insist on ideological purity, resist change, etc. " 'Overbounded' systems show *less* boundary permeability than is optimal for the system's relationship with its environment," Alderfer points out, and they face the threat of losing their capacity to respond to environmental changes. They tend to show unequivocal and uncompromising clarity about their goals, to exhibit highly centralized and monolithic authority relations, to restrict the free flow of information and inhibit criticism. "In overbounded systems people feel confined, constrained and restricted. Incumbents experience lack

98 Organizational Analysis

of creativity and stimulation, especially at lower levels in the organization where the full force of the organizational structure affects the individual" (1980, p. 272). Such systems, he adds, often show a typically positive balance of feelings, so long as survival is not threatened. But this is "partially the result of repressive forces within the system. The effect of a monolithic authority structure mutes … criticism and tends to direct negative affect outward rather than inward" (p. 274). Along somewhat similar lines, Rustin (1985) has applied Simmel's critique of secret societies to psychoanalytic institutions.

The description of the overbounded system is also consistent with the historic myths of psychoanalysis as a beleaguered and socially subversive movement. An organization that is established in opposition to established social values and that faces relentless hostility without and defection within has to develop strong and impermeable boundaries. It must defend itself at all costs; its very survival seems continually at stake.

But, I believe, the real danger against which the overbounded analytic systems are defending is not external or objective. It is the psychological power of the pair. The systems have to be rigid, confining, and authoritarian because the primary allegiances of its members are to the psychoanalytic pairs of which they are a part and to the lineages, the interlocking chains of pairs, of which they are descendants.

This is not to say that these pairs are, in fact, more real or more defining of the essence of psychoanalysis than are the organizations that give rise to them and to which in turn they report. On the contrary, I incline to Bion's view that "the individual cannot help being a member of a group." The odd thing is that the analyst, perhaps more than any other professional – particularly any other professional as dependent as analysts are upon training, professional development and recognition, referrals, etc. – can see himself "in such a way as to give reality to the idea that he does not belong to a group at all."

To understand this more fully, I believe, requires that we add to the defensive importance of the pair in psychoanalytic organizations a better understanding of some other anti-organizational aspects of psychoanalytic tradition and culture. But before going on to address that, I think we can see at this point more clearly how these dynamics of analytic organizations contribute to the social defense of intolerance. On the one hand, the very looseness of the felt tie to the organizational systems of psychoanalysis, the primacy of the involvement in the pair, generates greater ambivalence at best and resentment at worst about the constraints of organizational life; the organization is seen more easily as intrusive and becomes more readily the object of attack. At the same time, as one's own organization or faction is still needed as a source of recognition and support, other competing organizations or factions become targets for that displaced resentment. Moreover, the very sharpness and tightness of the boundaries that the organization sets up defensively to protect itself from the ambivalence of its members creates a clear boundary across which it becomes easier to project hostility and, of course, makes it more necessary that members find outlets for their hostility elsewhere than in their analytic factions or institutes.

Psychoanalytic Culture

There is, I think, a third set of factors embedded in generally unacknowledged aspects of psychoanalytic culture, a culture that tends to devalue the larger world to which it sees itself opposed and superior. Analysts often view the institutional world of business and government organizations, from which they have turned away in choosing this profession, with wary detachment if not contempt. Individually, they tend to adopt positions of superiority, even arrogance, toward those who do the work of management, even those who do their own administrative work. There is a certain privileged sense of immunity they feel from the ambition, envy, competition, and turbulence of the world. Collectively, they tend to exempt themselves from scrutiny and judgment, justifying authoritarian and secretive policies by virtue of their deeper insights or greater responsibilities; on the other hand, they feel victimized by those same practices.

Such attitudes and values originated with Freud, I believe, and are sustained by identifications and idealizations of him. For many years, Freud has been seen as a contemporary Copernicus, who shifted the center of the world, or Marx, who exposed the true basis of its ideals, or Einstein, who discovered its unifying principle. I don't mean to question the historic value of Freud's work, but I do mean to point out the impact of having such an heroic icon looming over the profession, an icon who described repeatedly his isolated opposition to the world.

"I understood that from now onwards I was one of those who have 'disturbed the sleep of the world'" (Freud, 1914). "I was completely isolated. In Vienna, I was shunned," he wrote of his early years. And later: "In Europe I felt as though I was despised" (Freud, 1925).

Freud's ambivalence toward the very institution he needed to establish as part of the world he scorned can be seen as the thread that runs through the early history of the psychoanalytic movement. In the early years he described his inward estrangement from the group he gathered around himself in Vienna: "I could not succeed in establishing among its members the friendly relations that ought to obtain between men who are all engaged upon the same difficult work; nor was I able to stifle the disputes about priority for which there were so many opportunities under these conditions of work in common" (Freud, 1914, p. 25). He suggests but does not embrace responsibility for what appears to be a bewildering curse. At another point he observed wearily, "to stir up contradiction and arouse bitterness is the inevitable fate of psychoanalysis" (p. 8). And later, justifying the choice of Jung as his successor: "I saw that there was a long road ahead, and I felt oppressed by the thought that the duty of being a leader should fall to me so late in life" (p. 43). He was 54 at this time, as Strachey notes.

His initial failure to establish Jung as his heir led to the creation of the Committee, "a band of brothers" (Grosskurth, 1991), as a means of controlling the burgeoning movement. At Freud's insistence, the Committee operated secretly, while the International Psychoanalytic Association and its congresses presented a more official public face to the world. But this attempt at control behind the scenes failed to prevent a series of defections following upon the earlier losses of Adler and Jung: Rank broke openly with Freud, Ferenczi was estranged at the time of his death, Jones built up a Kleinian faction in England.

Clearly Freud was well aware of the competition and hostility underlying such group arrangements. "Totem and Taboo" (1913) spells out clearly the problem of competition faced by the primal horde of brothers both among themselves and with the father. And it seems clear that the brothers/sons of psychoanalysis understood as well (Roustang, 1982). What I think was not understood in this collusion between the analytic sons and their father to control the movement from behind the scenes was how they enacted together an arrogant rejection of the

The Intolerance of Diversity in Institutes   101

larger world. The attempts of the sons to pair with the father and to secure for themselves a privileged position relegated the institutions they created and managed – the International as well as the local institutes – to a secondary status. The father's manipulation of his sons kept at bay the world that scorned him and which he scorned in return.

The dissolution of "the Committee" roughly coincided with the establishment of training policies through the International. The 1925 Bad Homburg Congress set up a committee to recommend and oversee training procedures for analytic institutes. At the same historical moment, Freud withdrew from public participation in institutional affairs. For some time he had held no official post in any of the psychoanalytic organizations, leaving that to his sons; from this point on he ceased attending the congresses. But the legacy had been established that would haunt the institutional life of psychoanalysis from then on: the true, uncompromising value of psychoanalysis was to be realized only on the "splendid isolation" (Freud, 1925, p. 22) of the analyst's lonely work; its institutional life was bound to be compromised, disappointing, corrupt, and successful only at the price of its own integrity. The message had been conveyed: Freud himself, the icon, had presided over only one failure after another in attempting to locate his contribution in the world.

This mythopoetic legacy derives additional force from the ways in which it resonates with actual practice. Psychoanalysis, of course, cultivates suspicion of avowed motives and self-reflection over action. It looks inward and backward, rather than outward and forward. Just as it seeks to uncover the illusions and fight the resistances of patients, it developed itself in opposition to prevailing institutions and social norms.

But the legacy of Freud's stance toward the world also resonates profoundly with important traditional practices and beliefs in psychoanalysis, which at this point have become stereotypes of orthodoxy – frequently more honored in the breach than actually observed, and certainly subject to substantial modification if not revision in many areas, yet still immediately recognized as hallmarks of traditional psychoanalytic thinking.

In traditional theory, for example, human behavior is not seen as grounded in social experience but rather in biological drives, drives that in their conflictful unfolding, their "vicissitudes," determine even the fate of civilization. Psychic reality, derivative of the drives, is distinct from social reality. In effect, Freud seeks to stand on a conceptual ground that exempts it from the influence of social forces.

Moreover, traditional theory parallels the hiddenness of this reality with the hiddenness of the analyst. A "blank screen," the analyst is urged to become invisible and, as a corollary to this, is instructed to become neutralized of the feelings and assumptions that govern the transference-ridden life of his patients.

Following from this is the assumption that analysts should be able to withstand conflict and temptation better than others. The training analyst, for example, as we have seen, should be able to withstand the pressure of seeking to convert his candidate/patient to his own analytic beliefs or should be free from the feelings that might cloud his judgment in reporting on his progress.

Traditional theory holds itself to a rigorous and uncompromising standard of scientific truth; symptomatic relief, cure, happiness are viewed as secondary goals, by-products. Patients may come for therapy, but the analyst is above all a scientist whose prime interest is studying human behavior. He is not to be swayed by the patient's needs or wants.

These stereotypical ideas have been significantly modified if not altered by most psychoanalysts in recent years. But my point is that they are of a piece with what I am trying to identify as a psychoanalytic *Weltanschauung* that places the analyst, in his own mind, apart from the world within which he lives and works. And I think it is no surprise that along with modifications of these stereotypical ideas in recent years has come a growing chorus of criticism, within the field, for its smug aloofness and indifference to critical reflection.

Earlier I noted the criticism that has been voiced about training practices. More recently and more broadly, Orgel (1990) noted the tendency in the profession to idealize and gloss over the errors of earlier generations of psychoanalytic leaders, including Freud, and pointed out their frequent narcissism, arrogance, and dogmatism, their insistence that they are above criticism, their aggressive behavior towards candidates, and their fomenting of dependent attachments.

At the same time, as Simon (1992) has recently noted, only lip service is paid to true scientific aims: "Our canons for use of evidence are sloppy and inconsistently applied, our commitment to serious empirical testing is weak. We rarely present our failures for communal discussion – we have no *Journal of Failed Cases*; only a few research-minded analysts are willing to survey the overall results of analytic treatment. We are prone to the undue influence of charismatic and persuasive leaders" (p. 966).

These criticisms from within the field derive in part certainly from the fact that psychoanalysis is under attack on many fronts, and no longer enjoys the privilege of its beleaguered past or more recent prosperous hegemony within the field of mental health. Masson (1990), a recent defector, writing with the vehemence of a disap-pointed convert, has aroused public controversy. But probably more important has been the challenges coming from biological psychia-try, academic psychology, changing reimbursement policies in health care, and competing methods of psychotherapy. The point here is that, under these pressures, psychoanalysis is beginning to acknowl-edge its position in and of the world. Its truths and methods no longer enjoy immunity.

But I think it is also time to acknowledge the role that this sense of privileged apartness has played in the history of psychoanalytic insti-tutional life. It has made it possible for analysts to maintain a sense of detachment from their own institutions, as if those very institutions were necessary concessions to existence in the world. Following Freud, they have found it difficult to assume true collective responsibility for their own organizational needs. Thus matching the almost exclusive attention to pairing relationships within the field, analysts have shown indifference, detachment, and disdain toward their own institutional position in the world.

The primary targets of that disdain, I think, have been psycho-analytic leaders themselves: whoever has aspired to become a son of Freud, to assume the mantle of leadership, has I think risked the subtle disparagement of their followers. If, as Orgel (1990) and Simon (1992) contend, psychoanalytic leadership has frequently been narcissistic, arrogant, and "overly-persuasive," and if, on the other hand, that kind of leadership has tended to be sheltered from overt criticism – fol-lowers have allowed themselves to be overly persuaded – one has to suspect the existence of a collusion. Leaders can lead, but the price of attempting to engage the world that Freud disdained and to create an organization that Freud failed to succeed in establishing is that those leaders will fail to engage the respect and support they need to fully succeed at their tasks.

If narcissists are attracted to leadership positions in psychoanalysis, could that be because they are particularly vulnerable to be exploited in the service of this collusion: will they buy into the prominence these roles afford and not probe too deeply into the underlying meaning of the support they are given or question too deeply the value of the tasks they are assigned to perform?

What I am suggesting, in short, is that an additional dynamic source of the virulent schisms and splits that beset psychoanalytic organizations derives from the bystanders, the psychoanalytic membership, who derisively watch their leaders sully and contaminate themselves in their ill-fated efforts to succeed where Freud failed, at tasks that Freud disdained. From the position they have taken up in their minds of being apart from the world of social reality – the world in which competition, compromise, and political conflict inevitably appear – they project their fear and hatred of that world into the leaders who dare to engage it. They unconsciously promote the very schisms that they also dread, because it confirms their sense that the world is a baffling, cruel, and ultimately inferior place, a place where they do not belong.

Conclusions

This exploration of the tensions embedded in psychoanalytic identity, psychoanalytic organizations, and psychoanalytic culture, I believe, accounts for the fragile nature of psychoanalytic institutions. When those institutions are subject to the stress of a particular conflict or controversy, threatening to alter the balance of ongoing power relationships, the membership resorts to the defensive response of splitting and schism.

The social defense of intolerance – which ultimately leads to splitting – is, in effect, the final common pathway in which defenses against the contradictions of the analyst's identity, the internal tensions of analytic institutions, and the marginality of psychoanalytic culture in relation to the world join together to proffer an illusory security of sectarian life. Virtually the entire history of psychoanalysis has been bedeviled by accusations and counter-accusations of "orthodoxy" and other forms of religious fanaticism. I don't think, in fact, that psychoanalysis is a form of religion, but I do think this constant looming threat of "orthodoxy" speaks to the apprehension that analysts have always had of how easy it is – almost how inevitable – to establish closed boundaries around the enterprise. In the task it sets itself of providing therapeutic interventions as well as in the task it faces of nurturing its own institutional development, psychoanalysis must be open to discovery and transformation through its encounters with reality; in that sense, it must be scientific (Kernberg, 1993). It is, on the other hand, constantly threatened by the danger of closed boundaries under the pressures I have attempted to point out; in that sense it is threatened – and, I think, knows itself to be threatened – by the danger of becoming a collection of cults.

In one way recent developments in psychoanalytic theory are helpful in lessening the underlying pressures I have been trying to describe. Increasingly, analysts seem to accept the multidimensional and indeterminate nature of reality; truth not only is seen as hypothetical but also contingent upon the particular stance of the agent who is seeking it. Thus the analyst increasingly accepts both the fact that an analysis is never concluded, the analysand is never conclusively analyzed, but also that, in a sense, each analyst provides his own analytic opportunity, with a unique collection of potentials and limits. This is a view of analysis as "action research," to borrow a term from organizational work. To the extent that this version of the analytic enterprise can be internalized by the psychoanalyst – made a part of training and valued as a part of analytic wisdom – the pressure to identify and punish deviants may diminish.

Along the same lines, I think that the analytic culture I have attempted to describe is also changing. Social reality has crashed in upon the International and American Psychoanalytic Associations in the form of an anti-trust suit; moreover, under the pressure of increasing competition from other forms of psychotherapy, analysts are grasping both the need for greater collaboration and the need for leaders they can support.

Finally, though, there is something of a prescription implied in this vision of the vicissitudes of psychoanalytic institutions. Psychoanalysis can broaden the scope of its vision to include its own institutional life. That is, it has the potential to build into its institutional structures the study of its own organizational conflicts and covert processes.

106 Organizational Analysis

At times, of course, particular and limited reforms in psychoanalytic training may be quite desirable for particular purposes. The introduction of different theoretical viewpoints into analytic curricula may help promote a greater acceptance of differences in analytic technique. The non-reporting by training analysts of the progress of candidates to training committees may be useful in making training analyses more authentic. Allowing candidates to select training analysts, or even supervising analysts, from other institutes may further reduce anxiety and conformity and may, also, foster an ecumenical spirit. But, I think, any such reform can easily be subverted into serving an end quite different from that intended (see Slavin, 1993). The analogy with symptom relief in psychoanalysis itself comes to mind. One may succeed in changing the patient's behavior, but the persisting pressure of the underlying conflict will cause a different and perhaps more virulent symptom to emerge.

The conflicts and anxieties I have described are deeply embedded in the texture of the psychoanalytic enterprise. As I have tried to suggest, the defensive maneuvers they have given rise to have been exceptionally virulent forms of intolerance sanctioned in the institutional history of psychoanalysis by its leaders, starting with Freud. But the underlying tensions persist in the work; they are part of it. The identity of the analyst will always crave certainty, and analysts will always be tempted to shore up that certainty at the expense of colleagues who think differently; moreover, colleagues will always invite scorn by clinging to limited views and being intolerant in turn. The analytic pair will always separate out from the analytic group to do its work, and the group will always feel threatened by the power of those pairing bonds. Finally, I think, the analyst will always seek to remove himself from the world he would rather understand than change; those who work with the wounded, by and large, prefer not to be at the front lines.

I believe that the only way these issues can be addressed adequately in the long run is by our analytic institutions themselves taking up a self-reflective, analytic stance toward their own internal conflicts and defensive maneuvers. That is, the hidden, covert aspects of our institutional relatedness might be made available to us to reflect upon and to consider as we work together.

There is a tradition of group and organizational analysis that has grown up out of psychoanalysis. Freud (1921) began it, of course, but Bion (1959) contributed the essential clinical observations that made it useful. This paper is an outgrowth of that tradition, and I have referred to some of its concepts, especially the concept of "social defenses" (Jaques, 1955; Menzies, 1967). This tradition remains available to psychoanalysis to further its own organizational work. This would require, of course, dismantling some of our institutions' more rigid and opaque boundaries, as Rickman (1951) suggested over 40 years ago. That is no easy matter, of course, as it would lead to more overt criticism, competition, and vulnerability in leaders. But that may be the only real alternative we have to enduring our institutional shortcomings.

A beginning might be to bring knowledge of this tradition into our psychoanalytic institutions through courses for candidates in the psychodynamics of organizations. Some forms of "executive education" might be designed for senior analysts within particular institutes. Consultation is also available from those trained in this tradition for organizations facing particular dilemmas. A major step would be the establishment of training programs for psychoanalytically oriented organizational consultation within analytic institutes.

It may sound implausible to think that our institutions would undertake self-analysis as a goal. But I do not think it is utopian to believe that they could bring about a greater tolerance for collaboration, given the fundamental vision of psychoanalysis as effecting transformation through insight.

Where brutalizing splitting was, there might organizational ego be.

References

Alderfer, C. P. (2011). *The Practice of Organizational Diagnosis*. New York: Oxford University Press.

Arlow, J. A. (1972). Some dilemmas in psychoanalytic education. *Journal of the American Psychoanalytic Association* 20, 556–66.

Balint, M. (1948). On the psychoanalytic training system. *International Journal of Psychoanalysis* 29, 163–73.

Balint, M. (1954). Analytic training and training analysis. *International Journal of Psychoanalysis* 35, 157–62.

Bibring, G. (1954). The training analysis and its place in psychoanalytic training. *International Journal of Psychoanalysis* 35, 169–73.

Bion, W. (1959). *Experiences in Groups*. New York: Basic Books.

Bollas, C. (1993). Preoccupation unto death. Paper delivered at the William Alanson White Institute, New York City, February 24, 1993.

108 Organizational Analysis

Buechler, S. (1988). Joining the psychoanalytic culture. *Contemporary Psychoanalysis* 24, 462–70.

Buechler, S. (1992). Stress in the personal and professional development of a psychoanalyst. *Journal of the American Academy of Psychoanalysis* 20, 183–91.

Cooper, A. (1986). Some limitations on therapeutic effectiveness: the "burn-out syndrome" in psychoanalysis. *Psychoanalytic Quarterly* 55, 576–98.

Dreyfus, P. (1978). Panel and open forum on the ego ideal of the psychoanalyst. *International Journal of Psychoanalysis* 59, 391–3.

Dulchin, J., & Segal, A. J. (1982a). The ambiguity of confidentiality in a psychoanalytic institute. *Psychiatry* 45, 13–25.

Dulchin, J., & Segal, A. J. (1982b). Third-party confidences: the uses of information in a psychoanalytic institute. *Psychiatry* 45, 27–37.

Eckhardt, M. H. (1978). Organizational schisms in American psychoanalysis. In J. M. Quen & E. T. Carlson (eds.), *American Psychoanalysis: Origins and Development* (pp. 141–61). New York: Brunner/Mazel.

Ellenberger, H. F. (1970). *The Discovery of the Unconscious*. New York: Basic Books.

Fine, R. (1979). *A History of Psychoanalysis*. New York: Columbia University Press.

Fleming, J. (1976). Report of the Ad Hoc Committee on Los Angeles. *Journal of the American Psychoanalytic Association* 24, 910–15.

Frattaroli, E. (1992). Orthodoxy and heresy in the history of psychoanalysis. In N. M. Szajnberg (ed.), *Educating the Emotions: Bruno Bettleheim and Psychoanalytic Development*. New York: Plenum Press.

Freud, A. (1966). The ideal psychoanalytic institute. In *The Writings of Anna Freud*, Vol. 7. New York: International Universities Press.

Freud, S. (1913). Totem and taboo. In J. Strachey (ed. and trans.), *The Standard Edition of the Complete Psychological Works of Sigmund Freud* (Vol. 13, pp. 1–162). London: Hogarth Press.

Freud, S. (1914). On the history of the psychoanalytic movement. In J. Strachey (ed. and trans.), *The Standard Edition of the Complete Psychological Works of Sigmund Freud* (Vol. 14, pp. 3–66). London: Hogarth Press.

Freud, S. (1921). Group psychology and the analysis of the ego. In J. Strachey (ed. and trans.), *The Standard Edition of the Complete Psychological Works of Sigmund Freud* (Vol. 18, pp. 67–143). London: Hogarth Press.

Freud, S. (1925). An autobiographical study. In J. Strachey (ed. and trans.), *The Standard Edition of the Complete Psychological Works of Sigmund Freud* (Vol. 20, pp. 3–74). London: Hogarth Press.

Friedman, L. (1988). *The Anatomy of Psychotherapy*. Hillsdale, NJ: Analytic Press.

Frosch, J. (1991). The New York Psychoanalytic civil wars. *Journal of the American Psychoanalytic Association* 39(4), 1037–64.

Gitelson, F. H. (1983). Identity crises: splits or compromises – adaptive or maladaptive. In E. D. Joseph & D. Widlocher (eds.), *The Identity of the Psychoanalyst* (pp. 157–80). New York: International Universities Press.

Glover, E. (1943). Response to memorandum by James Strachey. In P. King & R. Steiner (eds.), *The Freud-Klein Controversies, 1941–45*. London: Routledge.

Greenacre, P. (1966). Problems of training analysis. *Psychoanalytic Quarterly* 35, 540–67.

Grosskurth, P. (1991). *The Secret Ring: Freud's Inner Circle and the Politics of Psychoanalysis*. Reading, MA: Addison-Wesley.

Hinshelwood, R. D. (1985). Questions of training. *Free Associations* 2, 7–18.

Jaques, E. (1955). Social systems as defense against persecutory and depressive anxiety. In M. Klein, P. Heimann, & R. Money-Kyrle (eds.), *New Directions in Psycho-analysis*. London: Tavistock Publications.

Kernberg, O. F. (1986). Institutional problems of psychoanalytic education. *Journal of the American Psychoanalytic Association* 34(4), 799–834.

Kernberg, O. F. (1993). The current status of psychoanalysis. *Journal of the American Psychoanalytic Association* 41(1), 45–62.

King, P. (1983). Identity crises: splits or compromises – adaptive or maladaptive. In J. D. Edward & D. Widlocher (eds.), *The Identity of the Psychoanalyst* (pp. 181–94). New York: International Universities Press.

King, P. (1991). Conclusions. In P. King & R. Steiner (eds.), *The Freud–Klein Controversies* (p. 370). London: Routledge.

King, P. & Steiner, R. (eds.) (1991). *The Freud–Klein Controversies*. London: Routledge.

Klauber, J. (1983). The identity of the psychoanalyst. In E. D. Joseph & D. Widlocher (eds.), *The Identity of the Psychoanalyst* (pp. 41–50). New York: International Universities Press.

Levinson, H. (1990). Freud as entrepreneur. In *Clinical Approaches to the Study of Managerial and Organizational Dynamics*, Proceedings of the 4th Annual Symposium of the International Society for the Psychoanalytic Study of Organizations, Montreal, Quebec, Canada (pp. 227–50). Montreal: ISPSO and the Ecole des Haute Etudes Commercial de Montreal.

Lifschutz, J. E. (1976). A critique of the reporting and assessment in the training analysis. *Journal of the American Psychoanalytic Association* 24, 43–59.

Masson, J. M. (1990). *Final Analysis*. New York: Addison-Wesley.

Meisels, M. (1990). Introduction: the colorful background of the Clark Conference. In M. Meisels & E. Shapiro (eds.), *Tradition and Innovation in Psychoanalytic Education* (pp. 1–10). Hillsdale: Lawrence Erlbaum.

110 Organizational Analysis

Menzies, E. (1967). *The Functioning of Social Systems as Defense against Anxiety*. London: Tavistock Publications.

Millett, J. A. P. (1962). Changing faces of psychoanalytic eduction. In L. Salzman & J. H. Masserman (eds.), *Modern Concepts of Psychoanalysis* (p. 349). New York: Philosophical Library.

Morris, J. (1992). Psychoanalytic training today. *Journal of the American Psychoanalytic Association* 40(4), 1185–1210.

Oberndorf, C. (1953). *A History of Psychoanalysis in America*. New York: Grune & Stratton.

Orgel, S. (1978). Report from the seventh pre-Congress conference on training. *International Journal of Psychoanalysis* 59, 511–15.

Orgel, S. (1990). The future of psychoanalysis. *Psychoanalytic Quarterly* 59, 1–20.

Pollock, G. H. (1978). The Chicago Institute for Psychoanalysis from 1932 to the present. In J. M. Quen & E. T. Carlson (eds.), *American Psychoanalysis: Origins and Development*. New York: Brunner/Mazel.

Rickman, J. (1951). Reflections on the function and organization of a psychoanalytical society. *International Journal of Psychoanalysis* 32, 218–37.

Roustang, F. (1982). *Dire Mastery: Discipleship from Freud to Lacan*. Baltimore: Johns Hopkins University Press.

Rustin, M. (1985). The social organization of secrets: towards a sociology of psychoanalysis. *International Review of Psychoanalysis* 12, 143–60.

Sandler, A. M. (1990). Comments on varieties of psychoanalytic training in Europe. In M. Meisels & E. Shapiro (eds.), *Tradition and Innovation in Psychoanalytic Education* (p. 472). Hillsdale: Lawrence Erlbaum.

Schafer, R. (1979). On becoming a psychoanalyst of one persuasion or another. *Contemporary Psychoanalysis* 15, 345–60.

Simon, B. (1992). "Incest – see under Oedipus Complex": the history of an error in psychoanalysis. *Journal of the American Psychoanalytic Association* 40(4), 955–88.

Slavin, J. H. (1993). Revolution and counterrevolution: can reform be sustained in psychoanalytic training? Paper delivered at the Spring Meeting of the Division of Psychoanalysis (39), APA, April, 1993.

Stelzer, J. (1986). The formation and deformation of identity during psychoanalytic training. *Free Associations* 7, 59–74.

Thompson, C. (1958). A study of the emotional climate of psychoanalytic institutes. *Psychiatry* 21, 45–51.

Turkle, S. (1978). *Psychoanalytic Politics: Freud's French Revolution*. New York: Basic Books.

Wallerstein, R. S. (1978). Perspectives on psychoanalytic training around the world. *International Journal of Psychoanalysis* 59, 477–503.

Widlocher, D. (1978). The ego ideal of the psychoanalyst. *International Journal of Psychoanalysis* 59, 387–90.

Chapter Five

Psychoanalytic Training

The "Faculty System"

[Originally published as Psychoanalytic Training: The "Faculty System," *Psychoanalytic Inquiry*, vol. 24 (2004), pp. 51–70.]

The primary and ideal version of the task faced by training institutes is simple: to help aspiring candidates become competent. They receive assistance in developing their knowledge and skills as practitioners. But to look at the process of training more closely is to see a far more complex set of demands and expectations. Indeed, training as it is actually conducted in most institutes can easily appear inconsistent, contradictory, and, at times, self-defeating.

It has been cogently argued that candidates can become competent without formal training, that, indeed, training often inhibits or undermines competence. Lacan, most famously, took that position. In his perspective, it is inherently infantilizing to build into the process of professional training and certification the need to gain the approval of the father. Only the analyst himself, Lacan argued, can authentically proclaim his authority. Others, taking less uncompromising positions, argue that training as traditionally constituted undermines the creativity of candidates (Kernberg, 1999) or their independence and freedom to think (Hyman, 1990), etc.

Indeed, reinforcing these arguments is the indisputable fact that in the golden age of psychoanalysis training was considerably more haphazard and casual than it has become. Our efforts to become more systematic and thoughtful about training coincide with a general decline in our level of originality. Why has training, the development of competence, seemingly so clear and simple a task, become so complex and confusing?

The Three Systems of Psychoanalytic Training

Clearly, other factors are at work in the training process that compete with a single-minded devotion to the needs of candidates to develop into skilled practitioners. The most obvious one is the need of the profession itself to regulate access to the field, to monitor standards and control for competence. It is a means whereby unskilled or untalented candidates are screened out or, at least, held to standards well above what they might establish for themselves.

This has to do with the public face of the profession, the need to self-regulate in order to assure the public that individual practitioners are minimally competent. The professional authority of psychoanalysis depends on the confidence of the public in the field's ability to regulate itself and establish minimal standards of competence (Eisold, 1998; Chapter 2 in this volume). We might say that this is the primary and ideal version of the task faced by the profession, the process that leads to certification.

To be sure, the assessment of competence can be separated out from training – and sometimes is. In France, as Kernberg (2000) has recently pointed out, candidates train themselves individually and independently and then offer themselves for certification. In practice, however, there are pressures on both sides to align preparation and assessment. Assessment and certification can seem arbitrary and out of touch if it does not link to the expectations and actual experiences of those being assessed. On the other hand, training can seem irrelevant, idiosyncratic, and capricious if it doesn't realistically prepare candidates for certification. There is pressure on both sides to work toward some degree of coordination if not integration.

We have here, then, two overlapping systems involved in the training process. I call them "systems" because, in both cases, they consist of organized structures which marshal resources toward particular ends (see Miller & Rice, 1967). There is what we could call "the candidate system," focussed on candidates seeking help and guidance toward developing professional skills. And there is "the professional system," concerned with establishing standards and enforcing them in order to maintain and protect the professional authority of the discipline. In training as it is generally practiced, the two systems overlap, occasionally coming into conflict.

Supervision is a case in point. The supervising analyst has the job of teaching or guiding the supervisee to become a better practitioner. He also has the job of evaluating and reporting on the progress or shortcomings of the supervisee (much as training analysts also were once required to do). Frequently, supervision goes along well enough, despite the potential conflict between these two functions. The supervisee can trust enough that the supervisor has his interests and needs at heart; the training committee can trust enough that the supervisor has its values and standards in mind. One can reasonably believe that it is helpful to hold candidates to high standards, and candidates sometimes appreciate this and respond with greater efforts.

Kernberg (2000) has stressed the supervisory function as perhaps the best means of assuring quality control in training. But that depends, of course, on the supervisor's ability to manage this complex role. "We need to select supervisors who are knowledgeable, clear and direct in their interactions with candidates, able to be critical without becoming sadistic, respectful and open to different views, honest in their criticism and in being able to say no."

These personal qualities presumably will enable the supervisor to find his way through potentially his conflicting participation in the candidate and professional systems. He can help and he can monitor. But, in fact, as Kernberg's ideal list of personal qualities implied, the supervisor not infrequently feels the strain between these two overlapping systems in his role, more often than not siding with one aspect of the role, minimizing the other. Supervisors who tend to be empathic and supportive of candidates are often guided by an underlying assumption that virtually all candidates will eventually pass because initial standards in accepting candidates for training are high – or ought to be. The onus of maintaining professional standards, for them, falls largely on the admissions committee. Supervisors, on the other hand, who see themselves as guardians of the profession run the risk of being seen as punitive or obstructive; often feared by candidates, they run the risk of not being passed over by candidates who have a choice. Occasionally, of course, they are idealized and unduly venerated.

Clearly, supervisors may well bring the idealized qualities Kernberg identifies to their role, but they are inevitably pulled in different directions by the nature of the tasks they are assigned. And they have other motives as well. The important point that I want to emphasize,

114 Organizational Analysis

though, is that the supervisor – like the training analyst, the members of the training committee, the teaching faculty, and all the other senior analysts who staff the institute – are members of yet a third system, traditionally bound up with the functioning of our training institutes: the "faculty system." They play a crucial role, of course, because they actually do the work of training and evaluation. They serve on committees, attend meetings, debate issues, make judgments, establish policy, and so forth. And they do this with relatively little monetary compensation. To be sure, supervisors and training analysts are paid, though often at fees that are controlled and less than those charged the general public. Teachers are rarely paid, and administrators, if paid, receive fees well below what their clinical work could offer. Clearly, the compensation is of another kind.

There is an underground view of this – rarely spoken in public but, I believe, widely held – that the hierarchical control exercised by faculty throughout the history of psychoanalytic training is motivated by the craving for power. Szasz (1958), for example, noted that the progressive increase in the length and complexity of psychoanalytic training was accompanied by "a progressive increase in the power of the (analytic) teacher over his student" (p. 603). More recently, Wallerstein (1993), in his report on the Fifth IPA Conference on Training, noted that a number of commentators still see a contamination in the role of the training analyst stemming from their institutional power. (See also Cabernite, 1982.)

Balint (1948) called attention to the training system's fostering of dependency and idealization, a point elaborated at length and more forcefully by Roustang (1982). Arlow (1972) noted that the current system resembles indoctrination, a point reiterated by Kernberg (1986). Faculty members who have made it through training and through their apprenticeship years, achieving positions of dominance and control, identify with the aggressors that scrutinized and judged them. A training system provides for a steady and dependable supply of candidates that they, in turn, can scrutinize and judge. As a result of this repetitive pattern conformity is encouraged.

For the most part, this has tended to be viewed as an unfortunate but inescapable by-product of the system. The remedies usually advocated are a greater attention to transference in the training analysis and a greater scrupulousness in the selection of training analysts. The rationalization for continuing this system is that the senior and more experienced analysts are indispensable to the maintenance of standards. That is, the professional system demands that they continue to hold and exercise power over training because they are the ones with the most understanding of what constitutes professional competence. As Weinshel (1982) put it in remarks to the Board of Professional Standards he made in 1976: "the psychoanalytic organization may be the worst possible way to training for psychoanalysis except for all the other alternative ways that have been suggested" (p. 86). The cynical and often unspoken response to this, of course, is that any establishment would have to think this way in order to maintain its dominance. "Alternative ways" never really get a hearing from those whose interests might be threatened by change.

Faculty Power

Scrutinizing the history of psychoanalysis, one would have no difficulty identifying leaders, starting with Freud himself, who with seeming ruthlessness and arrogance have held on to their dominant positions and exerted control over psychoanalytic institutions (Roustang, 1982). But the existence of the faculty system would be incapable of achieving the acceptance it has were it not for the widespread support of senior faculty in establishing and maintaining it. That is, the power of the faculty that is being held onto in training is less about gaining material ends or supporting the ambitious claims of powerful leaders – though these are not irrelevant factors – than it is about maintaining control for those who are in positions of seniority. This control, however, is not about maintaining power for its own sake, I believe, as it is about providing for the psychological security of faculty.

In other words, the faculty system is an assembly of "social defenses" (Jacques, 1955; Menzies, 1967), a collectively elaborated organization of work relationships, seemingly rational and goal-oriented, but primarily devoted to defending against the various forms of anxiety encountered by faculty in task performance. I see it as a "system," like the candidate system and the professional system, because it too is a set of organized structures that marshal resources toward particular ends. In this case the structures are committees and procedures that select candidates and approve them, design curricula and assign faculty to courses, determine who will be training and supervising analysts, and decide who will occupy leadership positions. Its ostensible purpose is to ensure the strength and viability of the professional system while staffing and managing the candidate system. But the underlying purpose of this system is to provide stability, self-esteem, and status for faculty in their various roles.

In his last public address, Bernfeld (1962) made the point that the dominant training model was "faculty centered," not "student centered" as it claimed to be. But such voices have been few and far between – and without much effect, so powerful has been the need to affirm the correctness of the existing system and the traditional roles of those who support it. In 1954, Lewin and Ross noted with satisfaction that the Board on Professional Standards of the American Psychoanalytic Association succeeded and carried forward the work of the International Training Committee established in 1925, which "was formed and drew up a set of rules and standards which, except for details, are essentially those accepted today" (p. 6). At the same time, however, they noted that the institutes are the site of "novel conflict" hardly justifying such conviction: "The principles of psychoanalysis are being tested against the demands of education; the principles of education are being tested by psychoanalysis. An experiment of nature is being carried on in institute teaching" (p. 47).

The traditional "hallowed tripartite model" (Wallerstein, 1993, p. 175) – the Berlin or "Eitingon model" consisting of training analysis, supervision of control cases, and courses – continues to be repeatedly and ritually reaffirmed as if it were the tested and proven inevitably best means to develop competency. Indeed, it has been made into something of a shibboleth of training, as Kachele and Thoma (2000) noted, obscuring the fact that the original model differed in many respects from current practice and that, in reality, it assumes different forms throughout the world. But the existence of this asserted uniformity preserves the illusion of certainty along with the actual authority of those charged with maintaining it. Moreover, it discourages research into alternatives. A recent meeting of directors of training in the American Psychoanalytic Association, for example, concluded: "empirical research [about training] was not thought appropriate" (Ahmed, 1994).

The security for faculty that these assumptions defend has several dimensions, of course, and it will vary from person to person, but I think we can delineate its main features, the common elements that make it into an identifiable set of "social defenses." And, in so doing, we can begin to tease apart and discriminate what actually functions in the service of the other two systems and what, in fact, undermines and contaminates them.

Perhaps the most prominent source of anxiety defended against by the faculty system stems from the judgment and scrutiny that analysts as candidates have had to endure. The faculty system as it is generally constituted protects faculty from such scrutiny, defending faculty from the anxiety of being judged. Often under the guise of protecting confidentiality, faculty members do not have to explain or justify the decisions they make about candidates or, for that matter, each other. Candidates are accountable for their judgments with patients and with their teachers, often asked to justify or explore their decisions in order to get at their deeper, less apparent motivations. But once one has become a member of the faculty, little justification is required or even solicited for comparable assessments or decisions. In the past, it was often presumed that faculty members were thoroughly analyzed, unlikely to be prone to irrational behavior. These days, that presumption is less likely to be held, yet there is little pressure to open up the system to higher levels of accountability.

This is even more apparent when it comes to decisions that faculty make about each other in selecting training and supervising analysts. Weinshel (1982) noted how little research has been devoted to this process, particularly striking given how vital such decisions are to the future health of institutes. He concluded that "lack of 'hard' clinical data ... encourages a more insular and even solipsistic picture and conceptualization of the training analysis" (p. 434).

Striking too has been the resistance of faculty to presenting their own work. Long ago, Loewald cogently argued for the value of faculty offering case presentations to candidates, open to discussion and criticism. More recently, Kernberg reiterated the same point (1996). But Morris (1992) concluded in his generally optimistic survey of the "evolutionary" development of training practices that few institutes have adopted Loewald's suggestion. The clinical work of faculty continues to appear, by and large, protected by the highly edited and sharply focussed format of professional papers.

This touches on the second source of anxiety, the anxiety of ignorance – more precisely, the anxiety of acknowledging ignorance about something one claims to understand or feels one should understand. In a sense, although psychoanalysis is all about facing the unknown, collectively analysts themselves are often reluctant to confess to ignorance. Indeed, different analytic communities often organize around assertions of theoretical certainty and battle over claims to truth. Ignorance is located – or projected – into other camps (Rickman, 1951; Eisold, 1994). And, as has been pointed out, analytic training often comes to resemble a process of initiation or indoctrination.

A particular form of ignorance that analytic faculties collectively have had difficulty acknowledging is their skill in the task of selecting candidates. This may be less of a problem now as fewer apply; the task is simplified to weeding out the more obviously ill-equipped. But historically and still in some locations, this has been a troubling issue. At various points in our history, whole categories of applicants have been proscribed as unsuitable: women, homosexuals, non-medical practitioners, the disabled, those beyond a certain age, etc.

In an old study of the problem of making judgment among those deemed eligible, Holt and Luborsky (1955) concluded that "predictions from interviews [are] slightly better than chance" in making selections, and demonstrated that psychological testing significantly improved reliability. But that appears to have little impact on altering traditional reliance on faculty judgments, perhaps, in part, because the professional opinions of psychologists were easy to discount. More recently, Kappelle (1996) noted: "In selecting for psychoanalytic training, we are doing something we do not (precisely) know in order to achieve something we cannot (precisely) describe" (p. 1229). But he added, astutely, that it was unlikely that such findings would actually change institute practices.

A third source of anxiety that the faculty system defends against is the anxiety of change, which is, at root, the anxiety involved in acknowledging that something is inadequate and needs to be modified or altered. Some time ago, Arlow (1972) referred to a "cultural lag" in training, noting that little attention has been paid to a critical re-examination of training in the light of changes in theory and clinical practice over time. He wryly noted how unusual it was for a profession to devote itself primarily to studying texts over 50 years old.

Since then, I think, more substantial changes have been made in institute curricula. Indeed, the proliferation of different schools and the current pluralistic climate has led to a significant expansion of courses. But a constraining factor has been institute policies that often limit faculty roles to institute graduates; "outsiders" are rarely invited in to teach. As a result, institutes often lack the resources to cover such topics authoritatively. The alternative of faculty working together with candidates to learn about different approaches together has been seldom undertaken.

An additional issue stems from the fact that most current candidates face careers with few actual patients in psychoanalysis. This has highlighted the need for courses or programs addressing other forms of psychoanalytically oriented psychotherapy or applied psychoanalysis – but few institutes have responded to this current need. Kernberg (1993) has noted, in general, "the passivity of psychoanalytic institutes [in the American Psychoanalytic Association] consequent to their being subject to a standard organizational model related to their control by the Board of Professional Standards" (pp. 56–7). This is, no doubt, a highly significant factor, but, I believe, institute faculty members themselves have preferred to hold on to practices and skills with which they are familiar. The current system defends them against the need to venture into unknown territories that are unfamiliar and about which they may well feel inadequately prepared.

A fourth source of anxiety is threats to self-esteem. An aspect of training that has been widely noted is the tendency of candidates to protect and idealize their analysts and supervisors, and this has been correctly seen as having a stifling and inhibiting effect. What is less widely commented on – though I doubt it has gone unnoticed – is the tendency of faculty members to accept these idealized attributes as warranted by their superior experience and skills. That is, the "caste system" that has been widely commented upon in psychoanalytic institutes has, I think, the primary purpose of protecting the self-esteem of faculty in the higher castes by investing them with the presumption of superior judgment and skill. In such a system, even those senior analysts who disclaim superior wisdom or clinical skills end up getting additional credit for being so open and unpretentious.

120   Organizational Analysis

To be sure, experience often has the effect of making one not only more knowledgeable but also more balanced and nuanced in clinical work. Moreover, some subgroup of faculty has to have delegated to it the responsibility for managing their institutions and making the judgments essential to their functioning. The current hierarchical system, though, divides up the faculty in ways that suggest permanent differences in inherent abilities. Yet, while the governance structure of institutes states, in effect, that this is the case, and while those who occupy privileged positions within it enjoy the status and the opportunities it provides, few people actually believe that it represents what it claims to represent. The "caste system," by and large, has become an object of political manipulation and cynical assessment.

This, of course, is the difficulty with all "social defenses," particularly those that are not closely aligned with the demands of work: They work intermittently, imperfectly, selectively, and, more importantly, they interfere with the ability of the organization more rationally and adaptively to address its essential work. The "caste system," for example, protects self-esteem up to a point; it does not screen out awareness of other more critical or skeptical attitudes, especially on the part of one's colleagues. Defenses against the anxiety of ignorance do not prevent candidates from noticing egregious lapses of judgment made in the selection process, nor do defenses against change help candidates cope with the gap between their training and the professional opportunities that await them. And it is unlikely that faculty are totally unaware of the discontent of candidates or, even, unsympathetic.

This inefficiency of social defenses is particularly true of the fifth and last set that I want to discuss: defenses against the anxiety of professional responsibility. Faculty, of course, have a significant impact in shaping the future direction of the profession and a legitimate interest in doing so. Enjoying the status of their roles, the idealizations, and the potential for gratitude from candidates, they can indeed often think more freely about the larger needs of the profession and engage their roles as guardians of its future development more fully. But anxiety about the responsibility this entails has led, I believe, to a comparable set of defenses against engaging the problems.

Faculty often put up barriers between themselves and candidates, preventing them from learning from candidate experience and understanding their interests. Though it is not at all uncommon now for institute committees to have candidate representatives sitting on them, that is not always effective in encouraging candidates to discover their needs more fully and give active voice to them on those committees. Nor is it clear how effective this practice is in communicating to candidates at large the issues faced on an institute level. At best, I think, they simply offer an occasional additional perspective.

In recent years the American has debated "decoupling" certification from membership, that is, making full membership available to graduates – perhaps even candidates – who have not been certified (Curtis, 1992). The old system paralleled on a national level the status differences within institutes, and it was often defended on the same grounds, namely the need to maintain standards. In effect, enfranchisement in the organization was extended only to those who had been endorsed by it. As Kernberg (1993) has pointed out, this not only limited discussion and debate within the organization but also extended the process of infantilization and dependency for those aspiring to full membership.

In general, the role and even the significance of the faculty system as a part of training has been neglected. As the self-appointed and self-styled guardians of the profession and custodians of its institutions, faculty have been generally free from having their motives scrutinized – except, of course, for occasional attacks that could well be attributed to envy, paranoia, or competition on the part of insufficiently analyzed colleagues. The invisibility of the system, inlaid into the professional and candidate systems, however, has made the security it provides all the more dependable. Moreover, the general absence of discussion in the literature on training of faculty motivation in their various roles – all the more striking given the attention paid to the motivations of candidates to please and idealize their faculty members – has contributed significantly to this invisibility.

But recently there has been much more willingness to expose traditional practices to scrutiny. The general decline in the standing of psychoanalysis has promoted a new adaptive willingness to question long-standing assumptions not only about theory and clinical practice but training as well. As it becomes more and more apparent that senior faculty have not succeeded in defending psychoanalysis from erosion and attack, their stewardship has been questioned and new democratic practices and procedures are being introduced. Moreover, as psychoanalysis declines in popularity, fewer practitioners seek out the increasingly illusory security that faculty roles once offered. One might even say, in effect, that the dismantling of the faculty system as it has existed is now under way.

This may seem long overdue and the democratization of institute practices may be a very welcome correction to the secrecy and authoritarian control of the past. At the same time, though, it has profound implications for the future. Just as the faculty system was established without full attention being paid to how it functioned, now it is being altered without much attention paid to the effects. What will be the motivation for psychoanalytic faculty in the future? Where and how will institutional security be provided? Or should it be? What motivation could possibly take its place? These are vital questions to which I would now like to turn.

Some Suggestions

Standardization – the process in which procedures and norms become institutionalized – leads to predictability, easier replication, and a sense of stability. But it may not be what our psychoanalytic training institutes need at this point. If we are open to the idea of learning more about what we have thought we knew concerning psychoanalytic training and exploring potential new developments in psychoanalytic careers, we need to allow for a variety of new initiatives. Indeed, faced with the inherent conservative pull of social defenses, I believe, we need to encourage experimentation and change.

At the same time, collectively, we have to work at shoring up our professional authority. The warring of psychoanalytic factions and the thin record of outcome research for psychoanalytic treatments undermine public confidence in the field. With so many different schools of thought, it becomes more difficult to determine what clinical competence consists of even as it becomes more urgent to do so. We may not be able to find the "common ground" of clinical theory (Wallerstein, 1992), but that hardly absolves us of the need to work at clarifying the practices and skills specific to psychoanalysis that are effective (Eisold, 2000; Zeddies, 2000). Indeed, without clarity about those skills it is difficult to justify any training process. At the same time, without outcome studies we are all – practitioners, supervisors, directors of training – to some extent operating in the dark.

My first suggestion, then, is about differentiating and separating the training and professional systems. Establishing a field-wide credentialing system, independent of any psychoanalytic institute or existing professional organization, would help to free the professional system from supporting or advocating any particular approach to training. At the same time, it could allow us to face the public with a united stance. Such systems have been proposed and implemented in the past but without the widespread support that would be required to make them credible and effective.

Such a credentialing system would have several – I think, beneficial – effects. One would be to make it clear that an approved training program does not necessarily lead to successfully credentialed candidates, introducing a healthy note of uncertainty into something we ought to be uncertain about and encouraging candidates to be more free and flexible in preparing themselves for certification. This, in turn, would free existing professional organizations from the task of monitoring institutes as part of the professional system. They could, of course, continue to assess, advise, and guide institutes in their development and even accredit them as representing the particular standards or ideals their organization stands for, but, in that case, the accrediting process could be viewed as less adversarial and potentially more collaborative. What would be at stake, under such a system, would be the standing of the institute, not the candidates. The focus could become one of helping training institutes become more thoughtful and effective about training.

An additional effect of establishing such an independent credentialing body would be to charge it with the responsibility to think about psychoanalytic competence. Such an umbrella organization, of course, would have to be representative of the diversity in the field and, therefore, not tied to any particular set of preconceptions about what constitutes good analytic practice. It would, as a result, necessarily contain significant differences that engender conflict and debate, requiring it to develop the capacity to reflect on its own activity and engage in thoughtful discussion.

But while an independent credentialing organization is perhaps the field's most pressing need, given our currently existing set of institutional relationships, it is not likely that at the start it would have anything like the standing or resources it would eventually need to have. Indeed, initially, it is likely to reflect the lowest common denominator in our thinking; its standards would more likely reflect compromise than conviction. Its effectiveness and credibility would have to be built over time. Ultimately its success would depend on the willingness of existing organizations to invest it with authority and resources to do its job and on its ability to attract first-rate minds to staff it and to develop high-level research projects into therapeutic processes and outcomes.

My second suggestion is to involve candidates more fully in designing the shape of their training. It has not escaped the notice of several commentators that candidates are often highly experienced not only with clinical skills acquired in psychotherapy practices as psychiatrists, psychologists, and social workers, but also with life experience as job holders, spouses, and parents. Normally they could be expected to be serious and motivated to think about the training they need and are committed to undertaking, often at great expense and with considerable disruption to their lives.

To be sure, experienced analysts have learned something worth knowing from their experience. Their knowledge – and even their prejudices – are well worth consulting. I'm not suggesting by any means that this perspective is without value. Moreover, as the faculty, by and large, are needed to provide instruction and supervision, what they are interested in providing and what they consider worthwhile doing would need to be taken into account. No training program could possibly succeed without their support – indeed, without their enthusiasm and commitment. But I am suggesting that candidates have an important perspective on what they need from their training. Decisions about curriculum and supervision could be made jointly. Indeed the decision-making process might profit significantly from disagreement and debate.

In effect, I am suggesting that designs for training be openly negotiated between candidates and faculty. Such candidate participation in the management of institutes would go a long way, I believe, to making them more adaptive to current realities. More thoroughgoing and confidently voiced feedback on current practices could be a means of introducing some reality testing into decisions more often ruled by custom and prejudice. We might learn more about what actually works in developing competence and what support practitioners can actually use in their careers. I am not suggesting a laissez-faire approach to candidate choice in which they are simply offered more latitude in selecting courses. Rather, I am proposing more joint engagement and struggle to arrive at a workable consensus about what constitutes useful training.

It may well be that candidates would pressure institutes to pay more attention to psychoanalytically oriented psychotherapy (Kernberg, 1999), even forms of psychotherapy whose relationship to psychoanalysis has not been explored. They might want to learn about family and group treatments, as well as "coaching" for executives or psychodynamic forms of consulting to organizations. Their interest might well lead them to seek experience and expertise from faculty outside their institutes, and while this might be difficult for some institutes to accept, it might also set the stage for faculty to learn something new as well.

My third suggestion is to enlarge the concept of training to include life-long professional development. Some time ago, Wallerstein (1978) noted that postgraduate education programs, while strongly endorsed, have generally not been implemented. I suspect not much has changed since he made that observation. Despite lip service paid to the notion that candidates are not the only ones in need of learning, the faculty system, by and large, protects faculty from the kinds of scrutiny and evaluation essentially involved in all learning environments.

Fogel and Glick (1991) described a study group of senior analysts that was extremely valuable, often in unexpected ways. One suspects, however, that the value of the give and take in that group depended in part on the careful screening process that went into forming and maintaining it. No doubt a number of similar groups exist. And certainly peer supervision groups have become virtually normative for the isolated solo practitioner. In such cases, too, information about the groups generally is not widely distributed because, I think, many of the groups are protecting their composition. It is not only a matter of making sure that group members are truly interested in and engaged with the topics the groups are devoted to studying, but also making sure that destructive competition and gratuitous judgments are kept to a minimum. It can also be a means whereby pre-existing bonds that have little to do with learning needs are maintained, keeping out those who – for whatever reason – are unwanted.

Increasingly in America, states are requiring some form of continuing education for renewing licenses of professional practitioners, though the satisfying of such requirements is often perfunctory and doesn't actually require much learning to occur. Sorenson (2000) has described a compulsory postgraduate education system in an analytic institute. It may be that other institutes have successfully experimented with similar compulsory systems, but, of course, all compulsory systems – like state-mandated continuing professional education – easily lead to formulaic means of compliance.

A more drastic proposal is for periodic recertification (Gaskell, 1979) – a proposal that echoes Freud's (1937) call for periodic reanalysis, another idea that has not received widespread implementation but which, nonetheless, haunts the profession. Clearly, the pressure to create social defenses within the faculty system is so strong and insidious that it would take strong measures and policies that are unambiguous and well supported throughout the field to counteract it.

What will motivate members of institute faculties to keep learning and institutes to provide the resources to do so? To be sure, learning has rewards of its own. Clearly, we wouldn't provide training if we didn't think so. And just as clearly, the nature of psychoanalytic work continually pits us against unknown forces and inexhaustible defenses in our patients, not to mention in our own countertransferential responses. And lively, helpful new perspectives are being developed and written about. The full extent of the supervision and study groups, private courses and gatherings of peers, that currently exist is not fully known, but they testify to the need for learning that informs our work and the willingness of analysts to seek it out.

There is, moreover, a need to learn more about training itself. Few institutes offer courses in supervision or, even, help for instructors, though there is widespread acknowledgment that we have much to learn in these areas. We also, by and large, know very little about management, how to lead committees, meetings, or other groups of peers that institute life depends on; success in such management requires an understanding of not only work relationships but also the "basic assumptions" (Bion, 1961) they inevitably give rise to. Moreover, few of us know how to manage the complex ethical, fiduciary, legal, political, and professional demands of our institutions, and pay attention as well to the "social defenses" that are also constructed by participants in institutions in the process. It may not be easy for senior faculty members to acknowledge their need for learning of this kind, but the impetus toward providing opportunities to learn such skills might well come from the national level.

And then there is the proliferation of applied forms of psychoanalysis that institutes could help faculty members study: psychoanalytic perspectives on history and politics, as well as the arts. And there are areas of practice with families, groups, organizations, and communities that can be studied. Indeed, I think that many of us in the field do learn about these things and have expanded our interests and even our practices as a result. Largely, however, this takes place outside our institutes, and it is not unusual for colleagues to remain ignorant of what others are doing. Here an active effort at distributing information would be required.

What is needed here is a fundamental redefinition of psychoanalytic institutes as sites of learning throughout the psychoanalytic career. Such a redefinition would go a long way toward reshaping our understanding of the role of learner so that it resembles less and less the infantile and dependent forms we are most familiar with and, thereby, tend to recreate in our authority relations with one another. Continuing to work at that frontier might, in itself, teach us to be more effective and responsible citizens of our psychoanalytic communities – and that might also be something others could learn from our experience as well.

These suggestions might sound utopian, and, indeed, I am under no illusion about how receptive to proposals for radical change our field has been in the past or is likely to be now. At the same time, as Anna Freud (1966) noted in her comments on the "ideal" institute, the ideal "claims my interest only insofar as it is capable of becoming true" (p. 74). My point is that these suggestions flow from the analysis I have attempted to present. To the extent we can free ourselves from our collectively elaborated defensive prejudices about training, we will be more free to think about how to prepare ourselves and others for effective, lively, and interesting careers as psychoanalysts.

References

Ahmed, J. (1994). Meeting of directors of training institutes. *Bulletin of the International Psycho-Analytical Association* 75, 184–5.

Arlow, J. (1972). Some dilemmas in psychoanalytic education. *Journal of the American Psychoanalytic Association* 20, 556–66.

Balint, M. (1984). On the psychoanalytic training system. *International Journal of Psychoanalysis* 29, 163–73.

Bernfeld, S. (1962). On psychoanalytic training. *Psychoanalytic Quarterly* 31, 453–82.

Bion, W. R. (1961). *Experiences in Groups*. London: Tavistock.

Cabernite, L. (1982). The selection and functions of the training analyst in analytic training. *IRPA* 9, 398–417.

Curtis, H. C. (1992). Psychoanalytic ecumenism and varieties of psychoanalytic experience. *Journal of the American Psychoanalytic Association* 40, 643–63.

Eisold, K. (1994). The intolerance of diversity in psychoanalytic institutes. *International Journal of Psychoanalysis* 75(4), 785–800.

Eisold, K. (1998). The splitting of the New York Psychoanalytic and the construction of psychoanalytic authority. *International Journal of Psychoanalysis* 79(5), 871–85.

Eisold, K. (2000). The rediscovery of the unknown. *Contemporary Psychoanalysis* 36, 57–75.

Fogel, G. I., & Glick, R. (1991). The analyst's postgraduate development: rereading Freud and working theory through. *Psychoanalytic Quarterly* 60, 396–425.

Freud, A. (1966). The ideal psychoanalytic institute: a utopia. In *The Writings of Anna Freud* (Vol. VII, pp. 73–93). New York: International Universities Press.

Freud, S. (1937). Analysis terminable and interminable. In J. Strachey (ed. and trans.), *The Standard Edition of the Complete Psychological Works of Sigmund Freud* (Vol. 23, pp. 209–53). London: Hogarth Press.

Gaskell, H. (1979). Bridges to the future. *Journal of the American Psychoanalytic Association* 27, 3–25.

Holt, R. R., & Luborsky, L. (1955). The selection of candidates for psycho-analytic training. *Journal of the American Psychoanalytic Association* 3, 666–81.

Hyman, M. (1990). Institute training and its alternatives. In M. Meisels & E. Shapiro (eds.), *Tradition and Innovation in Psychoanalytic Education*. Hillsdale, NJ: Erlbaum.

Jaques, E. (1955). Social systems as a defense against persecutory and depressive anxiety. In M. Klein, P. Heimann, & R. E. Money-Kyrle (eds.), *New Directions in Psycho-analysis*. London: Tavistock.

Kachele, H., & Thoma, H. (2000). On the devaluation of the Eitingon-Freud model of psychoanalytic education. *International Journal of Psychoanalysis* 81, 806–7.

Kappelle, W. (1996). How useful is selection? *International Journal of Psychoanalysis* 77, 1213–32.

Kernberg, O. F. (1986). Institutional problems of psychoanalytic education. *Journal of the American Psychoanalytic Association* 34, 799–834.

Kernberg, O. F. (1993). The current status of psychoanalysis. *Journal of the American Psychoanalytic Association* 41, 45–62.

Kernberg, O. F. (1996). Thirty methods to destroy the creativity of psychoanalytic candidates. *International Journal of Psychoanalysis* 77, 1031–40.

Kernberg, O. F. (1999). Psychoanalysis, psychoanalytic psychotherapy, and supportive psychotherapy: contemporary controversies. *International Journal of Psychoanalysis* 80, 1075–91.

Kernberg, O. F. (2000). A concerned critique of psychoanalytic education. *International Journal of Psychoanalysis* 81(1), 97–120.

Lewin, B., & Ross, H. (1954). *Psychoanalytic Education in the United States.* New York: Norton.

Lifschutz, J. E. (1976). A critique of reporting and assessment in the training analysis. *Journal of the American Psychoanalytic Association* 24, 43–59.

Menzies, E. (1967). *The Functioning of Social Systems as Defense against Anxiety.* London: Tavistock Publications.

Miller, E. J., & Rice, A. K. (1967). *Systems of Organization.* London: Tavistock.

Morris, J. (1992). Psychoanalytic training today. *Journal of the American Psychoanalytic Association* 40, 1185–1210.

Rickman, J. (1951). Reflections on the function and organization of a psychoanalytical society. *International Journal of Psychoanalysis* 32, 218–37.

Roustang, F. (1982). *Dire Mastery: Discipleship from Freud to Lacan.* Baltimore: Johns Hopkins University Press.

Sorenson, R. (2000). Psychoanalytic institutions as religious denominations: fundamentalism, progeny, and on-going reformation. *Psychoanalytic Dialogues* 10(6), 847–74.

Szasz, T. S. (1958). Psycho-analytic training: a socio-psychological analysis of its history and present status. *International Journal of Psychoanalysis* 39, 598–613.

Wallerstein, R. (1978). Perspectives on psychoanalytic training around the world. *International Journal of Psychoanalysis* 59, 477–503.

Wallerstein, R. S. (ed.) (1992). *The Common Ground of Psychoanalysis.* Northvale, NJ: Aronson.

Wallerstein, R. (1993). Between chaos and petrification: a summary of the Fifth IPA Conference on Training. *International Journal of Psychoanalysis* 74, 165–78.

Weinshel, E. (1982). The functions of the training analysis and the selection of the training analyst. *IRPA* 9, 434–44.

Zeddies, T. J. (2000). Psychoanalytic praxis and the moral vision of psychoanalysis. *Contemporary Psychoanalysis* 36, 521–8.

Chapter Six

Institutional Conflicts in Jungian Analysis

[Originally published as Institutional Conflicts in Jungian Analysis, *Journal of Analytical Psychology*, vol. 46 (2001), pp. 335–53.]

The institutional life of analytical psychology has been beset by internal strife from the start.* This is hardly news to those participating in it; the splits within institutes leading to the establishments of new institutes, the controversies over the role of the Zurich Institute in the IAAP and its other component institutes, the difficulties in establishing coherence if not agreement within training institutes – all this is a familiar aspect of the professional life of a Jungian analyst, particularly for one who has assumed some management responsibility (Kirsch, 1995).

But, in the eyes of the educated public, these conflicts have been overridden by the conflict between Jungians and the mainstream Freudians. The Jungians are often still perceived as the splinter offshoots of an early psychoanalytic schism. Ellenberger (1970) vigorously protested this perception: "neither Adler nor Jung is a 'psychoanalytic deviant,' and their systems are not mere distortions of psychoanalysis" (p. 571). But this has had little impact. The psychoanalytic schism looms over subsequent developments, even for Jungians. Fordham put his view of it with exceptional bluntness: the notion of Jung's personal and scientific incompatibility with Freud "was a disaster, and in part an illusion,

---

* I wish to express a debt of gratitude to a number of Jungian analysts who have helped me materially in the preparation of this paper: John Beebe, Ann Casement, Moira Duckworth, Tom Kirsch, Andrew Samuels, Hester Solomon, Suzy Spradlin, and Martin Stone. Without their assistance, this paper would not only be considerably thinner in substance but also richer in error.

from which we suffer and will continue to do so until we have repaired the damage" (1961, p. 168).

The purpose of this paper, in a sense, is to align these two perspectives: The history and the internal conflicts of analytical psychology have been indelibly shaped by the circumstances of its origins out of – and continuing relationship to – psychoanalysis. For analytical psychology, psychoanalysis has been both powerfully influential and inimical; it represents both an established and competitive tradition of psychological treatment and an injurious source of disparagement and neglect. The effects of this on analytical psychology have been pervasive and deep, though not always easy to discern and, certainly, experienced very differently in different sectors of the Jungian community – the topic I intend to explore in this paper.

From the perspective of psychoanalysis, on the other hand, analytical psychology is a deviant and marginal presence; as such, it is not without influence or power (Gallant, 1996), but it is not generally included within its discussions and debates. The effects of this upon psychoanalysis are not insignificant, though unattended – a topic I explore in a parallel paper (see Chapter 7).

I

The early history of the conflict between Freud and Jung is probably too well known to require a retelling. But there are two important points about that history that, I believe, need emphasis. One has to do with the institutional basis of the original split, as opposed to the theoretical basis. The other is the "lesson" I believe Jung derived from that institutional split, and applied in his thinking about the institutional forms he needed to carry forward his work.

The Secret Committee was formed to displace Jung (Grosskurth, 1991, 1998). Jones proposed it in the summer of 1912, and Freud seized upon the idea. The problem being addressed by this plan was Jung's conduct as president of the International. In his letter suggesting this new "unofficial inner circle," Jones expressed his "pessimism" about the "men who must lead for the next thirty years," noting "Jung abdicates his throne" (Paskauskas, 1993, p. 146).

The immediate reference was to the fact that Jung had somewhat precipitously gone to America to deliver lectures and see patients,

132   Organizational Analysis

postponing the 1912 congress as a result. As Jones pointedly lamented, in that same letter to Freud, "so many put their own private personality first, in the foreground of importance, and relegate the cause to a subordinate position" (p. 145). (For an additional perspective on how IPA affairs may have contributed to tensions between Freud and Jung, see Kuhn, 1998.)

Jung had never been a particularly effective leader. As Freud confided to Ferenczi, four months after Jones's proposal: "I had deceived myself on one point, in that I had considered him to be a born leader who by means of his authority could spare others many errors ..." (Brabant et al., 1993, p. 434). And, indeed, Jung may have been charismatic, but he lacked the patience and the tact to actually run an organization. Almost from the start of his presidency, Jung had not only been dilatory in his duties but also adept at alienating the very people whose support he would have needed to cultivate in order to succeed at his job (Paskauskas, 1988; McLynn, 1996). And, not surprisingly, Jones was foremost among those who felt slighted by Jung.

That was the major issue: Jung's ability and willingness to function as the leader of Freud's movement and the willingness of Freud's other disciples to allow him to play that role – not theoretical conformity (see Stepansky, 1976). Freud was determined to replace Jung. Moreover, the members of the Secret Committee were fully engaged in their effort to displace their rival, and to ensure that no one else took his place. Immersed in their own suspicions and plots, Freud and his new Secret Committee quickly became riddled with paranoid fears about Jung's plans to take over the psychoanalytic movement; they seem to have projected their own ambitions and fears on to Jung himself, constructing an image of him as an ambitious and ruthless leader at a time when he was, in fact, surprised and hurt by the opposition he had engendered, ambivalently maintaining his separation from Freud, and struggling to keep himself together.

Freud wanted to maintain his ownership of psychoanalysis and, to that end, control his disciples (see Roustang, 1982). But while that was undoubtedly the case, it is important to bear in mind that both Alfred Adler and Jung were put forth as leaders of psychoanalytic institutions, successors to Freud, and that their ability to succeed depended on the willingness of others to follow them. In the case of Adler, I believe, his erstwhile followers brought him down, exploiting the issue of theoretical differences, in order to bring back Freud to take charge (Eisold, 1997; Chapter 1 in this volume). In the case of Jung, the loved and chosen "Crown Prince," it was a group of Freud's closest followers who banded together and – with Jung's own active cooperation – deposed him.

Jung was profoundly affected by these developments. As he put it in *Memories, Dreams, Reflections* (1961), "menaced by a psychosis," he struggled to hold himself together. In relatively short order, he resigned his editorship of the Jahrbuch, his presidency of the International, he abandoned the local society in Zurich he had founded, he resigned his university professorship, and he accepted Freud's proscription of the term "psychoanalysis."

When, in 1916, Jung emerged from his period of "disorientation" and "confusion," what had been the Psychoanalytic Society of Zurich seems to have dissolved into a series of informal and infrequent meetings. In its place he created a "Psychological Club," which he called retrospectively "a silent experiment in group psychology" (CW, 10, para. 887). Membership in the club was extended only to those who "demonstrated the ability to attend to the unconscious and had shown a realistic interest and displayed sensitivity in human relationships" (Samuels, 1994, p. 138).

As Jung put it in some notes he wrote prefacing a paper he presented to the club in 1916: "It is an attempt to work together as analyzed men ... We are acquainted in analysis up till now only with the function of the personal-collective (analyst and patient), just as we have learnt much about the individual function. But we know nothing about the collective function of individuals and its conditions. Because of this one must make this practical attempt, because no other opportunities to have this experience are present" (Shamdasani, 1998, p. 24). As Fordham put it much later: "it was to have no professional status, and membership was not a qualification to practice psychotherapy" (1979, p. 279). It was a group gathered together to support members in their own spiritual and psychological development. In doing so, they would also support Jung and provide a forum for him to present his thoughts. (For a more conspiratorial view, see Noll 1997.) The club, in this respect, couldn't be more different from the International Psychoanalytic Association or the Viennese Psychoanalytic Society.

In his new organization, by avoiding a professional focus and placing the emphasis entirely on mutual support and spiritual development, he hoped to avoid replicating the organizational dangers he knew. More importantly, I believe, he sought to create for himself a refuge from the trauma he had just endured in the IPA.

The club went through many vicissitudes, reflecting a lack of direction and purpose. "The impression one gets is of a marked lack of social cohesion" (Shamdasani, 1998, p. 76). And, indeed, Jung himself resigned from it for a period of two years. But no other formal organization existed, associated with Jung, until after World War II.

This informal arrangement had disadvantages. For one thing, it meant that it was extremely difficult to become accredited as a Jungian analyst. "How anyone became an analytic therapist in those days is vague and must be regarded largely as a matter of vocation, though there was an unwritten law that any person who wanted to be called a Jungian analyst was expected to go out to Zurich, make a relation with Jung himself, and undergo analysis with either himself or one or more of his close colleagues" (Fordham, 1979, p. 280). As a result, of course, while Jung may have explicitly disavowed the wish to set up a training program that encouraged the formation of "disciples," with such an informal method he, in fact, exerted sole control over those who wished to follow in his path.

In addition, as Samuels (1994) pointed out, this "cozy club setting" was "undoubtedly riddled by unresolved transferences and counter-transferences" (p. 139). Samuels added: "psychological concepts were employed to understand better what was going on among the often-warring members. One gets the impression from accounts of people who were there of a sort of therapeutic community" (p. 139).

It is easy to see that these circumstances – while difficult for his followers – were highly protective of Jung. While he may have set out deliberately to avoid the kind of professional competition and rivalries that had characterized psychoanalytic politics, in which he had participated actively, as well as curtail the idealizations of the leader which he felt Freud cultivated, he ended up in the "silent experiment" of the club creating an almost hermetically secure environment for himself.

I do not mean to imply that this was conscious plan on his part. In part, I believe, this reflected the need of a fragile ego in a period of recovery, when he was "menaced by a psychosis." We do not have definitive biographical information about Jung, especially in this period of his life, but there is reason to believe that he surrounded himself with devoted, mostly female acolytes, and with their assistance he nursed himself back to psychological health (McLynn, 1996). The founding of the club, with the help of Edith McCormick's money, may well have been part of this process.

These developments inevitably stamped the Jungians quite differently from the Freudians. While Jung may have continued to see himself as a scientist expanding the frontiers of human knowledge, and to have sought out opportunities to influence his medical colleagues, to the educated public his movement as a whole came to have an amateurish and mystical cast. Without formal training, his followers who wished to take up careers in psychotherapy lacked credentials and suffered by comparison with their psychoanalytic competitors. Moreover, those followers who had enthusiastic if undiscriminating interests in mystical and paranormal phenomena – and the money to indulge those interests – received considerable notoriety. In the eyes of the educated public, Freud may have been the tyrannical father but he stood for something and he had standards. Jung, by comparison, seemed dreamy, impulsive, and distant.

Throughout the 1920s and 1930s psychoanalysts set up training institutes in Berlin, Vienna, London, Budapest, New York, Chicago, Washington, and Boston. They added considerably to the number of their professional journals, established links to medical organizations, and they continued to organize international congresses. They worked strenuously to develop a professional identity. The Jungians, by contrast, expanded informally: "What tended to happen was that on completion of their analysis and studies in Zurich, people returned to their countries of origin where they set up a practice and in time organized clubs on the Zurich model ... By World War II there were clubs in London, New York, San Francisco, Los Angeles, Berlin, Rome, Paris and Basel, as well as in Zurich" (Samuels, 1994, p. 139). There were occasional "seminars," at which Jung spoke; and there were some regularly scheduled meetings, such as those at Eranos, but they were in general by invitation only. It was not until after World War II that there were Jungian training institutes. Kirsch (2000) has argued: "It was only with the founding of the International Association for Analytical Psychology (IAAP) in 1955 that the authority for accreditation was definitively transferred from Jung personally to a professional association" (p. 17).

II

This beginning institutional history of analytical psychology has had a profound effect upon its development. On the one hand, it started out predominantly and defiantly non-professional. On the other, it could be said that the psychoanalytic "shadow" of analytical psychology nonetheless persisted in the form of analysts who longed for training and the legitimacy of credentials. Many of them were psychiatrists committed to developing clinical practices, aware of the training and recognition that was available to their Freudian counterparts and increasingly aware of the shortcomings in their own professional preparation and standing.

Samuels (1994) has described this process of "professionalization." Typically, a medical group separated out from the club and then, after some period of conflict, gave rise to a society or institute devoted to professional training: "For example, in San Francisco, the club, founded in 1939, spawned the Medical Society of Analytical Psychology in 1943 and in 1963, after further developments, the C. G. Jung Institute of San Francisco was founded. In New York, the Jung Club was established in 1936, the Medical Society in 1946 and, after certain vicissitudes, professional training began in 1963. In Berlin, Paris and Rome, the formation of professional societies did not start until after World War II" (p. 139).

According to Fordham (1979), two groups in England were formed before World War II, by those interested in pursuing careers as Jungian analysts: a medical group, the Medical Society of Analytical Psychology, and a group of laymen. The war delayed plans, but they decided to amalgamate, under medical leadership, and seek Jung's approval. "In many ways the London analysts were doing just what Jung had sought to avoid, they were forming a school of analytical psychology. His agreement to what was being done was, however, gained and he became the first president, protesting, however, that he would not be able to take an active part in the proceedings of the

Society. Clearly he was ambivalent, and when he was written to about the starting of a clinic, he registered a vigorous protest, but here again was persuaded to let his name be used ... The C. G. Jung Clinic was thus started with the master's approval" (p. 283).

Elsewhere, however, Fordham makes it clear that a deliberate and controversial decision was made not to name the society after Jung: "I would not function as chairman nor help in building up the structure of the body, if the cult of Jung's personality was not firmly resisted" (Fordham, 1993, p. 133). No doubt this attitude contributed to the tensions that developed between the club and the society. On the one hand, according to Samuels, "There was a negative reaction by the general membership towards the professional analysts" (1994, p. 141). On the other: "one also gets the impression that the analysts were, by 1944, somehow ashamed of the club members" (p. 142). Plaut observed bluntly: "The Club had to be left behind or we would never have been taken seriously by the Freudians" (Samuels, 1989, p. 179).

As Samuels (1994) pointed out, "the Society of Analytical Psychology of London followed the British Psychoanalytical Society when it drew up its constitution in 1946 and the nomenclature is, in many respects, identical" (p. 146). Moreover, as criteria for training were developed, the society made several key controversial decisions in response to training needs that increased tensions not only between the society and the club but also within the society between older Zurich-trained analysts and the new group under Fordham's leadership: a focus on transference, regression, and infantile material; an increase in the number of analytic sessions per week; evaluation of candidates by the training analyst; and a minimizing of "education" by the analyst. All of these are quite understandable in the context of traditional psychoanalytic training practices – of which the Jungian analysts were quite aware – but they represented significant departures from traditional Jungian practice.

The Zurich Institute, on the other hand, established in 1947, became the repository of Jungian tradition. According to Kirsch: "The Zurich Institute was the place to train; here one could have analysis with a direct pupil of Jung, perhaps also see Jung himself, and the Institute in Zurich was certainly oriented towards international students" (1996, p. 573). Here, until recently, there was little if any influence from psychoanalytic practice.

138 Organizational Analysis

Thus the conflict between the club and the society in London paralleled a growing rift with Zurich. Essentially, at this stage, there was the London Society of Analytical Psychology, under Fordham's direction, attempting to develop the possibility of analytical psychology as a clinical discipline, learning from and maintaining contacts with psychoanalysts, and there was the Zurich Institute, attempting to base itself more purely on Jung's own clinical practices and beliefs.

Fordham (1993) described a kind of "identity crisis" for the society in its growing "lack of interest in the Zurich point of view," a state of affairs he tried to remedy by inviting prominent analysts from the Zurich Institute to come over to London to lecture. "But our members thought they were clinically naive and exhibited a derogatory and critical attitude, which created a bad atmosphere" (p. 129). The London Jungians, under Fordham, noted the clinical inadequacies of the Zurich Jungians, together with what they took to be an arrogance and inflated sense of authority. On the other hand, they faced the charge of being "anti-Jungian" (p. 131) and they were, in fact, prone to doubts about their own identity as Jungians.

The situation in London provided unique opportunities for these developments. The institutional connections between the Jungian analysts and the members of the British Psychoanalytical Society through the British Medical Society, as well as the links through the Tavistock Institute, made connections and collaboration possible. Fordham (1979), describing symposia organized by the Medical Section of the British Psychological Society in the 1950s on topics of overlapping interest to psychoanalysts and analytical psychologists, observed that "it began to appear that the old divisions between the two disciplines were in the process of dissolving because of the new thinking that was going occurring on both sides. Thus though the divisions are maintained formally their scientific basis is less meaningful" (p. 293). And this may have been furthered by the fact that the split between Freud and Jung, historically sited in Vienna and Zurich, found in London a more neutral territory for some degree of rapprochement.

At the same time, of course, such tendencies also created tensions and anxieties within each camp around their loyalties and identities. Some members of the British Psychoanalytical Society, having weathered the storm of their "controversial discussions," may have seen the problem of collaboration with the Jungians to be of relatively minor significance. Not surprisingly, the Kleinians and members of the Middle School led the way in exploring common ground with their Jungian colleagues; on the other hand, Glover, who resigned as a result of the "controversial discussions," led the opposition to collaboration with his *Freud or Jung* (1950). Eventually, the initiatives to explore common themes faded out.

Tensions within the SAP grew between those who, following Fordham, were interested in links with psychoanalysis, and those more loyal to Zurich. Adler and others, restive with Fordham's particular version of this accommodation to psychoanalysis, felt increasingly at odds with the policies of the SAP. According to one account, incensed by what he took to be a disparaging comment by Fordham about his interest in the "numinous" (Stone, 1998), he forced a break and formed the Association of Jungian Analysts (AJA) in 1976, for the purpose of teaching, as he put it, "Jung's psychology in an undiluted form" (Adler, 1979, p. 117; Casement, 1995). While this split has often been viewed as a matter of personalities, I think it is clear that it represented long simmering differences among those who attempted to work out links with psychoanalysis and traditional Jungian practice. There could not be easy solutions to these dilemmas.

This is all the clearer, I think, in the light of the subsequent split within the AJA. After 1976, most of those who returned to England after training in Zurich "gravitated instead to A.J.A." (Casement, 1995, p. 336), eventually insisting that those trained in Zurich automatically be granted full membership in the AJA. Adler resisted this move. But in 1982, a split in the AJA occurred and a new group, the Independent Group of Analytical Psychologists (IGAP), representing Jung's psychology in an even less diluted form, was formed. The IGAP, seeking support from other international colleagues, brought this dispute to the International Association for Analytical Psychology in 1983.

Formed in 1955 to link together and regulate the new Jungian training institutes, the IAAP was the logical place for the London professionals to go with their disputes. As Kirsch (1995) put it: "The IAAP ... represents the Jungian analytical psychology as a field of professional practice ... For those of us who do practice as analysts, rather than simply 'follow Jungian thought,' the IAAP has the function of saying, (1) we have at least gone through a certain common denominator of training, (2) we are recognized by our analytic community to be practitioners in good standing, (3) we have been touched at some recognizably deep level by what analytical psychology has to say" (p. 247).

At the 1983 Jerusalem congress, "AJA was faced with expulsion by a motion from the dissenting members of AJA, who had among their number half the founding members and half the existing membership" (Stone, 1998, p. 12; Casement, 1995, p. 337). The solution, eventually arrived at by the 1986 congress in Berlin, was to accredit not only the AJA, and the IGAP, but also the Jungian Division of the British Association of Psychotherapists (BAP), along with, of course, the SAP. Thus, four rival Jungian training societies in London came to be accredited, three of them representing points on a continuum from Jungian orthodoxy to psychoanalytic collaboration in their history of schisms.

The Jungian Section of the BAP, interestingly, held out for collaboration with psychoanalysis as they were institutionally committed to a structure in which Freudian and Jungian trainings coexisted in parallel. Indeed, they had already developed close ties with the SAP, and later with other Jungian trainings in London. In effect, they placed themselves in the group seeking collaboration. But, as Solomon has observed (personal communication, 1999), the theoretical and clinical collaboration has been, for the most part, one-sided: the Jungians have sought to incorporate Freudian ideas, while the Freudians have shown little if any reciprocal interest.

The tensions and rifts between the training institutes that surfaced so prominently in England are no less present in America, though they have taken somewhat different forms. Kirsch (1996) has noted that, as in England: "Over time, professional analytic societies emerged from their respective clubs. The process of separation between the two was often fraught with tension" (p. 570). As the professional societies developed and grew, this intensified internal conflicts and tension.

As in England, there is the continuing tension of relations with Zurich. Graduates of the Zurich Institute from America return with a kind of "psychic inflation": "Because they had drunk the waters at the source, they felt they really understood the collective unconscious in most of its aspects, and they especially believed they understood healing. These graduates seemed to have most of the answers, and they seemed sure that those of us who had not trained in Zurich had not really understood Jung" (Kirsch, 1995, p. 240). Consequently, "A tension often develops between the existing local group and the incoming Zurich graduate, and not infrequently a mutual suspiciousness ... Jealousy, envy, rivalry, and assertions as to who represents the true Jungian position quickly develop" (Kirsch, 1995, p. 243). This is intensified, as Kirsch also points out, by the fact that often the Americans who go to Zurich for training are those who were not qualified for training in America. Thus they come back, seeking qualification from their local colleagues, inflated by their journey to the source, and viewed with deep suspicion and reservation.

The special role of the Zurich Institute in this conflict derives from its role as the "Mecca" of analytical psychology. That is, much as the émigré Viennese analysts in England and America derived their special status as Freudian apostles, bearers of the charismatic authority of Freud (Eisold, 1998; Chapter 2 in this volume), the Zuricher's special status and organizational rights derived from an incompletely mourned attachment to Jung. Thus they were able to continue to assert a degree of control over the professionalization of Jungian analysis that was in direct conflict with the professional standards established elsewhere. And, I believe, just as the professional Jungian institutes could not let go of their incompletely mourned attachment to Jung, they were ambivalently bound to honor the special authority vested in Zurich. As a result, they felt obliged to come to terms with it on a case by case basis, as each Zurich graduate requested integration into and acceptance by the local community. In this way, repeatedly, the representative of Zurich was received back into the renegade community of professional analysts and the local community atoned for its independence and separate standards. Thus different sets of standards and professional expectations were allowed to coexist within Jungian institutes, feeding internal conflicts and promoting dissension.

This ambivalence extends, in America at least, to the IAAP itself. As Kirsch (1995) observed: "Currently there is no official, functioning national organization of Jungian analysts in the United States ... The IAAP has therefore an instant authority, which most American members tend to deny consciously" (p. 245). And it may be that this conscious denial of the authority of the IAAP in America is linked to the fact that it contains an institutional anomaly: that is, graduates of the Zurich Institute, regardless of their level of professional preparation, are automatically certified as Jungian analysts by the IAAP. Increasingly, American institutes providing training in analytical psychology require some form of clinical certification as a prerequisite for acceptance. Zurich does not.

Thus, in American institutes, conflict between the traditionalists or the "classicists," in Samuels's 1995 classification, and the "developmentalists," those influenced and seeking continuing affiliation with psychoanalysis, has tended to be contained within each institute (Samuels, 1985, 1996). There has not been a significant history of schism, but there has been substantial evidence of ambivalence and internal conflict painfully internalized. Different points of view coexist with thinly disguised hostility. This has, in its own way, often crippled the ability of institutes to develop and function effectively. Decisions are made and then undone as new factions come to power and refuse to implement them – or simply ignore and forget them. Members easily become burnt out, alienated, disaffected, and are reluctant to take on management responsibility under such circumstances. Often, as a result, the management function tends to be taken over by authoritarian leaders who step in and save the squabbling and ineffectual members from themselves.

III

Let us recapitulate this sequence of splits and delineate the process more closely.

The starting point is Jung's ouster from his leadership position and Freud's assertion of his ownership of psychoanalysis. This traumatic event led to a profound division in Jung's identity. On the one hand there is the part that could not be contained within psychoanalysis as shaped and controlled by Freud, the identity of the spiritual seeker, the explorer of myths and archetypes. This is the side of Jung that led him to the formation of his clubs, his "experiment," to the writing of his many books on symbols, and, eventually, to the seminars and other forums in which he assumed the role of teacher. This is the more public and known side of Jung.

The other side of Jung, the psychiatrist and psychotherapist, the wounded associate of Freud, developed in a more hidden and secretive manner, nurtured in the informal network of devoted followers, many of whom were non-professional women. In this more private world, he could support the belief – formed out of his traumatic relationship with psychoanalysis – that analysis ought to be a vocation, not a profession, a calling requiring special gifts of commitment and insight rather than training and evaluation. This informal organizational network depended on personal contact with Jung, who authorized individuals to practice through letters he wrote testifying to their psychological and spiritual development. In this sheltered world, he could also seek to immunize himself against the tensions and conflicts of transference and countertransference by cultivating his special, idealized position, by advocating multiple simultaneous treatments, by asserting the privileged privacy of the analytic relationship, and by severely restricting his public communications on the subject of treatment.

At the same time, this side of Jung, rooted in an empirical and scientific background, was experienced and informed as a clinician and trainer. Ambivalent as he was about exploring transference and countertransference, he insisted on the need for analysts to be analyzed themselves. And though he opposed instituting formal training, he did eventually agree to the setting up of training institutes first in London and then in Zurich.

We have seen the tensions and conflicts between the clubs and professional institutes, reflecting this split between the two sides of Jung's professional identity. These splits were sustained and energized, of course, by the divergent and competing interests of the groups involved. Thus, while the splits may have originated in the division of Jung's identity, they came to have a life of their own as the professional psychotherapists struggled with the club members and spiritual followers over Jung's legacy. Moreover, as we have seen, there were tensions between the two groups that arose over the incompatibility of their different missions. For the professional therapists, the amateurish and enthusiastic club members were an embarrassment, compromising their claim to professional recognition. For the club members, the professionals' claim was an unwarranted usurpation of power, relegating them to the status of mere "patients."

This conflict was transferred to the various training institutes, as we have seen, struggling over their interest in (and loyalty to) Jung and their interest in (and competition with) psychoanalysis. In recent years, as Fordham observed, there has been "new thinking." Parallels between Kleinian and other object relations theorists continue to be explored (Astor, 1995; Solomon, 1997; Knox, 1997, 1999), while other parallels with Winnicott and Bion are developed (Samuels, 1995). In America the influence of Kohut has been noted along with that of recent object relations theory via the work of Grotstein and Ogden (Kirsch, 1996). At the same time, new thinking has led to reformulations of such traditional Jungian notions as archetypes, making them more accessible to and compatible with contemporary mainstream psychoanalytic thinking.

Moreover, in America, the old proscription of the term "psychoanalysis" has been eroded: the copyright appears to have lapsed. Currently, the C. G. Jung Institutes of New York, Chicago, and Los Angeles are component societies of the National Association for the Advancement of Psychoanalysis – as is the Alfred Adler Institute in New York – which means that they sought and received accreditation as "psychoanalytic" institutes. I don't believe this implies that the identities of these institutes as organizational parts of analytical psychology no longer matter, but there is a larger – and older – identity they are reclaiming. In 1996, an entire issue of *The Psychoanalytic Review* was devoted to "Post-Jungian Thought," and *Psychoanalytic Dialogues* has featured a post-Jungian issue in May/June 2000.

But as Kirsch noted in his address to a 1996 conference in Sebasco, Maine, organized by the *Journal of Analytical Psychology* to explore links with psychoanalysis: "As psychoanalysts in general have so little knowledge of Jung and the Jungian literature, there is the potential danger that our uniqueness could get lost. On the other hand, most of us have some working knowledge of psychoanalysis in its various forms and are only too happy to embrace large parts of it. Will it go the other way around?" (Kirsch, 1997, p. 24).

Recently, Samuels (1998) has suggested that the split throughout the worldwide Jungian community is becoming more pronounced. Whereas in 1996 he still saw three schools of Jungian thought, he now sees four: "The classical and developmental schools have stayed pretty much as they were ... But there are two new schools to consider, each of which is an extreme version of one of the two hitherto existing schools, classical and developmental. I call these two extreme versions Jungian fundamentalism on the one hand and Jungian merger with psychoanalysis on the other." In the illustrative examples Samuels provides, the Jungian fundamentalist is ignorant of some of Freud's most basic cases, while the Jungian psychoanalyst follows a model of treatment that focuses almost entirely on process and ignores content.

While the classical and developmental schools have fought with each other, they at least retained some understanding of each other's positions. In the process Samuels describes, the extreme fundamentalist and psychoanalytic schools are not only thoroughly alienated from each other, but also they appear to have encapsulated themselves. In one, Freud has disappeared; for the other, Jung's interest in depth psychology is of uncertain relevance.

External factors have severely exacerbated these conflicts. In England, the split in the United Kingdom Council for Psychotherapy (UKCP) leading to the formation of the British Confederation of Psychotherapists (BCP) has driven a further wedge between the SAP and BAP, on the one hand, and the AJA and the IGAP on the other (Casement, 1995). This, in turn, has challenged and significantly eroded the good will that had begun to develop in the Umbrella Group, formed to link the existing four Jungian institutes in London (Stone, 1998). Again, the underlying issue has to do with professional standing and status. In this era of increasing competition among mental health practitioners, it has become more important to be – and to appear to be – more rigorous and demanding in maintaining standards of training in order to maintain one's competitive edge. Those traditionally more rigorous in their standards for training – and, moreover, more closely associated with psychoanalysis in their institutional development – are at pains to distinguish themselves from those who appear to be less so.

The comparable issue in the United States is the increasing requirement of state governments that mental health practitioners be licensed. In order to comply, institutes will face pressures not only to alter admissions policies of long standing, accepting only those who will be eligible for licensure, but also to de-authorize some faculty members and supervisors who currently occupy training roles but do not meet state requirements. Increasing competition and success inevitably lead to stricter standards for training and greater regulation.

This significantly impacts the underlying fundamental issue for Jungians about their own identity. The original division in Jung himself between the spiritual seeker and healer and the professional therapist, subsequently played out within and between institutes over the issues of their identities and missions, is now perpetuated and exacerbated by competition in the marketplace and state regulation. It becomes extremely difficult for individual practitioners to work out their own theoretical and clinical syntheses, much less seek and find help from others, without closing themselves off in their own institutional enclaves. Positions become concretized and entrenched as factions define themselves in opposition to other factions.

IV

This situation defines a growing crisis for analytical psychology. On the one hand, a greater degree of creative and innovative thinking is called for; frank discussion, debate and dialogue are required in order to foster new adaptations. On the other hand, institutes are often immobilized by internal conflict and threatened by increasing competition and external regulation. As a result, they are rendered less able to collaborate.

I think that members of Jungian institutes have to work at these dilemmas collectively in order to reach a workable understanding, if not consensus. The issues need to be clearly and unapologetically defined, and then wrestled with and debated openly. This process cannot be easy. Training institutes, at best, are vulnerable organizations. They depend on voluntary donations of time, effort, and money. Moreover, they contain powerful lineages and pairings between analysts and supervisors, on the one hand, and trainees, on the other, that elicit loyalties and passions far more powerful than those elicited by the institution as a whole; as a result, it is easy for institute members to minimize the importance of their institutes to themselves and to split off or withdraw from active participation (Allphin, 1999; Eisold, 1994). It is often difficult to differentiate the real issues at stake from the "social defenses" (Menzies, 1967) that have been erected to contain anxiety and protect existing conditions of emotional stability. The process of undoing defenses cannot be undergone without considerable anxiety, much less conflict and pain.

Let me try to give some more specific examples of the kinds of issues raised by this fundamental ambiguity within the professional identity of Jungian analysts. Stone and Duckworth (1999) have raised the question of frequency of treatment in analytical psychology: What is the actual impact of different frequencies on patient outcomes? This question, as discussed above, has been largely determined by the training policies of the various institutes in which different Jungian analysts have trained; those policies, in turn, have been shaped by the ways those institutes have been influenced by mainstream psychoanalysis and the pressures of the marketplace. Thus traditional assumptions about frequency, which are allied to different forms of professional identity, inevitably shape the issue – and promote controversy. Can it become possible on the basis of reasoned theoretical discussions and actual clinical experience to develop a distinctively Jungian set of perspectives on this issue? I do not mean by this that there should be a Jungian rule on frequency. Rather, might it be possible to develop a set of questions or considerations to think this matter through so that informed conversations including informed disagreements might be sustained?

Let me raise another issue. In evaluating candidates during training, inevitably, questions will be raised about the emotional capacity of some candidates to practice. If the orientation of the evaluator is one of spiritual healing, the tendency may well be to see the candidate as a struggling "soul" requiring patience, acceptance, and encouragement. The obligation of the community to sustain and refrain from abandoning its members may be stressed. If the orientation, on the other hand, is that of a "professional," more likely the candidate will be assigned a DSM IV diagnosis for a character disorder and placed on probation, remanded to an experienced supervisor, or simply dismissed. The need of the community to sustain its professional reputation, in this case, may seem paramount. These are different points of view – both of which can be justified – but they will inevitably lead to conflict among those holding responsibility for making such decisions. Again, would it be possible to develop reasoned conversations on such issues so that those holding different perspectives are not demonized or cast into subversive roles?

A final example: An education or curriculum committee charged with developing an educational plan for candidates in training has to be informed by an understanding of the mission or overriding purpose of the institute. What are the aims of training? What kind or kinds of practitioners does the institute try to develop? Competing factions within an institute with different points of view can agree to divide up the pie, so to speak, each faction gaining some control over the final product. This will curtail and postpone controversy, but it will also ensure a poorly integrated curriculum as well as confused and alienated candidates who will carry on the disputes of their analysts and supervisors.

Members of an organization need to share a common view of the organizational purpose if they are to work together. Hopefully, they will disagree about how to interpret it in particular cases; they will stress the importance of different aspects of it and bring to it different skills and values. But if they can agree on the aim of the organization, they can find the way to work together.

And, no doubt, sharply different and competing points of view will emerge in different institutes. Analytical psychology may become more openly pluralistic, as psychoanalysis has become pluralistic. Samuels (1995) has argued that this does not mean they need to be tamely inclusive. Indeed, this may enable them to become more frankly combative: "Through competition and agreement with others we may come to know ourselves and our ideas better and more deeply" (p. 34). That, in turn, opens up the possibility of becoming once again more competitive with psychoanalysis – but openly and in a spirit of mutual development.

The alternative to confronting and working through these disagreements is the continuing fragmentation of the Jungian community and the progressive weakening of many institutes. To be sure, some institutes will survive, but the current larger institutional framework that supports and sustains them will be eroded. Psychoanalysis, as well, is under attack and facing comparable strains. Our current social and economic climate is not hospitable to prolonged and deep psychological treatments. Internal conflict and weakness will only lessen the capacity of institutes to adapt creatively and survive with integrity.

In a sense, the divisions in Jung's identity provided and still provides analytical psychology with a unique opportunity to develop "new thinking" about dynamic psychotherapy. If psychoanalysis suffered from too great a degree of authoritarian centralized control and homogeneity, analytical psychology was set an opposite problem. New pathways were opened up, but often they led through uncharted territory. Jung, brilliant as he was, was hampered in his ability to provide guidance and control. Little wonder, then, his followers fell to squabbling and splintering along the way. But that was then.

References

Adler, G. (1979). *Dynamics of the Self*. London: Coventure.

Allphin, C. (1999). Complexities and paradoxes in our organizational life. *Journal of Analytical Psychology* 44: 249–58.

Astor, J. (1995). *Michael Fordham: Innovations in Analytical Psychology*. London: Routledge.

Brabant, E., Falzeder, E., & Giampieri-Deutsch, P. (1993). *The Correspondence of Sigmund Freud and Sandor Ferenczi*, Vol. 1: *1908–1914*. Cambridge, MA: Harvard University Press.

Casement, A. (1995). A brief history of Jungian splits in the United Kingdom. *Journal of Analytical Psychology* 40, 327–42.

Eisold, K. (1994). The intolerance of diversity in psychoanalytic institutes. *International Journal of Psychoanalysis* 75(4), 785–800.

Eisold, K. (1997). Freud as leader: the early years of the Viennese Society. *International Journal of Psychoanalysis* 78(1), 87–104.

Eisold, K. (1998). The splitting of the New York Psychoanalytic Society and the construction of analytic authority. *International Journal of Psychoanalysis* 79(5), 871–85.

Ellenberger, H. (1970). *The Discovery of the Unconscious*. New York: Basic Books.

Fordham, M. (1961). Obituary: C. G. Jung. *British Journal of Medical Psychology* 34(3–4).

Fordham, M. (1974). Memories and thoughts about C. G. Jung. *Journal of Analytical Psychology* 20, 102–13.

Fordham, M. (1979). Analytical psychology in England. *Journal of Analytical Psychology* 24, 279–97.

Fordham, M. (1993). *The Making of an Analyst: A Memoir*. London: Free Association Books.

Freud, S. (1914). On the history of the psychoanalytic movement. In J. Strachey (ed. and trans.), *The Standard Edition of the Complete Psychological Works of Sigmund Freud* (Vol. 14, pp. 3–66). London: Hogarth Press.

Gallant, C. (1996). *Tabooed Jung*. New York: New York University Press.

Glover, E. (1950). *Freud or Jung?* Evanston, IL: Northwestern University Press.

Grosskurth, P. (1991). *The Secret Ring*. Reading, MA: Addison-Wesley.

Grosskurth, P. (1998). Psychoanalysis: a dysfunctional family. *Journal of Analytical Psychology* 43(1), 87–95.

Jung, C. G. (1960). The stages of life. In *Collected Works* (Vol. 8), 387–403. Princeton: Princeton University Press.

Jung, C. G. (1961). *Memories, Dreams, Reflections.* New York: Random House.

Kirsch, T. B. (1995). IAAP and Jungian identity: a president's reflections. *Journal of Analytical Psychology* 40, 235–48.

Kirsch, T. B. (1996). A brief history of analytical psychology. *The Psychoanalytic Review* 83(4), 569–77.

Kirsch, T. B. (1997). Response to John Beebe. *Journal of Analytical Psychology* 42, 21–4.

Kirsch, T. B. (1998). Family matters. *Journal of Analytical Psychology* 43, 77–85.

Kirsch, T. B. (2000). *The Jungians: A Comparative and Historical Perspective.* London: Routledge.

Knox, J. (1997). Internal objects: a theoretical analysis of Jungian and Kleinian models. *Journal of Analytical Psychology* 42, 653–66.

Knox, J. (1999). The relevance of attachment theory to a contemporary Jungian view of the internal world: internal working models, implicit memory and internal objects. *Journal of Analytical Psychology* 44, 511–30.

Kuhn, P.(1998). "A pretty piece of treachery": the strange case of Dr Stekel and Sigmund Freud. *International Journal of Psychoanalysis* 79(6), 1151–71.

McGuire, W. (ed.) (1988). *The Freud/Jung Letters: The Correspondence Between Sigmund Freud and C. G. Jung.* Cambridge, MA: Harvard University Press.

McLynn, F. (1996). *Carl Gustav Jung.* New York: St. Martin's Press.

Menzies, E. (1967). *The Functioning of Social Systems as Defense against Anxiety.* London: Tavistock Publications.

Noll, R. (1994). *The Jung Cult.* New York: Free Press.

Noll, R. (1997). *The Aryan Christ: The Secret Life of Carl Jung.* New York: Random House.

Paskauskas, A. A. (1988). Freud's break with Jung. *Free Associations* 11, 7–34.

Paskauskas, R. A. (ed.) (1993). *The Complete Correspondence between Sigmund Freud and Ernest Jones.* Cambridge, MA: Harvard University Press.

Peck, J. (1997). Jung in the U.S.A. *San Francisco Jung Institute Library Journal* 15(4), 53–65.

Roazen, P. (1984). *Freud and His Followers.* New York: New York University Press.

Roustang, F. (1982). *Dire Mastery: Discipleship from Freud to Lacan.* Baltimore: Johns Hopkins University Press.

Samuels, A. (1985). *Jung and the Post-Jungians.* London: Routledge & Kegan Paul.

Samuels, A. (1989). Fred Plaut in conversation with Andrew Samuels. *Journal of Analytical Psychology* 34, 159–83.

Samuels, A. (1994). The professionalization of Carl G. Jung's analytical psychology clubs. *Journal of the History of the Behavioral Sciences* 30, 138–47.

Samuels, A. (1995). Pluralism and psychotherapy. *Australian Journal of Psychotherapy* 14(1–2), 31–44.

Samuels, A. (1996). Jung's return from banishment. *The Psychoanalytic Review* 83(4), 469–89.

Samuels, A. (1998). Will the Post-Jungians survive? in A. Casement (ed.), *The Post-Jungians Today*. London: Routledge.

Shamdasani, S. (1994). Introduction: the censure of the speculative. In S. Shamdasani & M. Munchow (eds.), *Speculations after Freud: Psychoanalysis, Philosophy and Culture*. London: Routledge.

Shamdasani, S. (1998). *Cult Fictions: C. G. Jung and the Founding of Analytical Psychology*. London: Routledge.

Solomon, H. M. (1997). The developmental school. In P. Young-Eisendrath & T. Dawson (eds.), *The Cambridge Companion to Jung* (pp. 128–75). Cambridge: Cambridge Univeristy Press.

Stepansky, P. (1976). The empiricist as rebel: Jung, Freud, and the burdens of discipleship. *Journal of the History of the Behavioral Sciences* 12, 216–39.

Stone, M. (1998). Splits between Jungian groups: diversity and division. In *Festschrift for the Association of Jungian Analysts 21st Anniversary* (pp. 139–56). London: Association of Jungian Analysts.

Stone, M., & Duckworth, M. (1999). The issue of frequency in the analytic process. Workshop at Exchanging Subjects: Contemporary Perspectives on Unconscious Processes and Analytic Method, The Third Annual Conference sponsored by the Journal of Analytical Psychology, Merida, Mexico, March 10–14, 1999.

Symington, N. (1986). *The Analytic Experience: Lectures from the Tavistock*. London: Free Association Books.

Young-Eisendrath, P. (1995). Struggling with Jung. *Round Table Review*, March–April, 1995.

Chapter Seven

Jung, Jungians, and Psychoanalysis

[Originally published as Jung, Jungians, and Psychoanalysis, *Psychoanalytic Psychology*, vol. 19 (2002), pp. 501–24.]

I

Who owns psychoanalysis? The question may seem absurd to us now, and yet the issue of proprietorship and control of the copyright has been an intricate and pervasive part of our history. In his "History of the Psychoanalytic Movement," Freud (1914/1966) asserted bluntly: "psycho-analysis is my creation ... I consider myself justified in maintaining that even today no one can know better than I do what psycho-analysis is, how it differs from other ways of investigating the life of the mind, and precisely what should be called psycho-analysis and what would be better described by some other name" (p. 7). He emphatically made the point that Adler and Jung should stop using the term. And, indeed, they did.

The myth that grew up around Freud as the isolated and courageous hero (Sulloway, 1979) legitimized his ownership: He was the conquistador who first set foot upon the territory of psychoanalysis, the Copernicus who first observed its distant movements, the Newton who first elucidated its laws. He encouraged that myth by repeatedly stressing the courage required to hold firm to the stark truths of psychoanalysis in the face of the resistances and opposition of society. In his "Autobiographical Study" (1925/1966) Freud restated his conviction that Adler's and Jung's defections were motivated by the "temptation ... of being freed from ... the repellent findings of psychoanalysis" (p. 52).

The myth of the hero became the myth of the movement. Freud wrote Ferenczi: "Of course, everything that strives to get away from our truths has public approval in its favor ... We are in possession of the truth" (Brabant et al., 1993, pp. 482–3). To Abraham: "recognition will come only for the next generation. But we have the incomparable satisfaction of having made the first discoveries" (Abraham & Freud, 1966, p. 111).

The claim required an institutional basis. "There should be some headquarters whose business it would be to declare: 'All this nonsense is nothing to do with analysis; this is not psycho-analysis.'" So wrote Freud in 1914 (1914, p. 43), explaining his motive in forming the International Psychoanalytic Association. Earlier, before the threat of Adler's and Jung's "defections," he had similarly claimed that the International was founded "to repudiate responsibility for what is done by those who do not belong to us and yet call their medical procedure 'psycho-analysis'" (Freud, 1910, p. 227).

By the public, Freud may have been seen as autocratic or authoritarian, but there was no doubt that he was and remained the dominant figure – victor, leader, and proprietor. Adler and Jung continued to be defined by their relationship to the central, heroic enterprise from which they "defected." Paradoxically, they were cast out of the psychoanalytic band and, yet, perpetually linked to it as "deviants," "former disciples," derivative figures. Protesting this continuing linkage, Ellenberger (1970) stressed the point that both Adler and Jung had developed some of their key ideas before being swept up in the psychoanalytic movement and that they evolved quite differently from Freud and each other: "Contrary to popular assumption, neither Adler nor Jung is a 'psychoanalytic deviant,' and their systems are not mere distortions of psychoanalysis" (p. 571). But this remains a lonely point of view.

Indeed, Adler himself responded to his "expulsion" by naming the alternate society he founded the Society for Free Psychoanalytic Research. He was stunned and deeply hurt by Freud's ad hominum attacks on his "petty outbursts of malice" and "uncontrolled craving for priority" (Freud, 1914/1966, p. 51). But, in his injured pride, he stressed the point that this was an institutional issue not a personal one.

If Adler's response to Freud's declaration of ownership was defiant, he nevertheless agreed to give up the term "psychoanalysis."

Jung, by contrast, at first entirely withdrew from organizational life, resigning all institutional positions after resigning as president of the International Psychoanalytic Association, including his university professorship, abandoning the Zurich Psychoanalytic Society, and only gradually finding a way back into organizational life as an "analytical psychologist."

"By common consent, Jung never got over the trauma of his break with Freud," wrote a recent biographer (McLynn, 1996, p. 420). He himself suggested in *Memories, Dreams, Reflections* (1961) that he underwent a profound disorientation, "menaced by a psychosis" (p. 176). I think we can understand this disorientation as representing a cleavage in Jung's identity. No doubt there was a confusing and troubled working out of his relationship to Freud as a father, but also there was conflict among the identities he had attempted to weld together as a psychoanalyst. As Ellenberger (1970) pointed out – and as Taylor (1996, 1998) and Shamdasani (1998) more recently elaborated – Jung brought to psychoanalysis not only considerable standing as a psychiatrist, a standing that so impressed Freud, but also he brought significantly developed interests and orientations that linked him with others outside psychoanalysis. To put it perhaps over-simply, there was the identity of a psychiatrist and psychologist, linked to Freud, committed to working professionally with patients, and there was the identity of a spiritual seeker, drawn to the study of religious myth and linked to the long line of Protestant ministers from which he had descended.

But the important point here is that his experience with Freud and the International Psychoanalytic Association inevitably had profound organizational consequences as well. After reorienting himself and his thoughts, following the break with Freud, Jung also had to develop the organizational structures and policies that would carry his work forward. Those structures had to be responsive to the particular needs and qualities of his ideas and his identity. Inevitably, they reflected his traumatic experiences with the organizations of psychoanalysis he left behind. And as they developed, they continued to bear the imprint of that traumatic break and to exhibit a complex, conflicted, and ambiguous relationship with psychoanalysis. In a parallel paper, I focus on the impact of that split on the institutional development of analytical psychology (Eisold, 2001; Chapter 6 in this volume), the effects of which are still powerfully felt today.

Here I want to focus on the effects of that split on psychoanalysis. Freud's determination to exclude Jung and his followers did not abate, and many of his loyal followers enthusiastically kept up the struggle. The International, formed to defend against "deviants," is still not open to Jung's followers. Indeed, I think, many in the psychoanalytic mainstream do not even recognize it as an issue to be concerned with; they "own" the copyright to the term "psychoanalysis" that Jung gave up the right to use. In a sense, they would agree with Ellenberger that Jung is not a psychoanalytic "deviant," though he may once have been. They see him as a somewhat mystical, somewhat eccentric – if popular – writer on myths and dreams. They may be well aware that there are Jungian institutes and Jungian practitioners, but, generally, that is viewed as having no relevance.

In effect, the struggle against Jung initiated by Freud has become more subtle, more embedded in everyday assumptions. Like Foucault, we could view this as a struggle to dominate and control the discourse: Language now, itself, keeps analytical psychology outside. But I will argue that the open war has been succeeded by the entrenched, invisible warfare of social defenses aimed at maintaining vestigial boundaries around psychoanalysis, of containing threats to its integrity and core assumptions. Many "deviants" followed Jung. Indeed, a central portion of the history of psychoanalysis can be read as the story of such "defectors" as Horney, Sullivan, Thompson, Fromm, Lacan, and others, key figures suffering fates narrowly avoided by others such as Ferenczi, Klein, and Kohut. None of them were forced to abandon the term "psychoanalysis," no doubt emboldened and warned by the examples of Adler and Jung, though many of them were subject to the same charge of watering down psychoanalysis to make it more acceptable to the public. It has been said of most of them, at one point or another, "This is not psychoanalysis." But their use of the term was never successfully proscribed. Jung remains the warning figure who went too far, the one who defines the dangerous boundary of what is acceptable.

II

In 1916, when Jung emerged from his period of "disorientation" and "confusion," the organization he founded to support and advance his work was a "Psychological Club." Retrospectively, he called it "a silent experiment in group psychology" (CW, 10, para 887). In a paper he presented to the club in 1916, he wrote: "It is an attempt to work together as analyzed men ... We are acquainted in analysis up till now only with the function of the personal-collective (analyst and patient), just as we have learnt much about the individual function. But we know nothing about the collective function of individuals and its conditions" (Shamdasani, 1998, p. 24). As Fordham put it much later: "it was to have no professional status, and membership was not a qualification to practice psychotherapy" (1979, p. 279). It was a group gathered together to support members in their own spiritual and psychological development. In doing so, they would also support Jung and provide a forum for him to present his thoughts.

This club has been called a "cult" (Noll, 1994, 1997), and, indeed, in its blending of mystical and German "volkisch" elements together with the reverence for Jung's idealized position in it, the club bears some resemblance to a cult. But it seems more likely that the club actually suffered from a lack of clear focus, permitting it to resemble, as one member wrote at the time, sometimes a "madhouse" and sometimes something "occult-sectarian" (Shamdasani, 1998, p. 78). It was convivial and social. A library was organized. There were lectures and discussions; every two weeks or so Jung met there with a group of senior analysts.

Responding to his recent experience of the professional structures of psychoanalysis, structures dominated by a strong leader, Jung was determinedly informal and non-professional. As Fordham (1979) put it: "Jung did not want to form a school of Jungian analysts, and, indeed, no formal training was ever instituted by him. He had witnessed that particular development in psychoanalysis; he did not like it and he did not want to repeat it" (p. 280).

Indeed, not only had he witnessed psychoanalytic politics first hand as the first president of the IPA, he had been the object of an organizational plot to displace and discredit him. The summer before his personal break with Freud, Jones had proposed a secret committee that would operate outside of the formal structures of the International (Grosskurth, 1991). In his letter proposing the "unofficial inner circle," Jones expressed his "pessimism" about the "men who must lead for the next thirty years," noting "Jung abdicates his throne" (Paskauskas, 1993, p. 146). The reference was to the fact that Jung had suddenly gone to America to deliver lectures and see patients, postponing the 1912 congress as a result. Jones pointedly lamented, in that same letter to Freud, "so many put their own private personality first, in the foreground of importance, and relegate the cause to a subordinate position" (p. 145).

As Grosskurth (1998) put it: the Secret Committee's "implicit raison d'etre was to expel Jung, the Outsider, from the psychoanalytic movement" (p. 91). Immersed in their own suspicions and plots, they became riddled with paranoid fears about Jung's plans to take over the psychoanalytic movement.

For his part, Jung seems to have had little idea of the campaign being mounted against him. He did not know that he had been supplanted by the Secret Committee, that his authority had been undermined. When Freud and his close followers abstained from voting for him in his second term as president, he appeared to be genuinely surprised and hurt (Jones, 1955). He was obviously deeply offended the following month when he heard that Freud doubted his good faith in his conduct as editor of the Jahrbuch, and he precipitously resigned (Paskauskas, 1988, p. 28). As it turned out, Jung not only had no interest in a fight but, as ever, little interest in running an organization. In April 1914, he resigned as president.

The issue was loyalty, the willingness of Freud's followers to defer to his leadership, to confirm his ownership of psychoanalysis. But while it was undoubtedly the case that Freud wanted to maintain his ownership of psychoanalysis (see Roustang, 1982), it is important to bear in mind that it was Freud himself who put forth both Adler and Jung as his successors. Their ability to succeed depended on the willingness of others to follow them. In the case of Adler, I believe, his erstwhile followers brought him down, exploiting the issue of theoretical differences, in order to induce Freud to take charge (Eisold, 1997; Chapter 1 in this volume). In the case of Jung, the loved and chosen "Crown Prince," it was a group of Freud's closest followers who banded together and – with Jung's own active cooperation – deposed him.

This was the experience that lay behind Jung's decision to set up his club. In his new organization, by avoiding a professional focus and placing the emphasis entirely on mutual support and spiritual development, he hoped, consciously at least, to avoid recreating the organizational dangers he had come to know first hand. He also created for himself an institutional refuge. No other formal organization existed, associated with Jung, until the founding of the Jung Institute in 1948.

"How anyone became an analytic therapist in those days is vague and must be regarded largely as a matter of vocation, though there was an unwritten law that any person who wanted to be called a Jungian analyst was expected to go out to Zurich, make a relation with Jung himself, and undergo analysis with either himself or one or more of his close colleagues" (Fordham, 1979, p. 280). At some point, Jung would indicate that he felt the person was ready to practice and wrote a letter to that effect. Samuels (1994) pointed out, this "cozy club setting" was "undoubtedly riddled by unresolved transferences and countertransferences ... One gets the impression from accounts of people who were there of a sort of therapeutic community" (p. 139).

Thus, setting out deliberately to avoid the kind of professional competition and rivalries that had characterized psychoanalytic politics, Jung ended up in the "silent experiment" of the club creating an almost hermetically secure environment for himself. By rejecting formal training, he avoided the possibility of creating rivals. And by not exploring transference, he ensured his preeminent, idealized status.

In part, I believe, this reflected the need of a fragile ego in a period of recovery, when he was "menaced by a psychosis." But it also represented a choice about the nature of the movement he wished to establish. The stress was on exploration of myths and religions, on education in occult traditions of symbolism, and on articulating the notion of spiritual development. Only secondarily was there a focus on the preparation of careers in psychotherapy.

III

When formal professional training in analytical psychology began, following World War II, it emerged with Jung's reluctant agreement. Aging and ill, he was persuaded to give his consent. Moreover, professional training had to establish itself in the institutional space that had been created in the intervening years, the space between Jung's psychological clubs and the highly professionalized world of psychoanalysis. Inevitably, it was forced to be in competition with both.

The development that Jung resisted, thus, took two opposing courses, represented by the two training institutions that were the first to be established: The Zurich Institute, founded in 1947, in the city where Jung continued to live, stayed close to his informal methods and to the ethos of the clubs, stressing education in myth and symbols. The other, the Society for Analytical Psychology (SAP), sited in London, founded in 1946, looked to psychoanalysis for models of training and professional links.

According to Fordham (1979), the chairman of the SAP: "In many ways the London analysts were doing just what Jung had sought to avoid ... His agreement to what was being done was, however, gained and he became the first president, protesting, however, that he would not be able to take an active part in the proceedings of the Society. No doubt he was ambivalent, and when he was written to about the starting of a clinic, he registered a vigorous protest, but here again was persuaded to let his name be used ... The C. G. Jung Clinic was thus started with the master's approval" (p. 283).

As Samuels (1994) noted, "the Society of Analytical Psychology of London followed the British Psychoanalytical Society when it drew up its constitution in 1946 and the nomenclature is, in many respects identical" (p. 146). In addition, the society made several key controversial decisions that were based on the practices of the British Psychoanalytical Society and which, as a result, increased tensions not only between the society and the club but also within the society between older Zurich-trained analysts and the new group under Fordham's leadership: a focus on transference, regression, and infantile material; an increase in the number of analytic sessions per week; evaluation of candidates by the training analyst; and a minimizing of "education" by the analyst. All of these represented significant departures from Jungian traditions.

The Jungians in England also actively explored parallels between their theories and methods and those of Klein (Fordham, 1993; Astor, 1995) as well as Winnicott and Bion (Samuels, 1985). The institutional connections between the Jungian analysts and the members of the British Psychoanalytical Society through the British Medical Society, as well as the links through the Tavistock Institute, made additional connections and collaboration possible. Fordham (1979) noted, "it began to appear that the old divisions between the two disciplines were in the process of dissolving because of the new thinking that was occurring on both sides. Thus though the divisions are maintained formally their scientific basis is less meaningful" (p. 293).

In his obituary of Jung, Fordham declared forcefully that he believed that the notion of Jung's personal and scientific incompatibility with Freud "was a disaster, and in part an illusion, from which we suffer and will continue to do so until we have repaired the damage" (1961, p. 168). It could be said that in the manner in which Fordham took up the job of establishing training for analytical psychologists he aimed precisely to repair the damage.

The Zurich Institute, on the other hand, established in 1947, became the repository of Jungian tradition, the Mecca attracting international students. According to Kirsch: "The Zurich Institute was the place to train; here one could have analysis with a direct pupil of Jung, perhaps also see Jung himself, and the Institute in Zurich was certainly oriented towards international students" (1996, p. 573). There was little if any influence from psychoanalytic practice. Indeed, it "was set up on the model of a European university with lectures, seminars, and finally exams" (Kirsch, 1995, p. 237). Multiple overlapping analyses were conducted, and a primary stress on dreams and myth was maintained.

The founding of these two centers of training inaugurated the complex and strife-torn institutional history of analytical psychology in the postwar era. In America, the battles of Jungian orthodoxy versus psychoanalytic influence have tended to be fought within institutes. As in England, many mental health professionals have sought training, many of them influenced by the theories and practices of mainstream psychoanalysis. Moreover, in recent years, a number of American Jungians have moved toward reclaiming the term "psychoanalysis." Currently, the C. G. Jung Institutes of New York, Chicago, and Los Angeles are component societies of the National Association for the Advancement of Psychoanalysis – as is the Alfred Adler Institute in New York – which means that they sought and received accreditation as "psychoanalytic" institutes. I do not believe this implies that the identities of these institutes as organizational parts of analytical psychology no longer matter, but there is a larger – and older – identity they are reclaiming.

Furthermore, the American Jungians, under the auspices of the *Journal of Analytical Psychology*, organized a series of conferences to explore areas of common or overlapping interest with mainstream Freudians. Conferences were held at Sebasco, Maine in 1996 and 1997; a third was held in Merida. A similar event was held in England to explore differences between contemporary Jungians and psychoanalysts (Astor, 1998).

As Kirsch noted in his address to a 1996 conference in Sebasco: "As psychoanalysts in general have so little knowledge of Jung and the Jungian literature, there is the potential danger that our uniqueness could get lost. On the other hand, most of us have some working knowledge of psychoanalysis in its various forms and are only too happy to embrace large parts of it. Will it go the other way around?" (Kirsch, 1997, p. 24).

IV

Symington (1986) has declared emphatically: "We of the Freudian school who have rejected Jung have been impoverished thereby" (p. 226). But what, in fact, has psychoanalysis lost by this continuing proprietary exclusion of the Jungians?

The question can be viewed in two ways. What are the potential links that are not being explored? Samuels (1996) has attempted a list of such topics, and the recent conferences in London, Sebasco, and Merida sought to identify such common ground. Earlier Scott (1978) attempted a sketch of this terrain, but, significantly, in a talk to a Jungian group published in a Jungian journal. More recently, *Psychoanalytic Dialogues* has published an issue on the Post-Jungians, and this journal has published a lengthy article by three prominent American Jungians on "What Freudians can learn from Jung."

But exploring potential links is an enormous and complex task, one requiring considerable depth of knowledge in two different traditions and two realms of clinical practice. It also requires a desire on both sides to bridge the gap, a desire that clearly many Jungians have evidenced over the years but one that has been notably lacking among mainstream psychoanalysts. I believe that this lack of desire reflects not

162 Organizational Analysis

simply ignorance of Jungian thought and what it might have to offer mainstream psychoanalysis but also considerable resistance. Despite the current ecumenical climate and interest in pluralism, analytical psychology by and large continues to be the object of a pervasive disparagement and neglect, amounting to a "social defense" (Menzies, 1967), a collectively elaborated set of assumptions and behaviors that subtly but firmly protects mainstream psychoanalysis from the anxiety of questioning some of its deepest and most pervasive affiliations. This "social defense," I believe, is what lay behind Wallerstein's remarkable statement excluding the Jungians from the contemporary effort to define a psychoanalytic "common ground." As a number of Jungians have pointed out (Samuels, 1996; Kirsch, 2000), Wallerstein ostensibly based his statement on the flimsy evidence of a doctoral dissertation. First-hand knowledge seemed irrelevant.

This brings us to the second way the question about the loss to psychoanalysis of this continuing exclusion can be raised: What has psychoanalysis used the figure of Jung to avoid? The wall of neglect and denial that has surrounded the contributions of Jung and the Jungians to the psychoanalytic discourse has been used to warn potential other deviants, to confine and proscribe exploration within psychoanalysis itself. Significantly, of course, it has often been those treading on or near the ground Jung had trod who experience the danger that they, like him, might be seen as going "too far." They too could be proscribed.

There have been a number of significant personal relationships that have allowed communication and influence to occur across this barrier, but even those are poorly known and have led to very little public acknowledgment. This is the hallmark of a social defense. It is not actually about the encounter with the proscribed matter. It is about the maintenance of the solidarity of the group and the preservation of one's relationship to it. It is a powerful collusion constituted of small acts of avoidance, distraction, and rationalization.

Acknowledging this, Winnicott (1964) exclaimed forcefully in his review of *Memories, Dreams, Reflections*: "If we fail to come to terms with Jung we are self proclaimed partisans, partisans in a false cause" (p. 450). And, indeed, his own coming to terms with Jung in that review aroused a disturbing identification, expressed in a remarkable dream of his own which he came to feel he had dreamt "for Jung and for some of my patients, as well as for myself" (Winnicott, 1963,

p. 229). His account of the dream is abstract, lacking the details that could suggest specific associations, but he leaves no doubt about its impact: "1. There was absolute destruction, and I was part of the world and of all people, and therefore I was being destroyed ... 2. Then there was absolute destruction, and I was the destructive agent ... 3 ... in the dream I awakened. As I awakened I knew that I had dreamed both (1) and (2)" (p. 228). Winnicott linked this dream to the genesis of his late seminal paper, "The Use of the Object," in which he described the vital sigificance of the child's acting on and living through its destructive impulses, learning that both the object survives as well as himself.

We cannot know for sure what Winnicott meant in claiming that he dreamt this dream "for Jung." But it is worth noting that the act of writing the review aroused in him such powerful aggressive feelings and fear that it led to a burst of creative insight as well as a strongly worded challenge to his colleagues not to remain "partisans in a false cause." It speaks, I believe, to the power that lies in social defenses and the terror aroused in confronting them.

I identify three areas of exploration in psychoanalysis, where the threat of Jung's example discouraged and intimidated new developments: Work on symbols, most usually manifest in dreams; work on identity and lifelong development; and, finally, "synchronicity," uncanny correspondences in human experience. In what follows, what I say can only be suggestive and incomplete – and easily challenged. As we know from our own clinical experience, it is difficult to identify definitively areas that have been avoided, split off, or denied. Nor am I arguing that these are the only areas where the social defense mobilized around the figure of Jung has discouraged exploration. But these are areas where the evidence is strong.

Symbols and Dreams

This is the topic Jung pursued during the period of his growing alienation from Freud in the book that has since become known as *Symbols of Transformation*. For his part, during this period, Freud was spurred on to write "Totem and Taboo," his own version of the origins of religious practices. The competition was friendly, at this point, if fierce, but it brought them together in acknowledging the kind of phenomena that Jung, later, referred to as "archetypes." That is, Freud depended on the argument of a phylogenetic inheritance to account for "the assumption of a collective mind" (1913/1966, p. 158). Jung's argument was different, but they both were interested in the phenomenon of symbols that had the quality of universals, that did not arise directly from individual experience.

In his *Interpretation of Dreams* – but in a passage added in 1911, during the period of this competition – Freud first elaborated the point that dream symbolism pre-existed individual experience: "how irresistibly one is driven to accept it in many cases" (p. 359).

Jung's explorations were indeed far-reaching, examining myths and religious rituals in order to develop and elaborate a thoroughgoing grammar of symbols. Jones (1916), at a strategic moment following the break between Freud and Jung, attacked him for abandoning "the methods and canons of science," to wander "in a perfect maze of mysticism, occultism, and theosophy" (p. 136). He warned psychoanalysts, in effect, to stick to the narrow range – and, indeed, it became a realm of inquiry that mainstream psychoanalysis has tended to avoid. Thus, as Fromm pointed out (1951), dream interpretation has tended to go in two opposing and mutually exclusive directions: Jung developed the notion of an autonomous realm of archetypes reflecting transcendent aspirations in the psyche, while Freud adhered to the notion that the symbolism of dreams reflected infantile, sexual urges. As Laplanche and Pontalis (1973) pointed out: "Whereas the symbols discovered by psychoanalysis are very numerous, the range of things they symbolize is very narrow" (p. 444).

For the English "developmental" Jungians, Klein's interest in phantasy, symbolization, and inner objects provided renewed opportunities to explore links with Jung's ideas about myths, symbols, and archetypes. Fordham, for example, wrote: "I discovered analogies between what Jung found in myths and what Klein found in small children's fantasies about their mother's bodies" (1993, p. 66). As we have seen, the postwar years in London, when training in analytical psychology first got under way, were years of ferment and interaction. Mainstream psychoanalysts participated in some beginning dialogues with their Jungian colleagues (Scott, 1978), and many Jungians opened themselves up to learning from psychoanalysis about child development and transference, topics neglected if not avoided by Jung.

It was in this context that Glover wrote and published his polemical *Freud or Jung* (1950). Clearly, he felt the danger that in this climate Jung was at risk of being more accepted than at any previous time in England. In a prominent footnote, he observed: "In the writer's view this Kleinian system constitutes a deviation from Freudian principles and practice, combining it is interesting to note, some of the errors of both Rank and Jung" (p. 21).

The potential of such criticism, I believe, inhibited psychoanalytic developments in dream interpretation. Friedman and Goldstein (1964) in their critical review of Jung's psychology noted this area of "definite interest" in Jung's work: "the study of comparative mythology and of the parallels between mythological and individual dreams and fantasies ... material which is rarely referred to in psychoanalytic writings" (p. 196). Meltzer noted in his groundbreaking *Dream-Life* (1984) that there has been a corresponding paucity of significant work on dreams in the psychoanalytic literature: "It is an enigma of psycho-analytical history that the theory of dreams ... should have been preserved throughout the years in word while dishonoured in deed in every session where a dream plays a part" (p. 14). In attempting to develop a more adequate theory based on the centrality of emotional experience and symbol formation, influenced by Bion's work on thinking, Meltzer once again aroused the interest of Jungians who saw an approach that linked up with their clinical and theoretical work (Fordham, 1995). But Meltzer himself did not credit Jung, nor did he seem in any way to come to his theory by way of Jungian connections. Indeed, his few references to Jung seem designed to establish the point of their differences.

The point I am making is precisely about the absence of such references. Psychoanalysts, going out on a limb to develop new approaches in such controversial areas, have felt hardly able to afford associating themselves with the original apostate. Indeed, to assert a critical difference with Jung can been seen to affirm that they are still loyal to the mainstream. Casement suggested such a point at the London meeting organized by the SAP: he wondered "whether every Freud in history needs a Jung 'to represent the thinking that goes beyond one person'" (Astor, 1998).

It is perhaps worth adding that, among Jungians, work on archetypes and symbols has not remained static or without controversy.

Contemporary Jungians are increasingly less likely to see symbols as direct reflections of transcendent reality. Polly Young-Eisendrath, writing from a postmodern perspective, has commented: "Constructivism does not reject universals such as archetypes or universal emotions, but it assumes that both the concepts and the experiences to which they refer come directly from human interpretation. That is, archetypes do not move and shape human consciousness; nor are we caught in morphogenic structures" (1995, p. 5).

Acknowledging these developments in the Jungian community more recently, Modell noted in a paper originally presented at the first Sebasco conference: "This interaction of private metaphor and cultural symbols may prove to be an area of fruitful collaboration between Freudian and Jungian psychoanalysts" (1997, p. 116). But it still remains to be seen if such collaboration is possible.

Identity and Lifelong Development

Jung's notion of lifelong "individuation," together with his notions of typologies of the self, provided a framework for his beginning speculations on adult development (Jung, 1933). Winnicott (1970) pointed out that "Jung usefully drew our attention to the fact that human beings ... do go on growing in all respects, right up to the moment of death" (p. 284). As Staude (1981) suggested, these speculations probably had their beginnings in Jung's own need to understand the extraordinary transformations of his own midlife crisis, the developments that led to his break with Freud, and the need to set out on his own adult pathway.

Erikson (1968), probably the psychoanalytic mainstream's best-known student of the life cycle, noted the clinical discoveries of Jung in this area but in a curiously indirect manner: "in the inventory of our patients' ideal and evil prototypes we probably also meet face to face the clinical facts on which Jung based his theory of inherited protoypes ('archetypes')" (p. 58). He added: "As though in fear of endangering a common group identity based on an identification with Freud's personal greatness, psychoanalytic observers chose to ignore not only Jung's excesses but also the kind of universal fact he had, indeed, observed" (pp. 58–9).

Erikson's recent biographer has called attention to the fact that, "It took years before Erikson could speak publicly about an ... important (and perhaps more 'heretical') influence on his life, the Jungian analyst Joseph Wheelright" (Friedman, 1999, p. 163). It was only at the point where his own reputation was securely established did he venture some tentative acknowledgment of the important role in the development of his own thinking played by Jungian ideas (Erikson, 1982).

Levinson, in his groundbreaking work on the male midlife crisis, was able to go further, calling Jung "the father of the modern study of adult development" (1978, p. 4). But, no doubt, Levinson was helped by the fact that he had no "common group identity" as a psychoanalyst to preserve, though he places his own work squarely in "the intellectual tradition formed by Freud, Jung and Erikson" (p. 5).

This is an area that has been explored in our literature by a number of writers and researchers, reflecting its clinical importance. But it has also aroused significant wariness on the part of psychoanalytic commentators. Vaillant's book *Adaptation to Life* (1977), based on a longitudinal study at Harvard, places itself in the Ericksonian tradition, and cites Jung's contributions. Colarusso and Nemiroff (1981), similarly, place their work in the tradition of Freud, Jung, and Erikson, adding to their list of progenitors the anthropologist Van Gennep. Emde (1985), too, notes the core contribution of Jung's work on individuation, Erikson's work on stages, adding Kohut's work on the self. But he also notes that in this area: "findings ... may be difficult for the psychoanalyst to assimilate" (p. 109).

The difficulty is that the concept of developmental stages throughout life does not easily fit the more traditional notion of intrapsychic conflict working itself out in individual and, often, highly idiosyncratic ways throughout adulthood. Indeed, as Abrams (1990) has suggested in his thoughtful review of the subject, any elaborated notion of development poses a threat to mainstream assumptions: "In such an approach, the therapist's stance may have to be different from what is customary in analysis, the unfolding treatment process would have to be different, and in all likelihood the mode of therapeutic action would also be different. It would be unwise to call such an approach 'psychoanalysis'" (p. 673). Others have expressed similar reservations. In a review of Colarusso and Nemiroff's book, Solomon (1982) noted: "psychoanalysts ... will find the book of limited value because of the insufficient elaboration of the intrapsychic ramifications of the developmental issues being considered," adding that it was "more appropriate to psychotherapy than to psychoanalysis" (p. 662).

No doubt, those engaged in substantial research projects in this realm worry less about their fidelity to privileged mainstream concepts, just as they worry less about acknowledging their indebtedness to Jung. Those who derive their primary identities from the world of psychoanalysis, however, walk a tighter line. Pollack and Greenspan's multivolume compilation of articles on the stages of life, *The Course of Life* (1988–93), avoids a theoretical frame and, except for the final volume on old age, does not reference Jung. Settlage et al. (1988) in their comprehensive review article on the subject entirely omit any reference to Jung.

Synchronicity

This is, perhaps, the most difficult topic to discuss because it so readily brings to mind the occult. And yet there is, in fact, so much "uncanny" material that many of us encounter in the course of our clinical work that we are at a loss to explain. "Synchronicity" – in Jung's (1935) terms a "connecting principle" that is neither causal nor merely chance – is hardly an explanatory concept. Still it creates space in clinical dialogue to acknowledge the presence of correspondences and seeming linkages that appear to have meaning, that are charged with significance, though we have no current way of explaining how or why that could be so.

The notion of "unconscious communication" occupies a somewhat analogous position in classical theory. Freud (1912/1966) used the analogy of the telephone: the analyst "must turn his own unconscious like a receptive organ towards the transmitting unconscious of the patient" (p. 115). Mechanisms such as projective identification, postural mimesis, and role responsiveness have been put forward to explain such processes, but the fact of the matter is that we seldom understand how we intuit what we know. Abend comments: "Surely, every practicing analyst has had many experiences that remind him of Freud's telephone analogy, but we are not very comfortable with mystical explanations of unconscious communication" (1989, p. 388). Freud himself, however, was not averse to the notion of thought transfer, and Deutsch (1926), elaborating on his comments and her own experiences of telepathy, wrote: "analytic experiences confirm that 'occult' powers are to be sought in the depth of psychic life" (p. 146).

Deutsch's quotation marks around "occult," however, speak to a certain reticence in embracing such phenomena, a reticence that continues to inform psychoanalytic writings. Nelson (1969) noted the "ostracism of colleagues who take parapsychology seriously" (p. 4). Farrell (1983) commented that telepathy is "treated like a skeleton in our closet" (p. 79). Mayer (1996a) has described a study group of the American Psychoanalytic Association formed to discuss personal experiences of uncanny knowledge not accounted for by our "public theories." "Some of those [more personal] schemata have been frankly disturbing to the analysts describing them and are based on experiences they have found exceedingly unsettling to disclose among colleagues. When spelled out, they suggest possible implications for psychoanalytic knowledge which are ... potentially radical" (p. 191).

She has gone on to describe convincing research suggesting that not only is thought transfer common and demonstrable but also that thoughts have external effects on inanimate matter. "Psychoanalysts belong in the dialogues these investigators are undertaking, and we belong as well in the effort to render comprehensible and non-anomalous what currently appears anomalous in the effects they are examining" (Mayer, 1996b, p. 723). At the same time, again, she acknowledges how difficult it is to engage such material: "I think we may need to re-cast certain of our conventions regarding what we find believable" (p. 724).

The history of applied psychoanalysis provides additional examples of uncanny phenomena. In "Group Relations Conferences," for example, designed to study the behavior of large systems (Miller, 1989), one repeatedly sees striking parallels in the behavior of different parts of the system. Common themes emerge in seemingly unrelated groups; individuals are put forth to enact behaviors on behalf of others without any conscious knowledge of what they are doing; member groups will mirror the staff without either group being aware of what is happening.

The point I am making is that those who have studied such processes must pay attention to what actually occurs without worrying about how it could be explained. To those unfamiliar with the methodology or experience of such conferences, such correspondences will appear uncanny or simply accidental. We may resort to such explanatory concepts as "parallel process" or "mirroring" or "projective identification" – but the fact of the matter is that we do not know how such connections occur. With inadequate experience, they could be overlooked or dismissed.

A second example comes from the work of Gordon Lawrence on "Social Dreaming" (Lawrence, 1998). Lawrence devised a methodology in which a "matrix" of individuals reports out its dreams and, then, associates to the dreams presented. The point is not to interpret the dreams but to allow, so to speak, dreams to speak to dreams. What he has found is that uncanny parallels and correspondences in the dreams begin to emerge. One becomes aware of a level on which, it could be said, our individual dreams are linked collectively.

Again, we may resort to some such idea as "unconscious communication" to explain such uncanny "synchronicities." Bion's (1970) introduction of the concept of O, "the unknown and the unknowable," has been frequently invoked to justify such an expanded version of the unconscious. But the point is that we profit in learning about our collective behavior by keeping our minds open to the meaningfulness of events we cannot explain.

Jung's concept of synchronicity is by no means an exactly parallel notion. Nor, I think, would it be accurate to attribute the reticence of psychoanalysts to openly embrace uncanny or anomalous phenomena exclusively to their association to Jung. And yet, I believe, there is no doubt that those psychoanalysts who are interested in exploring these ideas and experiences know about the work of Jung and avoid referencing it. The effort to gain a respectful hearing from one's colleagues for such unconventional thoughts could only be compromised by association to Jung and Jungians. And yet, as a result, the community of inquiry into such phenomena is unquestionably narrowed and constrained.

V

I believe there is less interest now in attempting to define psychoanalysis (Cooper, 1997). The ground has shifted to reconceptualizing psychoanalysis as a pluralistic endeavor. Following Wallerstein's classic question "One Psychoanalysis or Many?" – a question that seemed inevitable to pose but increasingly impossible to answer – the question we might now ask is this: In what sense is it "One" and in what sense is it "Many"?

In some measure, this is a matter of political expediency. If there is no longer the possibility of integrating or synthesizing the divergent schools of psychoanalysis, to find "the common ground," it becomes increasingly necessary to find a political solution, a form of coexistence. The model of competing interest groups within a democratic state, under these circumstances, becomes attractive. Berlin (1990) has argued compellingly for such a form of politics: "an uneasy equilibrium, which is constantly threatened and in constant need of repair" (p. 19).

And, yet, there are dangers in such a solution for psychoanalysis: it can become eclectic, abandoning the effort to reconcile competing theories, or it can become relativistic, abandoning theory altogether. Perhaps an even greater danger is that the professional identity of a psychoanalyst under such circumstances becomes virtually impossible to sustain. What forms of practice or set of skills can one hold on to as essential to one's professional identity?

But there are signs that pluralism might be more integrated into the fabric of psychoanalytic thought and clinical experience. Two proposals have recently been put forth – interestingly, one from the mainstream and one from the Jungians.

In her researches into the actual beliefs and practices held by analysts of different analytic communities, Hamilton (1996) demonstrated not only the variety of forms the actual practice of psychoanalysis takes, even within the mainstream, but also the role of the local community in shaping and sustaining that variety: "analysts think and practice much more loosely than they publicly claim. They are guided preconsciously by many dimensions" (pp. 3–4).

For her, the key concept is the preconscious, analogous to Winnicott's "transitional space," the third area of the mind in which creative ambiguity and play are sustained. Her argument is that this is the area of the mind in which analysts do much of their thinking, a realm of "muddled overlaps and uncomfortable, precarious coexistence of parts of belief systems" (p. 3). But, far from being a liability or simple embarrassment, such pluralistic complexity and potential confusion in the mind of the analyst is an asset because it matches the ambiguity of mental experience. The greater danger is that of a precise theoretical map that misleads with too much definition and clarity about a territory that does not lend itself to map-making in any traditional sense.

Where Hamilton argues for taking up an analytic stance in the pre-conscious, where creative ambiguity and conflict can be sustained, Samuels (1989) argues that the pluralism of theories matches the pluralism of the psyche. That is, the mind requires different and conflicting theories because it is itself composed of different and competing selves. The clinician approaching this complex and seemingly contradictory set of clinical phenomena is helped by having a diversity of theories to guide him.

For Samuels, the danger is not only a hierarchical view of the mind, matched by efforts to establish a theoretical hierarchy, but any view of consensus that minimizes conflict and contradiction. "The more integrated and professional the training programme, the greater the denial of pluralism" (1995, p. 41).

The proposals of Samuels and Hamilton overlap in key respects and, yet, emphasize different phenomena. Both suggest ways in which pluralism can become a more viable option for psychoanalysis – and, I believe, they open the way for additional speculation and theorizing so that pluralism does not remain simply a politically expedient solution.

Shamdasani, introducing a collection of papers originally commissioned for a conference at the Freud Museum, commented: "psychoanalysis is not One, cannot be owned, or adequately appropriated ... its heterogeneity renders impossible any pluralist, all-encompassing programme, or attempt at unification" (1994, p. xv). But this heterogeneity is difficult to live with, confusing to keep in mind, impossible to enjoy.

In its beginning years, psychoanalysis could not sustain such diversity. Adler, Jung, and their followers were victims of that failure. Now, however, it might be possible to conceive of it as one potentially encompassing if, at times, contentious, even acrimonious, conversation – that is, if psychoanalysts of different schools were able to enter into it.

References

Abend, S. (1989). Countertransference and analytic technique. *Psychoanalytic Quarterly* 58, 374–95.

Abraham, H. C., & Freud, E. L. (1966). *A Psychoanalytic Dialogue: The Letters of Sigmund Freud and Karl Abraham, 1907–1926*. New York: Basic Books.

Abrams, S. (1990). The psychoanalytic process: the developmental and the integrative. *Psychoanalytic Quarterly* 59, 650–77.

Adler, G. (1967). Methods of treatment in Analytical Psychology. In B. Wolman (ed.), *Psychoanalytical Techniques*. New York: Basic Books.

Adler, G. (1979). *Dynamics of the Self*. London: Coventure.

Astor, J. (1995). *Michael Fordham: Innovations in Analytical Psychology*. London: Routledge.

Astor, L. (1998). Some Jungian and Freudian perspectives on the Oedipus myth and beyond. *International Journal of Psycho-Analysis* 79, 697–712.

Berlin, I. (1990). The pursuit of the ideal. In H. Hardy (ed.), *The Crooked Timber of Humanity* (pp. 1–19). Princeton: Princeton University Press.

Bion, W. R. (1970). *Attention and Interpretation*. London: Tavistock Publications.

Brabant, E., Falzeder, E., & Giampieri-Deutsch, P. (1993). *The Correspondence of Sigmund Freud and Sandor Ferenczi*, Vol. 1: *1908–1914*. Cambridge, MA: Harvard University Press.

Casement, A. (1995). A brief history of Jungian splits in the United Kingdom. *Journal of Analytical Psychology* 40, 327–42.

Colarusso, C. A., & Nemiroff, R. A. (1981). *Adult Development: A New Dimension of Psychodynamic Theory and Practice*. New York: Plenum Press.

Cooper, A. M. (1997). Psychoanalytic education: past, present and future. Address to the Association for Psychoanalytic Medicine, November 4, 1997, New York.

Deutsch, H. (1926/1970). Occult processes occuring during psychoanalysis. In G. Devereau (ed.), *Psychoanalysis and the Occult*. New York: International Universities Press.

Eisold, K. (1994). The intolerance of diversity in psychoanalytic institutes. *International Journal of Psycho-Analysis* 75, 785–800.

Eisold, K. (1997). Freud as leader: the early years of the Viennese Society. *International Journal of Psycho-Analysis* 78, 87–104.

Eisold, K. (1998). The splitting of the New York Psychoanalytic Society and the construction of analytic authority. *International Journal of Psycho-Analysis* 79, 871–85.

Eisold, K. (2001). Institutional conflicts in Jungian analysis. *Journal of Analytical Psychology* 46, 335–53.

Ellenberger, H. (1970). *The Discovery of the Unconscious*. New York: Basic Books.

Emde, R. N. (1985). From adolescence to midlife: remodeling the structure of adult development. *Journal of the American Psychoanalytic Association* 33 (Suppl.), 59–112.

Erikson, E. H. (1968). *Identity: Youth and Crisis*. New York: W.W. Norton.

Erikson, E. H. (1982/1987). For Joseph Wheelwright, my Jungian friend. In S. Schlein (ed.), *A Way of Looking at Things: Selected Papers from 1930 to 1980* (pp. 713–15). New York: Norton.

Farrell, D. (1983). Freud's "thought transference," repression and the future of psychoanalysis. *International Journal of Psycho-Analysis* 64, 71–81.

Fordham, M. (1961). Obituary: C. G. Jung. *British Journal of Medical Psychology* 34, 3–4.

Fordham, M. (1974). Memories and thoughts about C. G. Jung. *Journal of Analytical Psychology* 20, 102–13.

Fordham, M. (1979). Analytical psychology in England. *Journal of Analytic Psychology* 24, 279–97.

Fordham, M. (1993). *The Making of an Analyst: A Memoir*. London: Free Association Books.

Fordham, M. (1995). *Innovations in Analytical Psychology*. London: Routledge.

Freud, S. (1910). "Wild" psychoanalysis. In J. Strachey (ed. and trans.), *The Standard Edition of the Complete Psychological Works of Sigmund Freud* (Vol. 11, pp. 219–27). London: Hogarth Press.

Freud, S. (1912). Recommendations to physicians practicing psycho-analysis. In J. Strachey (ed. and trans.), *The Standard Edition of the Complete Psychological Works of Sigmund Freud* (Vol. 12, pp. 109–20). London: Hogarth Press.

Freud, S. (1913). Totem and taboo. In J. Strachey (ed. and trans.), *The Standard Edition of the Complete Psychological Works of Sigmund Freud* (Vol. 13, pp. 1–162). London: Hogarth Press.

Freud, S. (1914). On the history of the psychoanalytic movement. In J. Strachey (ed. and trans.), *The Standard Edition of the Complete Psychological Works of Sigmund Freud* (Vol. 14, pp. 3–66). London: Hogarth Press.

Freud, S. (1925). An autobiographical study. In J. Strachey (ed. and trans.), *The Standard Edition of the Complete Psychological Works of Sigmund Freud* (Vol. 20, pp. 3–74). London: Hogarth Press.

Friedman, L. J. (1999). *Identity's Architect: A Biography of Erik H. Erikson*. New York: Scribner.

Friedman, P., & Goldstein, J. (1964). Some comments on the psychology of C. G. Jung. *Psychoanalytic Quarterly* 33, 194–225.

Fromm, E. (1951). *The Forgotten Language*. New York: Reinhardt.

Gallant, C. (1996). *Tabooed Jung*. New York: New York University Press.

Glover, E. (1950). *Freud or Jung*. Evanston, IL: Northwestern University Press.

Gould, R. L. (1972). The phases of adult life. *American Journal of Psychiatry* 129, 521–31.

Grosskurth, P. (1991). *The Secret Ring*. Reading, MA: Addison-Wesley.

Grosskurth, P. (1998). Psychoanalysis: a dysfunctional family. *Journal of Analytical Psychology* 43, 87–95.

Hamilton, V. (1996). *The Analyst's Preconscious*. Hillsdale, NJ: Analytic Press.

Hoffman, E. (1994). *The Drive for Self: Alfred Adler and the Founding of Individual Psychology*. Reading, MA: Addison-Wesley.

Jones, E. (1953–7). *The Life and Work of Sigmund Freud*. New York: Basic Books.

Jones, E. (1916/1948). The theory of symbols. In *Papers on Psychoanalysis*. London: Bailliere, Tindall & Cox.

Jung, C. G. (1933). The stages of life. In H. Read, M. Fordham, & G. Adler (eds.) and R. F. C. Hull (trans.), *The Collected Works of C. G. Jung* (Vol. 8), 387–403. Princeton, NJ: Princeton University Press.

Jung, C. G. (1935). Synchronicity: an acausal connecting principle. In H. Read, M. Fordham, & G. Adler (eds.) and R. F. C. Hull (trans.), *The Collected Works of C. G. Jung* (Vol. 8), 417–531. Princeton, NJ: Princeton University Press.

Jung, C. G. (1936–7). The concept of the collective unconscious. In H. Read, M. Fordham, & G. Adler (eds.) and R. F. C. Hull (trans.), *The Collected Works of C. G. Jung* (Vol. 9, i), 42–53. Princeton, NJ: Princeton University Press.

Jung, C. G. (1959). Introduction to Toni Wolff's "Studies in Jungian Psychology." In H. Read, M. Fordham, & G. Adler (eds.) and R. F. C. Hull (trans.), *The Collected Works of C. G. Jung* (Vol. 10). Princeton, NJ: Princeton University Press.

Jung, C. G. (1961). *Memories, Dreams, Reflections*, ed. A. Jaffe, trans. R. & C. Winston. New York: Random House.

Kerr, J. (1993). *A Most Dangerous Method: The Story of Jung, Freud and Sabina Spielrein*. New York: Knopf.

Kirsch, T. B. (1995). IAAP and Jungian identity: a president's reflections. *Journal of Analytical Psychology* 40, 235–48.

Kirsch, T. B. (1996). A brief history of analytical psychology. *The Psychoanalytic Review* 83, 569–77.

Kirsch, T. B. (1997). Response to John Beebe. *Journal of Analytic Psychology* 42, 21–24.

Kirsch, T. B. (2000). *The Jungians: A Comparative and Historical Perspective*. London: Routledge.

Laplanche, J., & Pontalis, J. B. (1973). *The Language of Psycho-Analysis.* New York: Norton.

Lawrence, W.G. (ed.) (1998). *Social Dreaming @ Work.* London: Karnac Books.

Levinson, D. L., et al. (1978). *The Seasons of a Man's Life.* New York: Knopf.

Levinson, H. (1994). The changing psychoanalytic organization and its influence on the ego ideal of psychoanalysis. *Psychoanalytic Psychology* 11, 233–49.

Maslow, A. (1962). Was Adler a disciple of Freud? a note. *Journal of Individual Psychology* 18, 125.

Mayer, E. L. (1996a). Changes in science and changing ideas about knowledge and authority in psychoanalysis. *Psychoanalytic Quarterly* 65, 158–200.

Mayer, E. L. (1996b). Subjectivity and intersubjectivity of clinical facts. *International Journal of Psycho-Analysis* 77, 709–37.

McGuire, W. (ed.) (1988). *The Freud/Jung Letters: The Correspondence between Sigmund Freud and C. G. Jung.* Cambridge, MA: Harvard University Press.

McLynn, F. (1996). *Carl Gustav Jung.* New York: St. Martin's Press.

Meltzer, D. (1984). *Dream-Life.* Perthshire: Clunie Press.

Menzies, I. (1967/1988). *The Functioning of Social Systems as Defense against Anxiety.* London: Tavistock Publications. Reprinted in *Containing Anxieties in Institutions.* London: Free Association Books, 1988.

Miller, E. (1989). *The "Leicester" Model: Experiential Study of Group and Organisational Processes.* Occasional Paper No. 10. London: Tavistock Publications.

Modell, A. H. (1997). The synergy of memory, affects and metaphor. *Journal of Analytic Psychology* 42, 105–17.

Nelson, M. C. (1969). Contribution on parapsychology: introduction. *The Psychoanalytic Review* 56, 3–8.

Nunberg, H., & Federn, E. (1967). *Minutes of the Vienna Psychoanalytic Society,* Vol. 2: *1908–1910.* New York: International Universities Press.

Noll, R. (1994). *The Jung Cult.* New York: Free Press.

Noll, R. (1997). *The Aryan Christ: The Secret Life of Carl Jung.* New York: Random House.

Paskauskas, A. A. (1988). Freud's break with Jung. *Free Associations* 11, 7–34.

Paskauskas, R. A. (ed.) (1993). *The Complete Correspondence between Sigmund Freud and Ernest Jones.* Cambridge, MA: Harvard University Press.

Peck, J. (1997). Jung in the U.S.A. *San Francisco Jung Institute Library Journal* 15, 53–65.

Pollock, G. H., & Greenspan, S. I. (1988–93). *The Course of Life,* 7 volumes. Madison, CT: International Universities Press.

Roazen, P. (1984). *Freud and His Followers.* New York: New York University Press.

Roustang, F. (1982). *Dire Mastery: Discipleship from Freud to Lacan.* Baltimore: Johns Hopkins University Press.

Samuels, A. (1985). *Jung and the Post-Jungians.* London: Routledge & Kegan Paul.

Samuels, A. (1989). Fred Plaut in conversation with Andrew Samuels. *Journal of Analytical Psychology* 34, 159–83.

Samuels, A. (1994). The professionalization of Carl G. Jung's analytical psychology clubs. *Journal of the History of the Behavioral Sciences* 30, 138–47.

Samuels, A. (1995). Pluralism and psychotherapy. *Australian Journal of Psychotherapy* 14, 31–44.

Samuels, A. (1996). Jung's return from banishment. *The Psychoanalytic Review* 83, 469–89.

Samuels, A. (1998). Will the Post-Jungians survive? In A. Casement (ed.), *The Post-Jungians Today.* London: Routledge.

Schwartz-Salant, N. (1982). *Narcissism and Character Transformation.* Toronto: Inner City Press.

Scott, W. C. M. (1978). Common problems concerning the views of Freud and Jung. *Journal of Analytic Psychology* 23, 303–14.

Settlage, C., et al. (1988). Conceptualizing adult development. *Journal of the American Psychoanalytic Association* 36, 347–69.

Shamdasani, S. (1994). Introduction: the censure of the speculative. In S. Shamdasani and M. Munchow (eds.), *Speculations after Freud: Psychoanalysis, Philosophy and Culture.* London: Routledge.

Shamdasani, S. (1998). *Cult Fictions: C. G. Jung and the Founding of Analytical Psychology.* London: Routledge.

Solomon, R. Z. (1982). Review of Adult Development: A New Dimension of Psychoanalytic Theory and Practice. *Psychoanalytic Quarterly* 51, 660–2.

Staude, J.-R. (1981). *The Adult Development of C. G. Jung.* London: Routledge & Kegan Paul.

Stepansky, P. (1976). The empiricist as rebel: Jung, Freud, and the burdens of discipleship. *Journal of the History of the Behavioral Sciences* 12, 216–39.

Stepansky, P. E. (1983a). *In Freud's Shadow: Adler in Context.* Hillsdale: Analytic Press.

Stepansky, P. E. (1983b). Perspectives on dissent: Adler, Kohut, and the idea of a psychoanalytic research tradition. *The Annual of Psychoanalysis* 11 (pp. 216–39). New York: International Universities Press.

Sulloway, F. J. (1979). *Freud, Biologist of the Mind.* New York: Basic Books.

Symington, N. (1986). *The Analytic Experience: Lectures from the Tavistock.* London: Free Association Books.

Taylor, E. (1996). The new Jung scholarship. *The Psychoanalytic Review* 83, 547–68.

Taylor, E. (1998). Jung before Freud, not Freud before Jung: the reception of Jung's work in American psychoanalytic circles between 1904 and 1909. *Journal of Analytical Psychology* 43, 97–114.

Vaillant, G. E. (1977). *Adaptation to Life*. Boston: Little, Brown, & Co.

Wallerstein, R. S. (1988). One psychoanalysis or many? *International Journal of Psycho-Analysis* 69, 5–21.

Wallerstein, R. S. (ed.) (1992). *The Common Ground of Psychoanalysis*. Northvale, NJ: Aronson.

Winnicott, D. W. (1963/1989). D.W.W.'s dream related to reviewing Jung. In C. Winnicott, R. Shepherd, & M. Davis (eds.), *Psychoanalytic Explorations*. Cambridge, MA: Harvard University Press.

Winnicott, D. W. (1964). Review of Memories, Dreams, Reflections. *International Journal of Psycho-Analysis* 45, 450–5.

Winnicott, D. W. (1970/1989). Individuation: a talk given to the Medical Section of the British Psychological Society, October 1970. In C. Winnicott, R. Shepherd, & M. Davis (eds.), *Psychoanalytic Explorations*. Cambridge, MA: Harvard University Press.

Young-Eisendrath, P. (1995). Struggling with Jung. *Round Table Review*, March–April.

Part Three

Problems of Professionalization

Chapter Eight

Psychoanalysis as a Profession
Past Failures and Future Possibilities

[Originally published as Psychoanalysis as a Profession: Past Failures and Future Possibilities, *Contemporary Psychoanalysis*, vol. 39 (2003), pp. 557–82.]

For Freud in 1937, psychoanalysis may have been one of the "impossible professions," along with teaching and politics, but it had unquestionably taken its place among the privileged occupations of the modern world. It was a profession.

Earlier, in 1916, it had been a "movement," earlier still a "cause." But gradually over the years it seemed to achieve the status for which it had slowly and inexorably striven. That is, like other professions, it possessed an esoteric and specialized body of knowledge, which it sought to develop and extend through journals, books, and conferences, it established institutes to train practitioners in the skillful use of that knowledge, it monitored standards of competence through professional associations, and it developed standards of ethical practice. As a result, psychoanalysts were coming to have a certain recognizable social identity and, like other professionals, lay claim to a corresponding social status.

The professionalization of psychoanalysis in this period paralleled the development of other professions out of relatively unorganized, unregulated, and vulnerable vocations. Social theorists in the earlier part of the century, such as Weber and Durkheim, essentially agreed with the professions' own self-assessment as self-regulating and stable occupations occupying a unique, privileged social position. For them, the idealized position of the professions stemmed in large part from the idea that professions took responsibility for their own development and practice, providing an alternative to the unbridled competition of the marketplace. And, no doubt, it was this idealized concept of the professions that Freud had in mind when he staked the claim of psychoanalysis.

But recent sociology of the professions questions this claim, calling attention to the "project" of professionalization, the process by means of which a practice or vocation acquires and sustains the status of a profession. They have stressed the benefits to practitioners of professionalization. As Macdonald (1995) recently put it, the question has changed, "from 'What part do the professions play in the established order of society?' to 'How do such occupations persuade society to grant them a privileged position?'" (p. xii).

Larson (1977), who spearheaded this shift, has pointed out that the issues of social status and market control are intimately linked: "all the devices mobilized for the construction of a professional market and the organization of the corresponding area of the social division of labor also serve the professions' drive towards respectability and social standing" (p. 66). Thus, as a result of a successful "professional project," practitioners enjoy social status as well as a high degree of control over their work and a certain independence in the marketplace.

As a result of such thinking, the very idea of a profession now is coming to be seen as a "folk concept," that is, a concept that has credibility and public acceptance but is lacking in scientific standing or logical clarity. As Freidson has put it: "One attempts to determine not so much what a profession is in an absolute sense as how people in a society determine who is a professional and who is not, how they 'make' or 'accomplish' professions by their activities, and what the consequences are for the way they see themselves and perform their work" (1986, pp. 35–6).

This approach to the professions illuminates the current dilemma of psychoanalysis. Rather than think of psychoanalysis as being a profession by definition, or by virtue of some inherent properties, we can examine how it has taken up – and currently takes up – its "professional project." Thus it can help us to see more clearly how psychoanalysis has failed – and continues to fail – at establishing itself in the eyes of the public as the profession Freud hoped and believed it had become.

I should say at the outset, however, that this is not an easy or comfortable topic to raise. I am a psychoanalyst myself, actively engaged in the management of the institute that trained me. I also teach and supervise. Moreover, I have consulted to several other institutes and other psychoanalytic organizations. Psychoanalysis, in short, is my world. Still, it is a world in serious – perhaps terminal – trouble. My struggle in this paper is to be direct and uncompromising in pointing out the shortcomings and contradictions that have undermined the pursuit of our professional standing. Not that we are entirely responsible for our current state of decline, but I believe it is essential to highlight what our responsibility for it has been. Having done that, I believe, we can address the question of remedies, a topic I take up in the final sections of this paper.

It did seem for a while as if, after an unprecedented and unexpected rise to prominence, psychoanalysis had in fact established a secure place for itself in the world of professions. It had unquestionable authority in the eyes of the public. Practices were full, and analysts migrated across the country and, indeed, across the world, setting up new training institutes. Professional associations proliferated, journals multiplied and expanded, and the publication of books testified to the increasing base of knowledge and skill practitioners could draw upon. In the 1950s, 1960s, and 1970s candidates vied for the opportunity to train.

Along with this startling success, though, was a history of internal conflict and dissent, suggesting the presence of underlying problems, but also compromising public respect. For one thing, the psychoanalytic past is littered with casualties, scapegoats who have been driven from their professional communities, labeled as deviants and rebels for developing new theories. Moreover, psychoanalytic institutes and other professional organizations have been repeatedly riven by destructive schisms, forcing the unwelcome analogy of religious wars.

And then the status of the profession began to crumble. Indeed, it seemed to fall as rapidly as it had risen, and for reasons just as difficult to discern. Freud became the target of criticisms for his theoretical shortcomings, his false scientific claims, for neglecting the impact of childhood trauma, for patronizing women. His human shortcomings were also exposed. And because during its period of success – indeed hegemony over competing theories and treatments for mental distress – psychoanalysts neglected to store up evidence of their therapeutic efficacy, they were scarcely able to defend themselves when skepticism began to surface. Indeed, for the most part, they seemed simply to deny the existence of the challenge to their status. Psychoanalysis, as a result, now suffers a dubious role in the eyes of a more skeptical public as well as challenges from a medical profession that questions its results.

But its status in the world of medicine is only a limited aspect of the problem. Freud always saw psychoanalysis as much more than treatment for mental disorders. Indeed, he complained repeatedly of the Americans, that they treated it as a mere "handmaiden of psychiatry." In his 1923 encyclopedia article, he defined psychoanalysis as three things: "the name (1) of a procedure for the investigation of mental processes which are almost inaccessible in any other way, (2) of a method (based on that investigation) for the treatment of neurotic disorders and (3) of a collection of psychological information obtained along those lines, which is gradually being accumulated into a new scientific discipline" (p. 235). The "new scientific discipline" was the knowledge base for the emergent new profession; its applications were wide and varied, as exemplified by his own writings on history, literature, anthropology, group process, biography, religion, and myth, as well as the psychopathology of everyday life.

The psychoanalyst was to be a generalist, applying his analytic skills in tracing the role of the unconscious in human behavior. Indeed, this was one of the critical reasons why, in Freud's mind, the question of lay analysis was so important. Indeed, I think it fair to say that all of those who closely identified psychoanalysis with medicine, who, in Knight's terms, saw it as a "specialty within a specialty" (1953, p. 213), borrowed the professional identity of medicine to cover their psychoanalytic identities and, in so doing, inadvertently undermined the efforts of psychoanalysis to establish a professional identity in its own right (Eisold, 1998; Chapter 2 in this volume).

This issue continues to play itself out as a kind of subversive leitmotif in the history of psychoanalysis. Psychologists in America, largely excluded by psychiatrists from participation in the professional life of mainstream psychoanalysis, developed their own distinct careers and professional identities as psychologist-psychoanalysts (Bornstein,

2001), as well as separate training, credentialing, and licensing procedures to support it. So did social workers. The result is a bewildering array of overlapping identities, professional associations, and competing claims. One has to be an insider to understand it all. Clearly, the public does not.

My aim here is to look at three tasks that psychoanalysis needed to address in order to succeed at its "professional project," three problems they failed adequately to resolve. The first is its fragmentation, its failure to present a united or at least coherent face to the public. The second is its inability to establish its professional authority in a consistent and convincing manner. The third is a persistent ambiguity about the nature of the service it offers to the public, the work it undertakes to provide. Taken together, these failures have undermined its success as a profession. Having examined these failures, then I will go on to reconsider how the professional project of psychoanalysis might be reconceived.

Fragmentation

Psychoanalysts have tended to isolate themselves in their professional communities. Their focus is inward. Freud, of course, modeled this, preoccupied as he was with establishing the shibboleths that would expose the internal enemies, discriminate those who belonged, the real psychoanalysts, from those who should be expelled.

This inward focus has led to an extraordinary history of schisms and splits, the institutional effects of which still divide the analytic landscape and prevent its professional organizations from speaking with one voice. In the 1940s in New York, two groups split off from the New York Psychoanalytic Society (see Frosch, 1991; Eckhardt, 1978). One group suffered two schisms in turn, leading to the formation of the William Alanson White Institute and to the Comprehensive Course in Psychoanalysis at the New York Medical College, a group which split yet again. The second group formed the Columbia Institute. At virtually the same time, the British Psychoanalytical Society narrowly averted a split by agreeing to form into virtually autonomous Kleinian and Freudian subgroups; subsequently a third or "Middle Group" separated out. In European institutes, schisms have occurred in Germany, Austria, France, Sweden, and Norway (Eckhardt, 1978).

186 Problems of Professionalization

In France, the controversies surrounding Lacan produced at least four surviving institutes (Turkle, 1978). Gitelson (1983), in addition, notes schisms that have occurred in Spain, Brazil, Mexico, Argentina, and Venezuela, as well as, in this country, in Washington/Baltimore, Philadelphia, Boston, Cleveland, and Los Angeles. Arlow (1972) refers to half a dozen splits in the American Psychoanalytic Association, as well as many narrowly averted splits, and adds to the census of developments in Columbia and Australia.

In addition, the exclusion of psychologists from the American Psychoanalytic Association led them to form the Division of Psychoanalysis (Division 39) of the American Psychological Association, an organization that further subdivided into warring sections. Social workers formed their own national organization. Other national professional organizations were formed, such as the American Academy of Psychoanalysis. Internationally, the International Federation of Psychoanalytic Societies rivals the International Psychoanalytic Association. And this is only a partial list.

Freud alone is not responsible for this history, of course, though by insisting on his proprietorship of psychoanalysis and establishing shibboleths of orthodoxy he set it firmly on this path. A major reason for this dramatic history of fragmentation is that the allegiances that analysts develop in their training tend to be to their analysts, supervisors, and teachers, a focus that encourages the projection of differences outward into rival analysts or other analytic communities. This has led to the development of a characteristic paranoid cast to the organizational world of psychoanalysis. Analysts have been, first and foremost, identified with their analytic lineages, secondarily with their local "schools" of psychoanalytic thought, lastly with the field as a whole.

Some belong to strict or strong schools: Kleinian, Lacanian, interpersonalists, ego psychologists, and so forth. Others are more eclectic, more accepting of the current pluralistic world. But in either case they have absorbed what they have been exposed to and trained to understand. Their interpretive frameworks, an aspect of their identifications with their analysts, supervisors, and teachers, bind them to their institutes. For analysts, what and how they think is who they are.

Thus, as they work with patients in their consulting rooms, they are powerfully bound to their local communities, on whom they also rely for referrals, for help with professional matters, for political collaboration in institute management, etc. But, even more importantly, as I have been trying to suggest, they rely on them because they are the groups to which they belong, the groups that sustain their identities, that keep them from being outcast, fragmented, alone. Even the most alienated and isolated analyst knows exactly from which professional group he is estranged.

The Italian psychoanalyst Nissan Momigliano provides a beautiful example of a moment in which she came in touch with this level of her clinical anxiety. Reflecting on the intense pressure she was subject to from a patient who demanded that she depart from her traditional practice of abstinence, she wrote: "It would, I felt, be an unbearable experience of defeat, failure, and surrender to someone I felt to be stronger than me ... and anxiety at the risk involved in abandoning something apparently safe and reliable, rather like the feelings of a climber who loses his foothold and begins to plunge headlong – in other words something reminiscent of entering an unknown dimension I was not sure I would be able to master or control and which therefore ultimately threatened a loss of identity" (Momigliano, 1992, p. 68).

To be sure, in describing this moment of terror, she does not explicitly refer to her community. Most of us, indeed, do not think of it that way. But that is what the risk of losing our footing ultimately is all about; that is the ground on which we stand. Another way of putting this is that analytic identities and theories have an important defensive aspect – but one that is often out of awareness because those identities are, by and large, not personally constructed by the analyst alone. They are provided by their training, imperceptibly woven into the way they have learned to think about their work.

The important point here, however, is that the defensive forces stemming from analytic identities also interfere with the ability to establish a collective professional identity. Wallerstein (1990) has called for the establishment of the "common ground" in clinical theories. It now seems far more likely that psychoanalysis is moving toward a pluralistic view of theoretical differences, a solution that is extremely attractive politically as a means of maximizing tolerance and minimizing the need to be defensive. But pluralism as an expedient solution to internal conflicts contains the danger that it perpetuates an image of psychoanalysis as inconsistent and irresolute – and expedient. Pluralism, in itself, hardly provides the united front of a coherent and confident profession.

The interlocking goals of a professional project are unity and monopoly (Macdonald, 1995). Unity means that the profession can speak convincingly with one voice to a public that can feel, as a result, confidence and trust in the profession's stewardship of its esoteric knowledge and expertise. Monopoly, correspondingly, means that the profession can impose its ways of doing business, including the setting of fees, on the public. Clearly, to the degree it is unified it can more easily impose monopolistic control. And often, then, it can persuade government to recognize and support that control.

But psychoanalysis has yet to demonstrate its ability to rise above the historic divisions that have conferred upon it, in the eyes of a bewildered public, the image of religious sectarianism.

Authority

In recent years, we have come to be far more sensitive to the fact that a false note is introduced into an analysis if interpretations are accepted simply on the basis of professional authority. Indeed, resistance to authority can be seen as an essential aspect of a patient's or a client's developing autonomy. On the other hand, the usefulness of professional authority is experienced in the rough patches of an analysis, particularly in managing a strong negative transference. In such phases, patients remember that they have experienced their analysts differently in the past, but they also recall that analysts are qualified professionals, and this lends a crucial element of doubt to their current experience and a willingness to go forward: "They must know what they are doing."

But far more importantly, if psychoanalysts did not have some form of credible authority, no one would come to them in the first place. Their professional authority is their collective credibility, their claim upon the public's trust, particularly in the face of competing professions and vocations.

Our psychoanalytic forebears worked hard to establish that authority by developing standards for training, rigorous procedures for certification, and professional organizations charged with monitoring the effectiveness of those standards and procedures. Indeed, that is a good part of what we look to professional organizations to do. It is not something professionals can do for themselves, as individuals.

Thus candidates are subject to the authority of their training and certifying institutions as part of the effort that needs to be mounted on behalf of the profession to establish and maintain its professional authority. This is all the more vitally important and difficult to achieve as psychoanalysis has, for the most part, charted an independent course outside universities and medical schools. The issue of lay analysis, in one sense, is the insistence that psychoanalysis is an independent profession that will have to establish its own professional authority.

But the professional authority of psychoanalysis is deeply flawed. In its early years, of course, it benefited from and relied upon the charismatic authority of Freud, aided by the strong, hidden management of the "secret committee." That phase was succeeded by the "apostolic era" in which his disciples, dispersed by Nazi persecution, spread the gospel throughout the world. But, as Weber pointed out, charismatic authority must eventually give way to technical authority for a profession to become established, and this is precisely where psychoanalysis has struggled indecisively.

Indeed, I don't think it is too much to say that psychoanalysis currently suffers from a crisis of authority pervading virtually all aspects of its work. Let me try to spell that out.

First of all, in the eyes of the public, not only does psychoanalysis present a fragmented and confused picture, rife with conflict and competing claims; it has not done a credible job of demonstrating its effectiveness. Research into the outcomes of psychoanalytic practice is thin and inconclusive.

In large part, of course, this stems from the fact that individual practitioners do not have the resources or the motivation to do research. The push for it and the support for it has to come from institutions, and there are few institutions that have been willing and able to do that, despite scattered and impressive examples of studies that have been done in academic settings. But, for the most part, psychoanalytic institutions have not taken up the challenge. During the period of greatest public recognition and success, most psychoanalysts were able to persuade themselves that indeed they were doing research of a sort with each patient, that psychoanalysis itself was all the research it needed. And, no doubt, individual case histories were often convincing to readers, filled with resonant meaning and emotional authenticity. But when the need arose to set those results against the achievements of biological psychiatry, psychoanalysis had very little to show apart from its stories of cure. It came to seem as if the emperor had no clothes.

Now the field is hard pressed to prove to a skeptical public what it can do. The best current research allows us to say is that psychotherapy seems to work, but we cannot convincingly assert that the talking cure is more effective than the behavioral cure, that individual help is better than group help, or that three or four times a week is better than once, or three years better than three months. The evidence is extremely thin.

A second point: The inability of psychoanalysis to claim authority from its results is paralleled by its growing inability to claim authority from its procedures for training and certification. The burden of managing these processes tends to fall to the senior, more established practitioners, who supervise, analyze, teach, examine, and ultimately approve new practitioners. To be sure, they often do their best to think carefully about candidates and what changes in the curriculum of institutes might be needed. But the fact of the matter is, there is very little evidence about how training works and few alternative models. Indeed, the field has fallen into the routine practice of replicating "the hallowed tri-partite" model (Wallerstein, 1993, p. 175) originally established 80 years ago, never seriously challenged or systematically studied. Most institutes simply go on doing what they have done before, what other institutes do, perhaps tinkering with the curriculum or the process of selecting faculty, etc. Few start out trying to think the process through freshly. The truth is that the regulation of psychoanalytic training and certification is largely a matter of convention.

As a result, institute training has become infiltrated over the years with assumptions and practices that are essentially social defenses, serving more to protect the psychoanalytic faculty (including training and supervising analysts) from anxiety than to advance the development of competencies in candidates (Eisold, 2004; Chapter 5 in this volume).

Let me briefly detail some of these social defenses. Institute faculty, by and large, do not need to explain or justify their decisions, as candidates must. It is presumed that their psychoanalytic competence protects them from irrationality in decision-making about selecting candidates, advancing them, or promoting themselves to advanced positions. Faculty, by and large, do not present their own work to candidates, despite repeated calls to do so. There is a well-established and recognized "caste system" in most institutes, in which senior analysts benefit from the presumption of superior competence in all areas of functioning. They also benefit from exclusive access to the pool of candidates who can patronize only them during their training. There is a pervasive passivity about even minor changes in procedures or curriculum. Finally, despite repeated recognition over the years that the current system fosters dependency (Balint, 1984), conformity (Arlow, 1972), and lack of creativity (Kernberg, 1996), there is extremely little movement toward self-reflection on why that is so or how it might be changed.

Thus the authority that senior faculty, training, and supervising analysts claim for themselves in managing the process of training and credentialing is often seen to be authoritarian. By "authoritarian" I simply mean authority not grounded in rational need, authority disconnected from the actual requirements of a particular task. Moreover, since it is extremely difficult to know the point at which adequate professional authority has been established through training and credentialing, as a result of which there are inevitably serious and valid disagreements about what is necessary to sustain it, virtually all aspects of the internal management of psychoanalysis can and will arouse fears and feelings of authoritarian control.

To summarize: Because there is inadequate demonstration of the effectiveness of psychoanalysis, because there is so little experimentation with training, because evaluation of the procedures used to assess competence is rare, because institutes and other professional organizations tend to be conservative in defending established practices, the authority of those charged with maintaining the professional authority of psychoanalysis is itself profoundly compromised. One repeatedly hears from one's colleagues private judgments about the motives of those who seek institutional authority, criticisms of the judgments that are made, skepticism about how institutes are run, and so forth. Indeed, the profession is riddled with alienation and privately expressed feelings of contempt.

On the larger stage, this plays itself out as competing forms of legitimization. Different professional and accrediting associations within psychoanalysis vie for recognition and, in the process, of course, undermine each other's credibility. Moreover, most forms of accreditation are tied to existing institutes. Thus individual practitioners are certified as practitioners on their successful completion of local standards. Guidelines for those standards may be set nationally or internationally, but it is the institutes that have to meet them, which are themselves accredited, and which become as a result essentially the gatekeepers to the profession. Rarely are candidates evaluated independently according to criteria based on competency. The effect of this is not only to perpetuate fragmentation in the field but to insure that candidates become dependent upon their institutes.

Could psychoanalysis develop a uniform credentialing process, apart from any existing professional association? Currently, efforts are being made toward this by many in leadership positions, but they are hamstrung by the existing web of political interests and alliances.

In the meanwhile, most practitioners enjoy a form of dual citizenship, in effect, that protects them in the eyes of the public and buffers them from the problem. Analysts who are psychiatrists, psychologists, and social workers are licensed by the state by virtue of their preanalytic professional training and credentialing procedures. They can afford, in effect, to neglect the question of their professional standing as psychoanalysts because their prior disciplines provide standing in the eyes of the public, the law, as well as insurance companies.

As a result of this complex and confused approach to professional authority, many psychoanalysts no longer value or even believe that there is such a thing as legitimate professional authority in their field and do not grasp the importance of their dependence upon it. And while the case can be made, particularly in a time such as ours where all forms of authority are problematic and highly contingent, the field languishes in its absence.

Our Task

Engineers build structures, physicians heal patients, lawyers represent clients before the law – but what do psychoanalysts do? At the very least, what do they aim to accomplish? As we have seen, a key aspect of all traditional professions is their guardianship of an esoteric body of knowledge, one that requires specialized training to master, certification procedures to judge competence in, and professional associations to continue developing. But, in each case, using that esoteric knowledge is a form of work. The public turns to a professional to perform some work he or she has become expert in by virtue of mastering that knowledge.

This may seem all too obvious and hardly worth stating, but it is an aspect of psychoanalysis that has remained muddled and obscure. The historic stress on correct theory and the subsequent organization of the discipline into different schools has emphasized the question of what psychoanalysts must believe in order to belong to their respective schools or to the field as a whole. To be sure, we could reframe that as an emphasis on how a psychoanalyst thinks, or how a particular school approaches human behavior. But in any event, psychoanalysts have not been able adequately to describe for themselves – or convey to the public – what as professionals they actually propose to do (Eisold, 2000; Zeddies, 2000).

To be sure, there are slogans to repeat when pressed, catchphrases based on statements made by Freud at different points in the development of his thinking. Reflecting the topographic perspective, for example, psychoanalysts can claim to "make the unconscious conscious," which can also be characterized as promoting "insight" or "overcoming resistance." The structural theory has given us: "where id was there shall ego be," or in terms of later structural theory, restoring the balance between the tripartite elements of the personality: id, ego, and super-ego. Object relations theory speaks of integrating split-off parts of the personality, Self Psychology of restoring developmental arrests. But all such formulaic statements are dependent upon a given theoretical framework to make sense.

In a somewhat different vein, Freud also said the goal of psychoanalysis is "replacing neurotic suffering with ordinary human misery." But virtually any psychotherapeutic process can be said to have such a modest aim. What actually sets psychoanalysis apart from other psychotherapies? The point is not that we do not have an answer to this question. We have too many answers. A recent issue of *The Psychoanalytic Quarterly* entitled "The Goals of Clinical Psychoanalysis" highlighted this dilemma. In reviewing the papers, Gabbard (2001a) noted a disturbing lack of agreement, adding: "we had better have some idea of which outcomes are unique to analysis if we are to retain credibility" (p. 188).

Here again, I believe that many psychoanalysts take refuge in the larger identity of psychotherapists. They can claim to cure or at least ameliorate mental or emotional suffering, and they can draw upon the large body of experience acquired in hospitals, clinics, community health services, and private practices, much of it heavily influenced by training in "psychoanalytically oriented psychotherapy," an even broader and vaguer concept than psychoanalysis itself. In so doing, however, they both adapt to the demands of the clinical work they are required to do and open themselves up to Freud's charge that they make psychoanalysis into a mere "handmaiden of psychiatry." They abandon what was for him the paramount goal of psychoanalysis, the amassing "of psychological information ... accumulated into a new scientific discipline" (Freud, 1923, p. 235) and his particular interest in applying psychoanalytic insights to literature, anthropology, society, etc.

Actually much can be said for abandoning Freud's goal. For one thing, it is now difficult to sustain the concept of psychoanalysis as a science. Psychoanalysis now is less certain of what kind of a discipline it is – indeed, what form of knowledge it possesses. For another, the focus on acquiring information has often been in conflict with the goal of helping patients or clients, as, indeed, Freud's own case histories make clear it often was for him. The scientific pretension of psychoanalysis has fed its lack of concern with finding evidence of its therapeutic efficacy. Historically, analysts have had difficulty, as Owen Renik (1998) has put it, of "getting real" in our work.

On the other hand, we cannot say what sets psychoanalysis apart from other practices or disciplines, what defines psychoanalysts or psychoanalytically oriented practitioners. Externally, as a result, psychoanalysis cannot clearly differentiate itself from the competition. The public is understandably confused.

But there are other consequences for this inability to define the work of psychoanalysis, consequences at least as damaging. I want to focus on two of them. The first has to do with understanding psychoanalytic competence. Without clarity about the nature of the work we engage in, and hence the skills it requires, the field is hampered in thinking about training and continuing professional development. The second has to do with the burgeoning fields of applied psychoanalysis. What is the meaning of a "psychoanalytic approach" or a "psychoanalytic orientation"?

As for training, let me state the obvious: If psychoanalysts cannot specify the nature of the work they do, how can they specify the actual competencies they try to train candidates to develop, much less continue to develop within themselves? And they are compromised when it comes to claiming the ability to evaluate and certify practitioners.

I am not saying that the field is riddled with incompetence as a result of lacking such clarity. On the contrary, I am often impressed with how seriously the task of training and evaluation is taken and how much time is devoted to scrutinizing the work of candidates and, even, the degree to which candidates benefit from their training.

But I am saying that, to a large extent, analysts are operating in the dark, relying on intuition and tradition to guide them in areas where they need to be sharper and more critical. The ritualistic reaffirmation of the "hallowed tripartite model" speaks to a self-imposed constraint in thinking of new ways of training much less addressing shortcomings in the current system (Kachele & Thoma, 2000). "At this time in our history, knowledge about what we need to teach neophyte psychotherapists is limited and infirm" (Matarazzo & Garner, 1992, p. 870), wrote two psychologists recently in a review of research on training. Moreover, there has been a striking absence of research into the effectiveness of decision-making about selecting and advancing candidates, much less promoting faculty to senior roles. (See Holt & Luborsky, 1955; Weinshel, 1982; Kappelle, 1996.) As a result, faculty are essentially "anointed," as Kirsner (2000) has pointed out.

My point here is that an absence of thought on the essential work of psychoanalysis contributes to this pattern of conservatism and resistance to change. Were the question to be raised in a serious and consistent way, it would be more difficult to assert that practitioners need to have certain number of hours of prescribed experiences or that they need to work with particular privileged experts or that they must be exposed to specific texts. The focus would shift to competence and effectiveness.

The second area where lack of clarity about the work of psychoanalysis has a significant impact is in its applications to other than individual therapeutic aims. "Applied psychoanalysis" takes many forms, but what concerns me here are the practices that involve working with others: "psychoanalytically oriented" individual or family therapy, psychoanalytic group work, the psychoanalytic study of organizations. What is "psychoanalytic" about such practices?

I suspect that there are many answers to this question, having to do with paying attention to unconscious motivation or unconscious fantasy, or transference and countertransference, or attunement to the suppressed emotional aspects of relationships, or diagnosing how anxiety and defenses against anxiety bring about resistance to change, and so forth. All of these are good answers – but, again, there are too many answers and too little consistency among them.

This mirrors the larger problem of psychoanalysis itself. If those working in applied forms of psychoanalysis cannot explain convincingly what it is they offer to do for their clients, they rely on good will, they cannot differentiate themselves from the competition, and they are impaired in understanding how their work fits in with or doesn't fit in with what others do. Without clarity about their work, they cannot assess their own competence in any meaningful way or carry on a helpful dialogue about the competencies they need to develop.

Antithesis

Having pushed the issue of the flawed professional project this far, an antithetical point of view now begins to come into view. Perhaps it was a mistake for psychoanalysis to have aspired to professional status as it did. Perhaps the project was misconceived from the start, put into motion before psychoanalysis could clarify the role it might actually play in the world.

In other words, Freud's 1923 threefold definition of psychoanalysis may have been premature, contaminated by the pressure to give an authoritative public endorsement to the particular form psychoanalysis had assumed at that point in its development. Perhaps the burgeoning "professional project" of psychoanalysis, as it was then seen, led Freud to attempt to describe and endorse the complex hybrid shape that had evolved, not the shape most suited to its real potential.

That is, he may have stressed the "treatment of neurotic disorders" – despite his misgivings about the medicalization of psychoanalysis – because that is what patients came to receive. His followers would have required that endorsement, as that was how they too earned their livings. And he stressed the accumulation of "psychological information" because, apart from the fact that he himself sought and believed he had found reliable knowledge of the unconscious, that "information" was the esoteric and specialized knowledge that any profession needed to have in order to stake its claim to professional status. Without a body of specialized knowledge there is no profession.

First and foremost, though, he identified the process of inquiry in his definition, the "procedure for the investigation of mental processes," because that is where he started and what underlay the complex range of discoveries and applications that intrigued him. By itself, however, that process may have seemed at once too radical, too subversive of social conventions, and too bare, too empty of applications.

As Laplanche and Pontalis (1973) have pointed out, the term "Psychoanalyse" first made its appearance in 1896, signaling Freud's abandonment of hypnotism and suggestion in favor of free association. That was before any of the psychoanalytic "discoveries" hardened into shibboleths. Indeed, the term can be taken to imply a continual probing beneath the surface, a potentially endless deconstruction of psychological certitude. Only now, after a hundred years of psychoanalytic practice, the technique of free association has evolved from "a procedure" to a diverse and rich collection of methods and techniques for uncovering neglected, suppressed, or inattended aspects of experience (see Rubovitz-Seitz, 1998).

If we can free ourselves of Freud's threefold definition and, for a moment, stand apart from our own enmeshment in the "profession" we have collectively brought about, it might be possible to see that it is this "procedure" of inquiry that, indeed, forms the central thread of psychoanalysis. (See Reisner, 1999.) This is what sets us apart from all other professions, the core activity defining the "psychoanalytic."

Uncovering the unwanted and disowned parts of individual experience opens up new understandings of our collective reality and inevitably takes us to new and frequently unwanted ideas. (See Benjamin, 1997.) Psychoanalysis in the beginning thrust Freud into the struggle against the sexual hypocrisy of his time, as a result of which he acquired a not unwelcome if somewhat uncomfortable reputation as an embattled social radical. As Jacoby (1983) has reminded us: "It is frequently forgotten (repressed?) that Freud himself championed a reform of sexual mores and codes" (p. 38, see Freud, 1908). And many others in the early movement found themselves espousing radical views of sexual conduct and associating with sexual reformers.

The point here is not that Freud was – or was not – a sexual reformer, but that the early work of psychoanalysis placed it on the edge where such a role almost came to seem inevitable. In exploring the unknown, many uncomfortable, censored, and disavowed aspects of human experience will be uncovered. Moreover, the process of inquiry will inevitably suggest new and sometimes radical theories of development, theories of psychic structure, theories of motives, meanings, and so forth. And, of course, those ideas will inevitably change under the pressure of continual probing, as they did for Freud who initially stressed the role of actual seduction in the etiology of hysteria, moved on to stress the role of fantasy, which led to the exploration of infantile sexuality, the hypothesis of libidinal energy, the drives, etc.

The important point here is that psychoanalysis continues a process of radical inquiry, struggling to clear away the encrustations of custom and conventional wisdom, of old habits, rationalizations, dogmas, and beliefs that obscure and circumscribe human experience.

The two other parts of Freud's definition (1923) introduced limitations and complexities into the psychoanalytic project that have bedeviled not only its own internal history but its relations with other disciplines and professions as well. Indeed, they have contributed to the isolation and arrogance the field still struggles to shake off.

We are familiar with the long history of conflict that the search to find and organize "a collection of psychological information" has led to. Detecting relevant information and assembling it into coherent theories has been an endless source of psychoanalytic battles, as different schools have fought over what information properly belongs to psychoanalysis and which explanatory constructs are most faithful to the tradition. But quite apart from these bitter struggles, the quest to assemble psychoanalytic information has isolated psychoanalysis from other disciplines, which on their own and in their own sometimes non-psychoanalytic ways have also been accumulating relevant and potentially useful information about human behavior. At one point,

Hartmann (1959) claimed, "psychoanalysis always aimed at a comprehensive general psychology" (p. 342), as if from the start it aspired to displace all other psychologies. As Kernberg has pointed out, though, it was "an illusion that we were a universal science when we were in fact totally isolated" (in Bergman, 2000, p. 230). The point is that psychoanalysis – if it does not have to maintain a claim to hegemony – can legitimately aspire to take its place among the "psychologies."

In recent years, the erosion of the boundary between the information of psychology and the more privileged information of psychoanalysis has begun to occur. Developmental psychology, attachment theory in particular, is a case in point. Slade (2000) recently noted the cost of Bowlby's isolation from the psychoanalytic establishment stemming from his departures from orthodox theory: "from the standpoint of psychoanalysis ... attachment theory all but ceased to exist for at least three decades" (p. 1148). Even infant observation at the start was highly controversial.

It goes the other way, as well. Psychoanalysts have begun to appreciate that other disciplines can provide support for some of their more fundamental guiding concepts and thus help to gain standing for psychoanalysis in the outside world. Westen (1998, 1999) has reviewed the relevant psychological research, but, as he points out, the data support some – by no means all – traditional ideas. We can't easily accept one side without the other.

The second part of Freud's definition, similarly, has led to the establishment of a self-defeating and confusing boundary: psychoanalysis as "a ... treatment of neurotic disorders." Though he himself, as we have seen, continually complained about the danger to psychoanalysis of being incorporated into psychiatry, he did include that therapeutic intent in his definition. And there were good reasons for his doing so. Apart from the fact that that was how analysts made their living, how the new profession sustained itself economically, it was also how he hoped to find new information as well as demonstrate the truth of the claims of discovery, through the psychic changes and cures that treatment brought about. Indeed, an extremely significant reason for the early acceptance of psychoanalysis among psychiatrists and neurologists was that it promised to be – and often was – an effective treatment at a time when there was virtually no serious competition. (See Hale, 1971.)

But that was before what Rieff (1966) has called the "Triumph of the Therapeutic," before the psychoanalytic movement was, as he put it, "ruined by the popular (and commercial) pressure upon it to help produce a symbolic for the reorganization of personality" (p. 21). Psychoanalysis came to be seen as psychotherapy, first and foremost, obscuring virtually all other aspects of its enterprise. Indeed, the analysis of its "failure" with which I began this paper is based on the widely held assumption that, as a profession, psychoanalysis is essentially that. The fragmented and competing schools represent different approaches to therapy, the shortcomings in its professional authority stem from failures to demonstrate therapeutic outcomes or effective training in providing therapy, and the ambiguity about its work speaks to the multiplicity of versions about its therapeutic goals.

In the "controversial discussions" that wracked the British Psycho-Analytic Society in the 1940s, however, it was a point of pride with both sides to stress their primary commitment to the "science" of psychoanalysis, their search for knowledge. Superior truth, not more effective cure, was the rallying cry of each camp (King & Steiner, 1991). Today, of course, such strident claims for truth are seldom made. Nor am I suggesting that psychoanalysis should resume its claims for scientific truth. But, clearly, the tables have turned. Now, instead of tension between truth and therapy, psychoanalysis struggles to establish and define its relation to "psychotherapy." Indeed, the effort to distinguish the two is the subject of virtually unending and inconclusive contemporary debate that is symptomatic, I believe, of an underlying contradiction.

Recently, Greenberg (2001) has pointed out the ongoing tension between the aim of psychoanalysis as an investigative activity, which he believes we can and do understand, and the nature of its therapeutic action, which we do not and, perhaps, cannot understand. He approvingly cites Michaels's straightforward characterization of the psychoanalytic goal of helping "patients appreciate the meaningfulness of their experience," especially, of course, disavowed or repudiated experience. He believes, correctly I think, that most analysts would agree with some such statement, a statement that closely parallels what I have suggested is the central thread of psychoanalysis stemming from the first part of Freud's 1923 definition. On the other hand, we cannot account for our therapeutic effects, though we debate it endlessly and tirelessly link concepts of therapeutic action to our various theories.

This is a strong argument for the value of our current pluralism. The tension of this disparity, he suggests, can be a source of creativity for the analyst, who needs to be continually alert to the different openings and strategies that might lead to change. But more important, here, is the underlying distinction between the psychoanalytic aim and the psychotherapeutic effect. From the perspective of the argument I am developing here, that discrepancy is an artifact of the underlying confusion in the relationship between psychoanalysis and psychotherapy. The question of therapeutic action is, of course, vital and important – but it is a question relevant to psychotherapy in general, and once psychotherapy has been disentangled from its complex and confusing relationship with psychoanalysis and more able to explore the variety of its approaches, I believe, it will be easier – if not easy – to address. But now, given our ignorance of therapeutic action, Greenberg (2001) stresses (his italics): "it is difficult to argue that *psychoanalysis has any unique place as a therapeutic modality.*"

In attempting so endlessly to differentiate itself from "psychotherapy," psychoanalysis is implicitly claiming a privileged status. Indeed, the continual efforts at differentiation not only place "psychotherapy" in the lesser role as the degraded "other" but also perpetuate the delusion that there is a single thing known as "psychotherapy" rather than a vast array of interesting and sometimes useful techniques that have evolved in response to a burgeoning social need. Only a resolute aversion from contemporary reality could sustain such an idea.

To summarize, Freud's definition of psychoanalysis as "a collection of psychological information" led to the establishment of a rigid boundary between psychology and psychoanalysis, which we are only recently coming to dismantle. And his definition of it as a "treatment for neurotic disorders" led to the virtually endless effort to define a boundary with "psychotherapy" in the attempt to sustain a privileged apartness. Loosening those boundaries will inevitably bring psychoanalysis closer to the larger worlds of psychology and psychotherapy, relieving it from the contradictions of its superior aloofness. It will also, I believe, help to clarify its primary mission.

A New Project?

If it were possible to agree on the essential psychoanalytic task of inquiry and exploration, how would that affect the nature of our "professional project"? What would psychoanalysis look like?

For one thing, such a psychoanalysis would have to see itself in the context of other professions and disciplines, abandoning its tendency toward isolation and aloofness, its tendency to see itself as uniquely qualified and hierarchically privileged. We would need to work at building links with other fields, demonstrating our willingness and interest in collaborating – and, of course, our ability to do so.

How, for example, could the "pure gold" of psychoanalytic inquiry link with therapeutic practice? Can we pry them apart, and maintain a meaningful relationship? Two possibilities come to mind. One has to do with psychoanalysis taking a critical – and self-critical – role within psychotherapy. Here it embraces medicine or, at least, the healing arts. The other has to do with its standing apart from medicine and psychotherapy as it is traditionally understood.

Thirty years ago, a group of sociologists (Henry, Sims, & Spray, 1971) argued in *The Fifth Profession* that social workers, psychologists, psychiatrists, and psychoanalysts together constitute the beginnings of a new emergent profession of psychotherapy. They found that not only did the work of the four professions overlap, but that there was significant overlap in their attitudes, values, and socio-economic backgrounds: "There are differences in ideology and in particular therapeutic activities, but they are minimal, and, far more important, they do not differ along lines of the professions of which these therapists are members ... their relevance to the production and final character of the psychotherapist is negligible" (p. 182).

This radical suggestion, so outmoded and impractical sounding, illustrates the degree to which psychoanalysis had become thoroughly identified as a branch of psychotherapy to those outside the field. But it also sets the stage for considering how it might fit in.

If we think of psychoanalytic training as providing particular skills in reflecting, questioning and self-questioning, constructing and deconstructing narratives, inherently perspectival, might it not offer to examine and reflect upon psychotherapeutic technique in general? Aware of the complexity and layering of human behavior, trained to appreciate the limits of all observation, the unexpected effects of any intervention, might not psychoanalysis, in short, take up a management or consultative role to the profession of psychotherapy?

Recent articles reviewing the history of psychoanalytic treatments for OCD, including such classic cases as Freud's Wolf Man, provide an example of what this might look like. "There is no avoiding the fact that the weight of clinical and research evidence on OCD is not favorable to psychoanalysis," concludes Esman (2001, p. 153). Biological and behavioral approaches are demonstrably more effective. But that does not mean that psychoanalytic thinking is without relevance. As Gabbard (2001b) pointed out, "The characterological features of individuals with OCD tend to undermine treatment in many cases" (p. 218). Work on the meaning of symptoms and family dynamics mobilized around specific resistances to treatment can often be crucial. He concludes: "OCD serves as a model illness to demonstrate the value of an integrated approach to the treatment of major psychiatric disorders" (p. 219).

With its awareness of the complexity of human behavior and its ability to shift perspectives, indeed, psychoanalysis may be the only mental health discipline able to take on the role of managing the complex and varying integration that each case would require. To be sure, such managers would have to be better informed than most psychoanalysts currently are about other forms of available treatment, but given their experience with pluralism and ambiguity they might best be able to take it on.

It is even more apparent in the realm of applied psychoanalysis that psychoanalysis offers not competing but supplementary perspectives on behavior. In group, family, and organizational work, psychoanalysis does not supplant other modalities, but offers additional perspectives through the clinical ability to reflect and reframe, taking into account such factors as the role of the observing instrument, the unconscious aspects of behavior, including conflict, the role of anxiety and defenses against anxiety, secondary gains, and so forth. Perhaps, most importantly, in these areas psychoanalysis offers its familiarity with ambiguity and uncertainty, an ability to tolerate not knowing, what has sometimes been called, after Keats, "negative capability."

The second answer points to a reframing of therapy itself, out of medicine altogether. Mitchell (1993) has suggested that the role of

204 Problems of Professionalization

contemporary psychoanalysis has shifted from the treatment of more or less well-defined clinical entities, as in Freud's day, to an exploration of the false adaptations people have made to their cultures: "what the patient needs is a revitalization and expansion of his own capacity to generate experience that feels fresh, meaningful, and valuable" (p. 24). And while this shift represents a development within psychoanalysis – he cites Loewald, Winnicott, Kohut, Bion, Bollas, Benjamin, etc. to bolster this point – he notes: "It is part of a search for a new context of meanings to house the psychoanalytic process" (p. 24).

This view of psychoanalysis addresses the need of patients for authentic and vital experience, increasingly rendered problematic by our highly organized, controlled, and competitive social order. It represents a shift away from the treatment of what has been called "mental illness" or discrete pathological entities. That shift also resembles, I believe, a view of psychoanalysis shared by those who have drawn parallels with religion. Symington (1994), for example, has argued that the primary issue addressed by psychoanalysis is narcissism, which he defines as "a deep emotional refusal in the face of crisis" (p. 123). The goal of psychoanalysis, for him, is to help the patient face up to the crisis, open himself to reality, a goal he sees as essentially "spiritual," having been carried by religion in the past.

My only point here is that one can see how this view links with the definition of the essential psychoanalytic task we have been pursuing. The search for the hidden, obscured aspects of human behavior clearly includes the search for spontaneous experience, for the authentic and real that lies behind contemporary false selves and compliant adaptations. And it is necessarily open-ended, not confined to particular symptoms and discrete goals. In that, as well, it addresses the criticisms of Cushman (1990, 1993), Jacoby (1983), and others concerning the collusion of psychoanalysis and psychotherapy with the contemporary social order – though, in so doing, it necessarily evokes serious questions about the degree of psychoanalysis's current engagement with the established mental health system.

Let me summarize. I am suggesting three pathways for a reconsidered psychoanalytic project: (1) The path of partner in the psychotherapies, offering the benefits of insight and inquiry in the treatment of psychiatric disorders; (2) A comparable partnership in the "applied" fields of organizational, family, and group work, allied with other disciplines and professions; (3) The path of inquiry into false adaptations, social identities that block authentic and full human experience. There may well be other paths to be charted, but I believe that we are already on these paths now and can take steps to clarify our goals.

For psychoanalysis to reposition itself with respect to psychotherapy and other professions would require internal changes. We would need to be more accepting of our divisions and differences, seeing that as a source of useful diversity in addressing a range of different problems with a range of different skills. In this, we might model a flexibility appropriate to professions that are facing rapidly changing and unstable circumstances and demands. We might also, then, model more appropriate versions of professional authority, based less on uniformity and control and more on collaborative and shared conversations and negotiations. (For a parallel in psychology, see Benjamin, 2001.) If we could be seen to be working with each other in reasonable competition, respecting the authority we have achieved in our respective areas of work, that would lend credibility to our claims for professional authority with the public.

On the other hand, for psychoanalysis to separate itself out from the psychotherapies, as a practice that addresses the search for authentic experience rather than providing cures for mental illness, it would require giving up the benefits of medicalization. That might mean abandoning the quest for outcome studies; success in the realm of real experience may prove difficult to measure. It would certainly mean abandoning the claim for reimbursement from third parties; we would not be dealing with traditional diagnostic categories.

Such a new "professional project," pursued along three such pathways, would require a renewed emphasis on training, the development of enlarged skills and competencies. Collaboration with other disciplines would require extended exposure to allied fields, not merely psychotherapy. Not only would training need to provide a more culturally diverse range of offerings, suggesting how psychoanalysis could be enriched by and could, in turn, enrich other disciplines; training would need to include exposure to other clinical areas as well, in larger systems such as groups, families, and organizations, in order to gain some familiarity with complex clinical phenomena.

But such a new "professional project" would be significantly enhanced if we were able to develop means of self-governance that were inclusive and cooperative, despite differences and disagreements (see Richards, 1999). Eventually, we might be able to put to rest the accusation that we are sectarian zealots engaged in self-perpetuating delusions.

Obviously much would have to change were psychoanalysis to redirect itself away from its "failed" current project. This could only be a sketch of what such a new project – and a new profession – might look like. But perhaps it could stimulate an engagement with alternative visions.

References

Arlow, J. A. (1972). Some dilemmas in psychoanalytic education. *Journal of the American Psychoanalytic Association* 20, 556–66.

Balint, M. (1984). On the psychoanalytic training system. *International Journal of Psycho-Analysis* 29, 163–73.

Benjamin, J. (1997). Psychoanalysis as a vocation. *Psychoanalytic Dialogues* 7, 781–802.

Benjamin, Jr., L. T. (2001). American psychology's struggles with its curriculum. *American Psychologist* 56, 735–42.

Bergmann, M. S. (ed.) (2000). *The Hartmann Era*. New York: Other Press.

Bornstein, R. F. (2001). The impending death of psychoanalysis. *Psychoanalytic Psychology* 88, 3–20.

Cushman, P. (1990). Why the self is empty: toward a historically situated psychology. *American Psychologist* 45, 599–611.

Cushman, P. (1993). Psychotherapy to 1992: an historically situated interpretation. In D. K. Freedheim (ed.), *History of Psychotherapy* (pp. 21–64). Washington, DC: American Psychological Association.

Eisold, K. (1994). The intolerance of diversity in psychoanalytic institutes. *International Journal of Psycho-Analysis* 75, 785–800.

Eisold, K. (1998). The splitting of the New York Psychoanalytic and the construction of psychoanalytic authority. *International Journal of Psycho-Analysis* 79, 871–85.

Eisold, K. (2000). The rediscovery of the unknown. *Contemporary Psychoanalysis* 36, 57–75.

Eisold, K. (2004). Psychoanalytic training: the "faculty system." *Psychoanalytic Inquiry* 24, 51–70.

Eckhardt, M. H. (1978). Organizational schisms in American psychoanalysis. In J. M. Quen & E. T. Carlson (eds.), *American Psychoanalysis: Origins and Development*. New York: Brunner/Mazel.

Esman, A. (2001). Obsessive-compulsive disorder: current views. *Psychoanalytic Inquiry* 21(2), 145–56.

Freidson, E. (1986). *Professional Powers*. Chicago: University of Chicago Press.

Freud, S. (1908). "Civilized" sexual morality and modern nervous illness. In J. Strachey (ed. and trans.), *The Standard Edition of the Complete Psychological Works of Sigmund Freud* (Vol. 9, pp. 177–204). London: Hogarth Press.

Freud, S. (1914). On the history of the psychoanalytic movement. In J. Strachey (ed. and trans.), *The Standard Edition of the Complete Psychological Works of Sigmund Freud* (Vol. 14, pp. 3–66). London: Hogarth Press.

Freud, S. (1923). Two encyclopaedia articles. In J. Strachey (ed. and trans.), *The Standard Edition of the Complete Psychological Works of Sigmund Freud* (Vol. 18, pp. 233–59). London: Hogarth Press.

Frosch, J. (1991). The New York Psychoanalytic civil wars. *Journal of the American Psychoanalytic Association* 39(4), 1037–64.

Gabbard, G. (2001a). Overview and commentary. *Psychoanalytic Quarterly* 70(1), 287–96.

Gabbard, G. (2001b). Psychoanalytically informed approaches to the treatment of obsessive-compulsive disorder. *Psychoanalytic Inquiry* 21(2), 208–21.

Gitelson, F. H. (1983). Identity crises: splits or compromises: adaptive or maladaptive. In E. D. Joseph & D. Widlocher (eds.), *The Identity of the Psychoanalyst* (pp. 157–80). New York: International Universities Press.

Greenberg, J. (2001). Psychoanalytic goals, therapeutic action, and the analyst's tension. The 44th Rado Lecture of the Columbia Center for Psychoanalytic Training and Research, New York City, June 5.

Hale, Jr., N. G. (1971). *Freud and the Americans*. New York: Oxford.

Hartmann, H. (1959). Psychoanalysis as a scientific theory. In *Essays in Ego Psychology* (pp. 318–50). New York: International Universities Press.

Henry, W. E., Sims, J. H., & Spray, S. L. (1971). *The Fifth Profession*. San Francisco: Jossey-Bass.

Holt, R. R., & Luborsky, L. (1955). The selection of candidates for psychoanalytic training. *Journal of the American Psychoanalytic Association* 3, 666–81.

Jacoby, R. (1983). *The Repression of Psychoanalysis*. Chicago: University of Chicago Press.

Kachele, H., & Thoma, H. (2000). On the devaluation of the Eitingon-Freud model of psychoanalytic education. *International Journal of Psycho-Analysis* 81, 806–7.

Kappelle, W. (1996). How useful is selection? *International Journal of Psycho-Analysis* 77, 1213–32.

208 Problems of Professionalization

Kernberg, O. F. (1996). Thirty methods to destroy the creativity of psycho-analytic candidates. *International Journal of Psycho-Analysis* 77, 1031–40.

King, P., & Steiner, R. (eds.) (1991). *The Freud–Klein Controversies*. London: Routledge.

Kirsner, D. (2000). *Unfree Associations: Inside Psychoanalytic Institutes*. London: Proces Press.

Knight, R. P. (1953). Present status of organized psychoanalysis in the United States. *Journal of the American Psychoanalytic Association* 1, 197–221.

Laplanche, J., & Pontalis, J. B. (1973). *The Language of Psycho-Analysis*. New York: W. W. Norton.

Larson, M. S. (1977). *The Rise of Professionalism*. London: University of California Press.

Macdonald, K. M. (1995). *The Sociology of the Professions*. London: Sage.

Matarazzo, R. G., & Garner, A. M. (1992). Research on training for psycho-therapy. In D. K. Freedheim (ed.), *History of Psychotherapy* (pp. 850–77). Washington, DC: American Psychological Association.

Mitchell, S. (1993). *Hope and Dread in Psychoanalysis*. New York: Basic Books.

Momigliano, L. N. (1992). *Continuity and Change in Psychoanalysis: Letters from Milan*. London: Karnac.

Reisner, S. (1999). Freud and psychoanalysis: into the 21st century. *Journal of the American Psychoanalytic Association* 47, 1037–60.

Renik, O. (1998). Getting real in analysis. *Psychoanalytic Quarterly* 67, 566–93.

Richards, A. D. (1999). A. A. Brill and the politics of exclusion. *Journal of the American Psychoanalytic Association* 47, 9–28.

Rieff, P. (1966). *The Triumph of the Therapeutic*. Chicago: University of Chicago Press.

Rubovitz-Seitz, P. F. D. (1998). *Depth-Psychological Understanding: The Methodologic Grounding of Clinical Interpretations*. Hillsdale, NJ: The Analytic Press.

Slade, A. (2000). The development and organization of attachment. *Journal of the American Psychoanalytic Association* 48, 1147–74.

Starr, P. (1982). *The Social Transformation of American Medicine*. New York: Basic Books.

Symington, N. (1994). *Emotion and Spirit*. London: Cassell.

Turkle, S. (1978). *Psychoanalytic Politics: Freud's French Revolution*. New York: Basic Books.

Wallerstein, R. (1990). Psychoanalysis: the common ground. *International Journal of Psycho-Analysis* 71, 3–20.

Wallerstein, R. (1993). Between chaos and petrification: a summary of the Fifth IPA Conference on Training. *International Journal of Psycho-Analysis* 74, 165–78.

Weinshel, E. (1982). The functions of the training analysis and the selection of the training analyst. *International Review of Psycho-Analysis* 9, 434–44.

Westen, D. (1998). The scientific legacy of Sigmund Freud: towards a psycho-dynamically informed psychological science. *Psychological Bulletin* 124(3), 333–71.

Westen, D. (1999). The scientific status of unconscious processes: is Freud really dead? *Journal of the American Psychoanalytic Association* 47, 1062–1106.

Zeddies, T. J. (2000). Psychoanalytic praxis and the moral vision of psycho-analysis. *Contemporary Psychoanalysis* 36, 521–8.

Chapter Nine

The Erosion of Our Profession

[Originally offered as a plenary talk at a conference at the Tavistock Centre, London, October 21, 2005, "Extension, Dilution and Survival." Published as The Erosion of Our Profession, *Psychoanalytic Psychology*, vol. 24 (2007), pp. 1–9.]

Two interlocking problems account for much of the erosion and demoralization we are experiencing in the profession of psycho-analytic psychotherapy. The first problem is the undermining of traditional professional relationships, as a result of profound social and economic forces affecting all of the professions. These changes are particularly critical in the service industries. (I say "industries" here to stress both the scale that our work has assumed and its role in the economy. I might have said "growth industries.") The psychological care we provide in our intimate relationships with patients is increasingly dominated by pressures for economy, effi-ciency, and control – pressures that place us at variance with trad-itional arrangements with clients that we once were able to take for granted.

The second underlying problem has to do with the relationship between psychotherapy and health care in general. Having come under the jurisdiction of medicine, psychotherapy now finds itself increasingly restricted in virtually every aspect of its work. On one level, we suffer from current draconian efforts to curtail the costs of health care. The alliance with medicine, which once enhanced our professional authority, now has become something of a handicap. On another level, we are often pressured into misrepresenting the nature of the work we do to fit expectations that our medical identity arouses.

We cannot simply decide to alter our professional identity, of course, but at least we might reflect on how that affects our ability to be understood and to be effective.

Problem One: The Professions

Professions as we know them have not always existed – and, very likely, they will not always continue to exist. The medieval world recognized three professions – law, medicine, and teaching – but the system of professions we know today was established during the latter half of the nineteenth century during the flowering of industrial capitalism. It was a means whereby providers of expert services, services based on esoteric knowledge and skills, were able to band together to gain control over the conditions of their work and establish a greater measure of autonomy and security for themselves.

Physicians, dentists, lawyers, accountants, architects, teachers, and others established professional associations in order to negotiate for themselves special relationships between their clients, the market, on the one hand, and government, on the other. In exchange for agreeing to regulate themselves stringently, setting up and monitoring standards for competence as well as ethical behavior, they were granted a considerable degree of autonomy, essentially a monopoly over the provision of services. Governments agreed to license professionals, prohibiting non-licensed professionals from practicing, turning over to the professions themselves the setting of standards, the management of training, the establishment of fees, and the monitoring of malfeasance.

Thus a middle ground in our economy was established that was relatively immune to the more destabilizing and destructive aspects of unbridled competition. Professionals came to enjoy a certain amount of economic security along with a pride in their ability to regulate themselves. And along with this came a certain social status. Educated, relatively independent, prosperous, needed and valued for their skills, they came to occupy a privileged station. Government could stay aloof from attempting to control matters they did not understand. And the public was able to enjoy relatively well-managed professional services with reasonable confidence.

This is the basic model. Different professions varied, of course, in how they worked this out in different countries, based on the specifics of local traditions and conditions. In Germany, for example, the independence and prestige of universities gave the medical profession a means of regulation and a status that no professional organization could compete with at the start of the twentieth century. Being a "doctor" conferred far less prestige than holding an academic position – a fact not lost on Freud, who always preferred the title of "Professor." In America, on the other hand, where universities lacked such status, physicians had a more difficult time establishing themselves as respected professionals. It was not until standards of education and practice were established in the early twentieth century, that the American Medical Association came to have unprecedented authority over the field (see Starr, 1982). This belated but highly successful development for American medicine helps to account for the tenacious insistence of the early American psychoanalysts, almost uniformly psychiatrists, that psychoanalysis had to be grounded in the newly prestigious profession of medicine. Without that, they feared, it would be associated with quackery, as were medical doctors before the profession had succeeded in establishing itself (Eisold, 1998; Chapter 2 in this volume).

Thus in different ways in different countries, the professions developed. But as this was happening, it came to seem that certain practitioners were inherently entitled to the privileges and status of a professional by virtue of their specialized knowledge. It was not seen as a bargain that had been struck, or an achievement that had been negotiated, but a reflection of the fact that professional services could be organized no other way.

The early theoreticians of professions, such as Max Weber, assumed so. And I think that most of us still do, assuming that by virtue of the kind of work we do we are "professionals." It is only in the last 25 to 30 years that sociologists of the professions began to examine more closely how professions came to be organized, reflected in the account I just gave (Larson, 1977; Macdonald, 1995). No doubt this new understanding of the "creation" of the current system of professions became possible because changes in the stability and structures of the professions themselves were well under way, as a result of which it was easier to see that the model was far from inevitable or sacrosanct.

But many of us, inside the professions, still tend to see the professions as fixed or essential. When we speak about what is happening to our profession, we tend to bring to the discussion an assumption that something pure, stable, and strong is being worn away, threatened, compromised. It may be the case that something valuable is being slowly debased, but I think it is important to see this in context. The economic forces that enabled the professions to establish themselves in the last century are now moving on, creating the conditions that make that way of providing services no longer feasible.

What is happening to our profession is happening to all professions, at different rates of change and in different ways, but inexorably. The market forces to which the model of the professions was originally a response have evolved so that economies of scale and the management of costs have become mandatory. Professionals no longer control the economics of their work. If we look at the professions of law or architecture or accounting, for example, increasingly we see huge multinational firms, recruiting "professionals" directly from graduate schools at competitive salaries. The legal structure of these enterprises may still bear some resemblance to the partnerships they started out being, but they no longer actually function as those partnerships did. Those professionals are now, by and large, employees. To be sure, there are the "boutique" firms, which have been able to carve out for themselves a market niche, remaining small and distinctive; but they are the exception, not the rule.

In short, the idea of protecting or preserving an established profession is no longer an adequate defense against these developments. Our identity as professionals provides us no leverage. To claim that some established professional ideal is being compromised carries no weight.

This is particularly true where costs are associated with social entitlements, such as workplace benefits and insurance coverage. Increasingly physicians do not go into private practice as they once did; either they join a group practice, which frequently evolves into a kind of clinic or specialized center, or they become employees of outpatient hospital services. The choice is to be entrepreneurial, if you can figure out an opportunity that has not already been exploited, or a worker in someone else's shop.

An article in *The Wall Street Journal* described a dramatic example of the economic benefits of medical entrepreneurship: "In a 2000 speech, neurosurgeon Larry Teuber rhetorically asked why doctors would want to open a hospital dedicated to surgery. 'Profit, profit, profit,' ran his answer. When it comes to taking business from general hospitals, 'you can't believe how easy it is,' he said." The *Journal* went on to note that he made $9 million when his company went public, while the local hospital, where he used to practice, posted an $8.3 million operating loss. The hospital claims that the "surgery center has siphoned away healthier – and more profitable – patients. Dr. Teuber says his rival's problems stem from poor management and inefficiency" (Armstrong, 2005, p. 1).

This may strike us as an extreme example, but put it beside what has become a standard practice in psychotherapy: relatively affluent patients end up in private practices, paying decent fees, while others are left to public services increasingly strapped to meet this need.

There is another aspect of this development that we need to take into account: what has become known as the "commodification" of services. That is, the treatments we provide, under the pressure of the marketplace, are increasingly viewed as products to be measured against other products rather than as unique, specialized relationships with clients. These commodities are broken down into components in order to be analyzed for cost, effectiveness, and consistency. In the more crude language of the market, this is known as "pricing," "value," and "quality control"; the total package is promoted as a "brand."

In our field, psychodynamic psychotherapy or psychoanalytic psychotherapy is in competition with cognitive behavioral therapy, psychopharmacological treatments, rational emotive therapy, EMDR, group therapy, etc. etc. Thus the relevant questions that are raised are about comparative outcomes, expense, and reliability. Increasingly we have treatment protocols, manualizations, best practices – all the bureaucratic apparatus that takes professional judgment out of the hands of practitioners, putting decisions into the hands of managers who are charged with implementing policies that seek to reconcile quality and profit.

Managers too must now inevitably raise the question of how much expensive training is required to provide adequate care. Do we really need Ph.D.s or prolonged apprenticeships? What is the evidence for the effectiveness of traditional trainings? Can cheaper labor do the work?

This is a radical departure from the traditional autonomy of the professional, exercising his or her own judgment about the needs of the patients, the skills he or she possesses to provide for them, and the training required to acquire them. The judgment of practitioners is no longer privileged. Decisions not only exist within narrow guidelines (such as length or frequency of sessions) but also often need to be justified to managers who have no specific competence apart from the formulas they must adhere to. At least this is the situation in America.

But no matter how insulting such procedures are to the self-esteem of the "professional," if we may still use the term, and no matter how liable they are to abuses in the name of profit, we have to acknowledge that these developments are not entirely bad. They stress efficiency and accountability, something our profession has tended to be lax about. The traditional complaint about professionals, in general, has been that either through self-interest or ignorance they abuse their trust, often too willing to promise what they cannot or will not actually deliver.

Psychoanalysis has a somewhat embarrassing history in this respect. I am sure we recall the days, if they are indeed over, when psychoanalysis was considered the treatment of choice for all patients, so long as they were "analyzable." Three, four, or five times a week, for an unspecified number of years, regardless of the complaint, was not only preferred and often mandated by professional organizations that viewed any other approach as a form of deviance or apostasy. Today, lengthy and frequent treatments will not be supported by insurance companies or the state, even if we could manage to find the way to rationalize them to ourselves as an ideal for most forms of mental distress.

On the other hand, or course, it is hardly better to have decisions about mental health driven by "profit, profit, profit," in the words of the American medical entrepreneur, or to have those who provide the service largely excluded from the decision-making process. I do not think that the abuses of the past account for these new developments, or justify them, but they do help us to understand some of the arguments used against traditional practices.

To summarize: the professions that we knew, that we grew up understanding, that we thought we joined – those professions no longer exist. We have licensure regulated by the state, but that no longer insures a professional monopoly over the provision of services. Increasingly, the state now takes on the role of gatekeeper to the profession and has its own agenda in seeking to ensure that costs are contained. The definition of essential services is no longer in the hands of practitioners. Increasingly, fees are set by others.

As a result, along with losing control over our economic conditions, our ability to make clinical judgments about treatment, and determine schedules, we have also lost much of the status and social respect we once enjoyed. We still have the ideas – if not ideals – of professional knowledge, skills, and ethical standards, but, to a large extent, we have become workers, mental health workers.

A blunt way of putting this is that now we still have the responsibilities and obligations of professionals but not the autonomy and privileges that once were part of the package. We are suffering from the cutbacks and economies that increasingly characterize all employees, particularly those providing social services. In the increasing gap between the richer and poorer members of society, we ourselves are among the losers.

Problem Two: The Link with Medicine

My second point is about the link between psychotherapy and medicine. Psychotherapy has come under the jurisdiction of medicine. Even if we are trained and licensed as psychologists, social workers, pastoral counselors, nurses, etc., as psychotherapists we are part of the health care industry, regulated by its procedures and expectations, reimbursable under medical insurance plans, covered by malpractice insurance, etc.

This was by no means inevitable. I am not at all sure that, at this stage of the process, it is reversible, but it is useful, I think, to grasp the fact that it is not essential. It is worth our while to reflect upon the professional space within which we now find ourselves housed.

The link with medicine was there in the beginning with Freud, a neurologist, developing psychoanalysis as a treatment for hysteria, a disorder that, under the influence of Charcot and others, had come to be generally considered a medical problem. Very quickly, Freud saw the danger of psychoanalysis becoming "a mere handmaiden of psychiatry," as he put it, and tried to set it up as an independent profession. But many of his medical followers combated him on the subject of "lay analysis," insisting that psychoanalysis needed to be under the control of physicians.

Freud lost on this issue, with the result that medicine gained jurisdiction over the new field, servicing the growing array of personal problems that the dislocations and stresses of industrialization helped to create. As a result, though we do now have many "lay" psychoanalysts and psychotherapists, all of us have become providers of medical services, adjuncts to the medical industry.

Earlier in the century, the greatest competition for the claim staked by neurologists, such as Freud, came from the clergy, whose social role as advisors and consolers to their parishioners inevitably suggested that they were the logical choice to take on this work. But other groups, as well, joined in the battle to assert jurisdiction.

As the sociologist Andrew Abbott (1988) pointed out: "The jurisdiction of personal problems was created, split, reattached to other jurisdictions, split in new ways, and reconceptualized a dozen times between 1860 and 1940. Groups associated with it subdivided, joined, then divided along new lines, both ideological and organizational" (p. 281). Neurologists competed with psychiatrists; Christian Scientists competed with evangelicals, electrotherapists competed with hydrotherapists; psychologists and social workers made concerted efforts to claim specific areas of work. At stake was the opportunity to get into a rapidly growing business and claim social importance.

In the 1920s and 1930s, the battle was joined by the newly established mental hygiene movement, developed to bring the benefits of scientific thinking to social problems, free from ideological and moralizing judgments. Framing mental problems as forms of disease, mental hygienists believed, helped patients to accept them as objective problems they needed to face, not as moral failings to be ashamed of. The concept of illness promised to take the stigma out of mental suffering, making it a problem, not a failing. But it also provided a boost to medicine as it competed against the clergy to establish jurisdiction over this burgeoning new field.

My point here is not to dwell on these historical developments but simply to make the point that the jurisdiction of medicine over psychotherapy was not inevitable. And just as it was by no means preordained that medicine should triumph in this battle, it is by no means required that it should continue to prevail. Indeed, now, there are powerful reasons for us to combat the identity that medicine fought so hard to achieve, and there are significant social factors to make change seem somewhat more likely.

Throughout our history, powerful critiques have been waged against this medical identity. In 1961 Thomas Szasz attacked the "myth of mental illness," arguing that psychotherapists are "shackled to the wrong conceptual framework and terminology" (1961, p. 4). And many have continued to protest what is frequently referred to as "the medical model," urging us to refer to "clients" instead of "patients," "problems in living" instead of "diseases," etc.

The medical concept of disease is actually complex and multifaceted, reducible to no simple physical condition, according to medical doctors who have wrestled with this problem. Indeed, one scholar has plausibly suggested a "sociopolitical definition" of disease, in which a disease is an "undesirable" condition that "it seems on balance ... physicians (or health professionals in general) and their technologies are more likely to be able to deal with it effectively than any of the alternatives, such as the criminal justice system (treating it as a crime), the church (treating it as a sin) or social work (treating it as a social problem)" (Kendell, 2004, p. 35). This pragmatic if not somewhat self-serving definition may be the best that can be offered, but it is certainly not without its shortcomings.

The concept of mental health is misleading for a number of reasons. It introduces the idea of normative functioning into human behavior, replacing traditional morality with a new set of standards about the "healthy personality" that we are hard put to justify. It also suggests a similarity between organic diseases, treatable by surgery and drugs, and the kinds of difficulties that clients experience. The increasing array of psychotropic medications reinforces that implication, arousing false hopes of palliatives if not actual cures. Moreover, in emulating medical procedures, we find ourselves often engaged in a collusion of bad faith, finding a diagnosis that will make a patient eligible for the care he has come to expect, that we think he should have, and that our managers want us to be able to provide.

More recently, the hermeneutical critiques of psychoanalytical claims to scientific status have reinforced the idea that the primary focus of our work is interpretation or understanding: narratives not diseases. Much of our work is about meaning: false beliefs, misconceptions, inadequate stories, unknown motivations, confusions, misattributions, etc. etc.

Let me take a moment to briefly survey the range of problems that are now addressed by psychotherapy, the range of issues under our jurisdiction.

Some problems are entirely about meaning: the work we do helping clients through difficult life transitions – the death of a spouse or close friend, divorce or other forms of separation, job loss, illness, and so forth. Though such problems of adjustment may provoke intense anxiety and depression, suggesting the temporary use of medication, by and large these problems are clearly not "illnesses," in any sense of the term, requiring medical attention. Closely related are family problems: marital disputes, child/parent conflicts, ageing parents, etc. People need considerable help in managing these issues or reaching painful decisions.

Here our old professional adversaries, the clergy, have a distinct advantage. No one would question the relevance of their interest in such matters or the appropriateness of their concern and desire to help, though their current levels of competence may leave much to be desired.

Our expertise as interpreters of experience becomes more clearly relevant with clients who suffer from self-defeating behaviors: the incapacity to sustain intimate relationships, the failure to pursue their own self-interests, to follow through on projects, to feel worthy of achievement, to confront others. There is a related set of clients who are unable to lead authentic lives.

Many of the problems we face in our daily work suggest that the body is profoundly involved in the symptom picture, and that, therefore, we are somewhat closer to the traditional concept of disease. Anorexia, for example, or OCD implicate the neurological and endocrine systems. It is hard to assert the sufficiency of working with narratives or interpretations when we know that drugs will often be powerfully effective in relieving depression or panic and that behavioral approaches are required to counteract deeply entrenched habits or powerful cravings.

And then there are patients who require more active management, severely depressed patients who cannot care for themselves or who are suicidal, schizophrenic, sociopathic.

This list is far from comprehensive, but sufficient, I think, to make the point that the complexity of what we are learning and discovering about human behavior suggests that there is no single approach that is adequate. This, in turn, implies that there is no single set of competencies, no single discipline that can hope to encompass all that is required. Neurologists have come back into the picture by virtue of the new discoveries being made into the functioning of the brain and nervous system. Behavioral psychologists have a role to play in reshaping destructive habits. Psychopharmacologists clearly have a powerful role to play by virtue of the complex array of new medications being developed for anxiety and depression. Traditional social workers often provide essential support. And, of course, psychotherapists continue to be essential, with their interpretive skills.

We have come full circle: beginning by questioning the location of psychotherapy in medicine, we are now questioning the location of psychotherapy in any single discipline, the adequacy of any existing profession to encompass the knowledge and skills required to deal with the realm of personal problems. Thirty years ago, a group of sociologists (Henry, Sims, & Spray, 1971) argued in *The Fifth Profession* that social workers, psychologists, psychiatrists, and psychoanalysts together constitute the beginnings of a new emergent profession of psychotherapy. They found that not only did the work of the four professions overlap, but also that there was significant overlap in their attitudes, values, and socio-economic backgrounds.

Professional jealousies and ideological differences kept that from happening, but it may be that now, in the face of adversity, such a radical idea may have more appeal. If so, it would not be an autonomous profession, as in the old model of the professions. The complexity of the work of psychotherapy suggests it would have to be a matrix organization drawing on an amalgam of skills, prepared to adapt to constantly changing conditions.

I doubt that what I am saying here is particularly new to those who struggle on a daily basis with these complexities. What would be new is reorganizing our profession to promote cooperation among relevant disciplines and to find the means to pay for it.

Some Concluding Thoughts

Let us assume that the economic forces reshaping our profession – and our society – cannot be challenged. The market is too strongly entrenched as our dominant ideology. Competition will prevail, services will continue to be commodified, and costs will continue to be questioned and cut.

We will have no choice but to become entrepreneurial in our thinking. That does not mean we have to be like the American surgeon with his battle cry of "profit, profit, profit," gleefully putting competing services out of business; but it does mean that we will need to decenter from our traditional orientation as professionals, defending our familiar privileges. Difficult and distasteful as it may be for many of us, we will have to think about ways of improving value and cutting costs.

Some trends in the commodification of services can be readily joined without compromise. It would be possible to set up specialized services to deal with complex clinical entities such as eating disorders, OCD, phobias, etc., where different sets of skills are brought together: psychopharmacology, behavior modification, nutrition, neurology, endocrinology, as well as psychotherapy. Such services could utilize best practices as well as perform ongoing research in order to establish and maintain a competitive advantage in the market. Services such as these ought to be managed by psychoanalytically oriented psychotherapists, I think, as they will have the best overview of the patient's relationship to the treatment process. But this would require, in turn, that psychotherapists develop managerial skills in coordinating teams.

Another set of commodities that could be developed is services for executives or managers contending with the complex and contradictory demands of their work. Frankly, I believe well-trained psychotherapists are best suited to do this work because they readily detect signs of unconscious anxiety and emotional conflict, but they can also help in grasping and reframing the meaning that clients attribute to their behavior and that of others. And they are less likely to be taken in by their clients' own preconceptions about their problems.

Much of this work today is in the hand of "coaches," who know the world of organizational life and business better than most of us, but do not know the intricacies of personality and behavior as we do. To compete in this field would require additional training, but there is no inherent reason why psychotherapists should not be able to grasp the cultural and psychodynamic issues pervading organizational life sufficiently to understand the context of work issues for clients.

Might it also be possible to provide "advisory services" to those facing disconcerting transitions in their lives: deaths, divorce, empty nests, etc.? I deliberately use the term "advisory" here because of the well-known aversion in our field to offering advice. But people want advice – or at least advice is what they seek, even though they usually still do not want to be told what to do. Can we envisage sophisticated "advice" that does not specify answers but helps clients think through their problems, clarifying their thoughts, assessing their strengths, becoming aware of some of the choices others have made in similar circumstance? Groups might be an option here.

Similar services might be made available for those who require counseling for problems with children, spouses, colleagues, friends, or parents, or for those going through difficult career transitions. Much of this kind of work now is lumped together under psychotherapy, but such problems can be separated out into particular services and characterized in ways that make them more readily accessible and acceptable to clients. If they were more clearly non-medical, they could be easier for clients to accept.

There will be continued pressure to make services broader and cheaper by minimizing the costs of training. Inevitably that will lead to the development of two tiers of competence: those who know enough and have the basic skills to provide direct services and those who can provide supervision, deal with thorny problems, and manage. There are many citizens who could provide useful services dealing with "problems in living" but who would profit immensely from having guidance and supervision: mothers, retired businessmen, refugees. To be in the supervisory tier in the provision of such services would require some additional training for psychotherapists.

All of these suggestions, however, would require reinvigorating our professional identity. I noted earlier that as professionals we have lost much of the control over the conditions of our work, along with the status, that have been the traditional hallmarks of professions. What has been left to us is the responsibility – but also the expertise. Society needs us because we have essential knowledge and skills that we have the obligation to protect and to employ. No matter how degraded and manipulated we may feel, we still know something that others do not know – and that they need.

Let me summarize. The problem we face now is twofold: First, we need to help the public understand better what it is we do, what the skills are that we employ in the service of alleviating emotional distress, the knowledge we have acquired and that we refine and use to train others. Linking it with medical skills may have seemed useful to us at one point in the past, but that point has gone. The link with medicine makes us seem relevant in emergencies, oriented to suffering and disease, part of pathology, not part of life.

The second has to do with our relationship with the public itself. Earlier I stressed our need to come to terms with the market in an age of heightened competition, and I think that that is an essential aspect of the economic reality we face. But the public is our market; our consumers are people who are confused and desperate, often frightened and helpless. It is true that we need to think of providing useful commodities to those consumers, but we also need to develop their trust in us so that they trust the services we provide.

Part of that is being clear about the first point, what it is we do. But part of that is also convincing the public that we are not indifferent and aloof, primarily concerned with our own status, salaries, working conditions, rather than their needs. In our present condition, mourning the erosion of our profession, preoccupied with losses of our social standing and control over our work, we do not present an attractive picture.

We do need decent working conditions, good salaries, respect, and a significant say in the work we perform. All workers are entitled to that, and our work is uniquely sensitive to those factors. Even if the model of the professions no longer holds as it did, the nature of our work itself requires these things. But times have changed, and we have to look to ourselves to make it happen.

References

Abbott, A. (1988). *The System of Professions*. Chicago: University of Chicago Press.

Armstrong, D. (2005). A surgeon earns riches, enmity by plucking profitable patients. *The Wall Street Journal*, New York, p. 1.

Eisold, K. (1998). The splitting of the New York Psychoanalytic and the construction of psychoanalytic authority. *International Journal of Psychoanalysis* 75, 785–800.

Henry, W. E., Sims, J. H., & Spray, S. L. (1971). *The Fifth Profession*. San Francisco: Jossey-Bass.

Kendell, R. E. (2004). The myth of mental illness. In J. A. Schaler (ed.), *Szasz under Fire* (pp. 27–48). Chicago: Open Court Press.

Larson, M. S. (1977). *The Rise of Professionalism*. London: University of California Press.

Macdonald, K. M. (1995). *The Sociology of the Professions*. London: Sage.

Starr, P. (1982). *The Social Transformation of American Medicine*. New York: Basic Books.

Szasz, T. (1961). *The Myth of Mental Illness*. New York: Harper & Row.

Chapter Ten

Succeeding at Succession

The Myth of Orestes

[Originally published as Succeeding at Succession: The Myth of Orestes, *Journal of Analytic Psychology*, vol. 53 (2008), pp. 619–32.]

The relationship of Laius and Oedipus seems an inescapable model for succession in psychoanalytic organizations. Not only is that myth enshrined in our thinking since Freud first proposed it to account for the hidden conflicts between fathers and sons, but all too often it seems to fit the facts of aggression and acrimony. But of all the destructive paternal actions in our psychoanalytic histories, which ones to single out: the crime of their presuming to analyze themselves or – worse – their own children; manipulating them into carrying out their wishes; pressuring their followers into becoming apostles; proscribing or punishing competition; refusing to let go? If all foundational acts are based on crime, as René Girard suggested (Girard, 1977), we have a wide variety of crimes by our founding fathers to choose from.

And then there is the effect upon the successors, destined to feel guilt for killing off their fathers. Are we doomed to identify with our aggressors, repeating what we do not understand, arrogant and self-defeating? Or, are we expected to expiate our sins, purging ourselves with acts of self-mutilation? Alternatively, do we live constricted, obedient lives, complying with old theories and methods, vying to be each more faithful and unoriginal than the next? Is our fate to suppress what we learn? Must we fail to grow and change?

Oedipus is our archetypal individual, and this is what we have learned to see in the depths of generational succession, the rivalries, fears, and hatreds that are the underpinnings of success. We never go beyond our fathers without exceptional cost. We never triumph as we hope we will – and sometimes believe we have.

There is substantial reason to see such patterns in the history of our profession. Freud insisted that psychoanalysis was *his* possession. In the midst of his conflict with Jung, he asserted that no one could know better than he what it was. Although he set up formal organizations that paid lip service to professional autonomy, he manipulated them behind the scenes, obsessed with maintaining control. The Secret Committee, for example, set up after Jung's "defection," ensured that his followers could compete with each other only by being more faithful and loyal; no one would be allowed to gain an advantage over any of his "brothers" (see Grosskurth, 1991). His anointed "apostles," following the Nazi diaspora, carrying his charismatic authority, spread his vision – and his control – throughout the world. His daughter devoted herself to guarding his legacy, and, like Antigone, protected him in his old age. Today, the system of training analysts – whatever else you may think of it – carries forward the control they initially exerted (Eisold, 1997; Chapter 1 in this volume).

And Jung, for his part, injured by his experience as the "Crown Prince," shied away from the institutional forms used by Freud and his successors to control its future. As a result of his aversion to institutions, grounded in large part on these experiences, Jung held tight personal control over the development of analytical psychology. As Michael Fordham described the days before formal training in analytical psychology was set up: "How anyone became an analytic therapist in those days is vague ... though there was an unwritten law that any person who wanted to be called a Jungian analyst was expected to go out to Zurich, make a relation with Jung himself, and undergo analysis with either himself or one or more of his close colleagues" (Fordham, 1979, p. 280). Jung, too, had his coterie of devoted followers, loyal to him alone, and bearing the stamp of his charismatic authority. As a result, such a personal method of authorization, designed to avoid institutional corruption, ensured that Jung and his close followers would be able to exert an extraordinary degree of control over the professional development of analytical psychology. They may have been more ambivalent about being "professional," but neither did they cede control (Eisold, 2001; Chapter 6 in this volume).

Both psychoanalysis and analytical psychology gradually emerged from these matrices of individual and family dynamics, but they have been crippled in their efforts to become autonomous professions. I will come back to this theme of the confounding effects of the personal and the professional, effects that can still be seen today in the way in which our professional training has been set up. But before I go into that, I would like to return to the Greeks and the guidance that their myths have to offer us in thinking about these issues.

The Myth of Orestes

There is another perspective on succession that I want to stress, the perspective of the community with its collective needs and obligations. A generation before Sophocles told the story of Oedipus and his disastrous triumph, Aeschylus gave an account of Orestes, the son of Agamemnon, caught in a comparable web of family conflict, suffering a similar fate.

Let me briefly recapitulate the myth behind Aeschylus' drama: Orestes murdered his mother, Clytemnestra, to avenge her murder of his father, Agamemnon, on his triumphant return from the Trojan War. Clytemnestra's murder of Agamemnon had been, in turn, an act of vengeance for his killing of their daughter, Iphigenia, whom Agamemnon had sacrificed in order to appease the gods as he set sail to lead the armada of Greek warriors against Troy. Clytemnestra cut down Agamemnon for his sacrifice of Iphigenia. Orestes, following the inexorable logic of dynastic justice, a dutiful son to his father, cut her down in turn.

Despite the similarities in these stories of family conflict, the piling up of paradoxes and horror, there are several key differences between the two myths. For one thing, Oedipus was blind to his own identity, and, along with Laius and Jocasta, blind to the consequences of his own actions. Sophocles, in an age that affirmed the value of the Delphic motto "Know Thyself," pointed out how impossible that goal could be, a point that Freud borrowed to underscore the role of the unconscious in our lives. The destiny of the house of Laius was sealed almost hermetically within the dense web of its opaque personal entanglements. The story of Oedipus starts with him as a king among his subjects, but ends with him alone, a single man.

Agamemnon's family, by contrast, enacted its destiny on the far broader stage of the Trojan War. Agamemnon was a world-historical

228 Problems of Professionalization

figure, perhaps not precisely as described by Aeschylus or Homer, but his actions had political meaning for all the Greeks. His kingdom, Mycenae, was a precursor of Athens, the dominant city state in Greece. Moreover, each of the characters, directed by the gods or driven by their duty and their rage, were fully aware of their actions. But perhaps the most important distinction is that the characters in Aeschylus' drama enacted a set of dilemmas that had political as well as personal significance. The story of Orestes is about the establishment of political justice – and this is the point of Aeschylus' narrative. Up until the moment Orestes fled the persecution of the Furies, justice was a personal obligation, a duty of individuals or of a ruler who, with luck, stood apart from the families he ruled. In the hands of families, it often was enmeshed with feuds and historic rivalries. Aeschylus recounts how it became the responsibility of the *polity*, the collective of all citizens.

Let me recount how this occurs in Aeschylus' trilogy. After murdering his mother, Orestes, tormented by the Furies, seeks refuge at the shrine of Apollo at Delphi. Apollo had supported Orestes' act; the gods could not let the murder of the legitimate ruler go unpunished. The authority of the state was at stake, as was theirs. The Furies represent a more primitive claim, the blood tie to the parent, the mother. That claim too could not go unavenged, or else the order of the family would be subverted. Apollo, the god of reason, powerless to quiet the Furies, sends Orestes to Athena, at her shrine in Athens, where the Furies continue to pursue him.

Athena, hearing the competing and mutually contradictory claims of Orestes and the Furies, establishes the first court of law, in effect, selecting 12 citizens to sit in judgment on the case. A tie vote forces Athena to cast the deciding ballot. She votes to absolve Orestes, who then departs to become king of Mycenae, as his father Agamemnon's successor. But, then, in the most significant development in the play, the avenging Furies threaten Athens with blights and plagues. Unappeased, their claim denied, they threaten the community that tolerated the crime – much as the citizens of Thebes were punished with plagues for the crimes of Oedipus. Athena remonstrates with them but, mindful of their power, she offers them a compromise: Orestes will be spared but they will be given an honored and permanent place in Athens, where the legitimacy of their claims will be recognized in annual ceremonies and sacrifices. Gradually, grudgingly, they come around to accepting her offer. The play ends as she herself leads them to their new sacred, underground dwelling.

What does this mean? First of all, Aeschylus grounds the Athenian legal system in this myth. That is, justice is no longer up to individuals to decide and implement. The burden of avenging the murder of the father no longer falls upon the shoulders of the son. There is now a larger and more important legal entity than the family, and it has mechanisms and procedures for carrying out its responsibilities. In this he acknowledges the development of the state out of perpetually warring feudal entities.

Secondly, he describes a crucial act of building a community. By telling the story of how the primitive Furies are transformed into the more benign Eumenides, he illustrates how communities grow and synthesize their competing array of needs. The Furies, for their part, accept a role and a place in the community; they are no longer disorganized and impulsive, random and destructive. But the community, for its part, must recognize their importance. Citizens must pay attention to their more primitive, unconscious needs and honor the place they occupy in the relationships they establish and maintain with each other.

The story of Orestes as told in Aeschylus' awe-inspiring trilogy is the myth of the state, of an organized community. On one level it is about the transformation of individual conscience into community justice. It is somewhat comparable to the shift from Old Testament Talionic Law to the New Testament concept of the Golden Rule in that it represents an advance in sophistication and, hence, a new set of complexities for those seeking to lead a just life. But it is fundamentally different in that it does not simply replace one moral imperative with another; it calls for a new process of negotiation, integration – and ambiguity.

In short, it inaugurates a rule of law, of man-made laws. It places the responsibility on the community, which means that the citizens of that community must not only follow the collective rules but also must participate in the formulation of those rules. Henceforth, conscience requires us to detach from our families, to become citizens, and as we become more independent, self-reliant, accountable, the state becomes more stable. The community is far from perfect. It will not always have Pallas Athena there to cast the decisive vote, and it will go on to commit such atrocious acts as condemning Socrates to death. But it does

230 Problems of Professionalization

acknowledge the new role of citizen, and it does not make a bogus appeal to transcendental truth.

Psychoanalysis has acquainted us with the reality that we are not as independent of our infantile pasts as we once believed, not as rational and free. The myth of Oedipus reminds us of these primitive and peremptory demands. But the myth of Orestes reminds us of the collective achievement that our adult roles represent and continually require of us. We may never escape the imprint of our families, but then neither can we evade the obligation to engage in the dialogues and struggles of our institutions, to be citizens of our political and professional communities. This is something that psychoanalysts, so preoccupied with uncovering the infantile, can forget.

Succession in Psychoanalysis

Let us look at our psychoanalytic institutions from this perspective, extrapolating from the myth of Orestes to find the lessons that can guide us as we seek to address the organizational dilemma of succession. There are three points to make.

First, we must create the mechanisms and procedures that will permit us, fairly and impartially, to make judgments on behalf of the community. As Athena created the institution of trial by jury to weigh the competing claims of Orestes and the Furies, we must create just and workable means to make our decisions and resolve our disputes. We cannot leave this up to individuals – or, to put this in language we will all understand, we cannot leave such judgments up to personal bargaining or to transference, to individuals who exert their influence either directly through power relations or unconsciously on the group.

Secondly, we have to build into our communities a respect for the darker, more primitive powers that lurk in us, and find ways of acknowledging them and integrating them into our institutional lives. The first problem is the simpler one, as it was for Orestes, the second more complex and difficult.

There is a third point: attention to the historical and social realities that form the context for our institutional lives. Agamemnon was responsible for the killing of Iphigenia, but he did it for reasons that were sanctioned by the gods: the campaign of the united Greeks to subdue the Trojans. Agamemnon's pride may have been involved, but so was his reputation as a leader. Moreover, the dominance of Greek culture and Greek power was at stake. The perspective of history does not allow us to claim that this was, in itself, a greater good, outweighing the carnage required to bring it about. Even the gods were divided on this issue. The point here is that the presence of such issues in the myth of Orestes distinguishes it from the myth of Oedipus. True, Oedipus was a king, and the health and well-being of his subjects was at stake. But Thebes was the stage on which the drama of Oedipus was enacted; in that respect, it was just another kingdom. A culture, a civilization, and the destiny of a people were not in the balance.

I have already begun my discussion about the first point, the role of the individual and personal in psychoanalytic succession, which is all about the destructive relevance of Oedipus. So long as individuals are able to stake proprietary claims to psychoanalysis, we will be subject to competition, murder, and betrayal. I noted earlier how Freud set up institutions but manipulated them behind the scenes. His followers trod the same path. My contention now is that so long as our psychoanalytic world continues to be dominated and riven by loyalties to old leaders, allegiances to particular theoretical schools, with their rival claims for truth, it will remain contaminated by the individual and personal. So long as we remain "tribal," so to speak, we will persecute our leaders and undermine their capacity to fulfill the obligations they have undertaken on our behalf.

The typical mechanism for succession in organizations today is the search committee, set up and authorized by the board or the executive committee, whichever body has the final authority to make the choice. The value of the search committee is that it brings into the process a representative sample of constituents of the community, sometimes called "stakeholders." The recommendation of the search committee, thus, is informed by the views of different sectors of the community and the final decision by the board is less likely to be perceived as arbitrary or ill-informed. At the same time, the decision rests with those who do have the legal authority. The main point is that the decision must be seen as legitimate, both formally and informally, by those who are affected by it, who have to live with it. If the leader is to be able to lead, he or she must be solidly authorized. And she or he needs to be able to lead the whole organization.

Several years ago, I was asked to advise someone who was the leading candidate to become director of a highly factionalized institute in New York. He believed, probably rightly, that he could force the decision in his favor. Behind the scenes politicking had given him the edge. I urged him to hold out, pointing to the fact – more obvious to me as an outsider – that being able to lead was more important in the long run than winning the contest to become the leader. I am not sure if it was my compelling logic that persuaded him, but he did refrain from pushing the issue. Subsequently, he himself, emphasizing the importance of the selection process to the institute over his own ambition, was able not only to negotiate a better contract for himself but also to gain the support from other factions he needed to govern successfully. In this case, it was the better strategy for him, but my larger point is that it was the better strategy for the institute to be more deliberative and inclusive. He got the job, but they got a director in whom they could have more confidence.

As in the Athenian trial by jury, a free and uncoerced process is essential for the resolution of conflict. That is not always possible to accomplish, of course, but it is certain that, without it, the conflicts will persist and they will affect the ability of the leader to fill his role successfully.

This is the relatively easy part. Harder to discern and harder yet to deal with are the deeper issues, buried with the Furies in the unconscious of the organization, carrying with it the power to tear it apart if they are not recognized and dealt with appropriately. These issues are hard to see from the perspective within our institutions, as they have always been, but not so difficult to see from without.

On a personal level, much is always at stake for individuals involved in such transitions. All the carefully cultivated means of influence and access to power in an established situation is jeopardized. I use "power" here advisedly. For all our paranoid sensitivities, there is actually not much power to be had in our institutions, if we understand power as the ability to get things done. Given the embedded routines of training, the limited scope of institute activities, their meager resources, there isn't much to accomplish that isn't restricted or predetermined.

But power is also about preventing things from getting done. In my experience today, this is actually the power that counts in our institutes and organizations, and this is where they come to grief. Power in the form of collusively managed "social defenses" is about protecting the faculty from exposure to the anxieties that might be aroused in the course of their work. (See Jacques, 1955; Menzies, 1967.) A "social defense" often looks like a rational or traditional procedure or policy, the way things are done in a given institution, but its hidden, real purpose is to contain and manage anxiety.

Let me briefly enumerate the threats that the traditional social defenses of institutes protect faculty from experiencing. I will then go on to look at each one in greater depth. (For a fuller account of these issues, see Eisold, 2004; Chapter 5 in this volume.) The first source of anxiety is the threat of judgment, of being assessed or evaluated as candidates are relentlessly scrutinized and judged in the course of their training. That scrutiny, by and large, ceases upon graduation – at least on a formal or public level. A second form of anxiety faculty are protected from is the anxiety of confronting their ignorance, the risks of not really knowing what they need to know in order to make sound judgments about candidates, about training, about each other. Third, there is the threat of adapting to the new, being forced to go beyond their carefully constructed and circumscribed areas of expertise. Finally, faculty are protecting against threats to their identity. The "caste system" in institutes and the idealization of senior analysts tend to immunize them against pressures to question who they have become, what role they really play in the ongoing life of the institution.

Let me begin with the anxiety of judgment. In contrast to candidates who are repeatedly asked to justify or explore their decisions in order to get at their less apparent motivations, faculty members require little justification for comparable assessments or decisions. In the past, it was often presumed that faculty members, being thoroughly analyzed, were unlikely to be prone to irrational behavior. Today, though that presumption is less convincing, there is little pressure to open up our systems to higher levels of accountability.

This is even more apparent when it comes to decisions that faculty make in selecting training and supervising analysts. Twenty-five years ago, Edward Weinshel (1982), an American analyst, noted how little research has been devoted to this process, particularly striking given how vital such decisions are to the future health of institutes. He concluded that "lack of 'hard' clinical data ... encourages a more insular

234 Problems of Professionalization

and even solipsistic picture and conceptualization of the training analysis" (Weinshel, 1982). Many others have made comparable points.

Striking too has been the resistance of faculty to presenting their own work. Long ago, Hans Loewald cogently argued for the value of faculty offering case presentations to candidates, open to discussion and criticism. But few institutes have adopted Loewald's suggestion, despite the fact that it has been echoed by many others, including Otto Kernberg (2000). The clinical work of faculty continues to appear, by and large, protected by the highly edited and restricted format of professional papers.

This touches on the second source of anxiety, the anxiety of ignorance – more precisely, the anxiety of acknowledging ignorance about something one claims to understand or feels one should understand. In a sense, although psychoanalysis is all about facing the unknown, analytic training often comes to resemble a process of initiation or indoctrination into received wisdom or truth.

A particular form of ignorance that analytic faculties collectively have is their skill in the task of selecting candidates. This may be less of a problem now as fewer apply; the task is simplified to weeding out the more obviously ill-equipped. But historically and still in some locations, this has been a troubling issue. At various points in our history, whole categories of applicants have been proscribed as unsuitable: women, homosexuals, non-medical practitioners, the disabled, those beyond a certain age, etc.

An old study of the problem (Holt & Luborsky, 1955) concluded that "predictions from interviews [are] slightly better than chance" in making selections, and demonstrated that psychological testing significantly improved reliability. But that appears to have little impact on altering traditional reliance on faculty judgments. More recently, the German analyst Kappelle noted: "In selecting for psychoanalytic training, we are doing something we do not (precisely) know in order to achieve something we cannot (precisely) describe." But he added, astutely, that it was unlikely that such findings would actually change institute practices (Kappelle, 1996).

A third source of anxiety that the faculty system defends against is the anxiety of change, which is, at root, the anxiety involved in acknowledging that something is inadequate and needs to be modified or altered. Thirty-five years ago, the American ego psychologist Jacob

Arlow referred to a "cultural lag" in training, noting that little attention has been paid to a critical re-examination of training in the light of changes in theory and clinical practice over time. He wryly noted how unusual it was for a profession to devote itself primarily to studying texts over 50 years old (Arlow, 1972).

Since then, the proliferation of different schools and the current pluralistic climate has led to a significant expansion of courses. But a constraining factor has been institute policies that often limit faculty roles to institute graduates; "outsiders" are rarely invited in to teach. As a result, institutes often lack the resources to cover such topics authoritatively.

An additional issue stems from the fact that most current candidates face careers with few actual patients in psychoanalysis. This has highlighted the need for courses or programs addressing other forms of psychoanalytically oriented psychotherapy or applied psychoanalysis – but few institutes have responded to this current need. I believe that institute faculty members themselves have preferred to hold on to practices and skills with which they are familiar. The current system defends them against the need to venture into unknown territories that are unfamiliar and about which they may well feel inadequately prepared.

A fourth source of anxiety is threats to self-esteem. An aspect of training that has been widely noted is the tendency of candidates to protect and idealize their analysts and supervisors, and this has been correctly seen as having a stifling and inhibiting effect. What is less widely commented on – though I doubt it has gone unnoticed – is the tendency of faculty members to accept these idealized attributes as warranted by their superior experience and skills. The "caste system" has, I think, the primary purpose of protecting the self-esteem of faculty in the higher castes by investing them with the presumption of superior judgment and skill. In such a system, even those rare senior analysts who disclaim superior wisdom end up getting additional credit for being so open and unpretentious.

To be sure, experience often has the effect of making one not only more knowledgeable but also more balanced and nuanced in clinical work. The current hierarchical system, however, divides up the faculty in ways that suggest permanent differences in inherent abilities. Yet, while those who occupy privileged positions within it enjoy the status and the opportunities it provides, few people actually believe that it represents what it claims to represent. The "caste system," by and large, has become an object of political manipulation and cynical assessment.

This, of course, is the difficulty with all "social defenses," particularly those that are not closely aligned with the demands of work: They function intermittently, imperfectly, selectively, and, more importantly, they interfere with the ability of the organization more rationally and adaptively to address its essential work. The "caste system," for example, protects self-esteem up to a point; it does not screen out awareness of other more critical or skeptical attitudes, especially on the part of one's colleagues. Defenses against the anxiety of ignorance do not prevent candidates from noticing egregious lapses of judgment made in the selection process, nor do defenses against change help candidates cope with the gap between their training and the professional opportunities that await them.

These are serious lapses in our training system, but, to repeat, they operate largely out of awareness. We would need to work to expose them, and dismantle the system of social defenses that keep them in place. We would need to visit our own Furies, where they dwell and continue to afflict us with the inconsistencies and rigidities that, usually, we walk past without noticing.

The Historical Context

But what about the larger world, the political and social environment that shapes our problems with succession? What are the wars in which we are engaged? The whole field of prolonged and intensive psychotherapeutic treatment – whether psychoanalysis or analytical psychology – is in serious decline. Several irreversible social trends have combined to bring this about. One is the vastly increased pressure of globalized competition. The drive for efficiency and economy has led to the commodification of services, so that cheaper and shorter services are driving out longer treatments that are less focussed. An allied trend is the pressure of time. Multiple sessions on the couch spread over many years are no longer acceptable, even to many who could afford them, or thinkable to those who could not. People now work harder, travel more, and struggle to preserve their discretionary time. A third change has been the loss of established and traditional forms of authority in government, religion, as well as the professions. People are skeptical of our promises of cure – or, on the other hand, all too gullible about alternative and easier treatments.

Our organizations feel this acutely as the numbers of candidates seeking training decline and our ability to choose among applicants lessens. More subtle are the effects on them of the changes in the careers they can look forward to. While we train them for lengthy, in-depth analytic treatments, most are not likely to have the opportunity to do that kind of work and will have to find ways of applying their knowledge and training to patients with less time and shorter treatments. Our institutes, oriented as they are to perpetuating old habits and distinctions, are threatened with becoming obsolete. Training analysts have standing even if they do not have work, and newly minted candidates look on their careers with a growing sense of powerlessness that only further alienates them from their institutes. (See Eisold, 2007; Chapter 9 in this volume.)

This is our equivalent to the Trojan War, the historical issue we face collectively. Absolved of the murder of his mother, the Furies placated, Orestes returned to assume his father's role as king of Mycenae. Mycenae was still awaiting its ruler. But our familiar world is fast disappearing. We urgently need leaders who will help us confront and deal with the fact that the profession we have known and devoted ourselves to mastering is falling apart.

There is an even deeper problem for us in facing these profound changes: our institutes were set up to avoid change. Isolated and self-contained, they were built to be immune to outside influence. They hire only their own graduates and promote only from within. Teachers and supervisors, by and large, know primarily what they have learned inside their organizations, and they perpetuate those bodies of knowledge and techniques. They are accountable to no outside authority, apart from those that they themselves support and maintain. Preoccupied with their own internal politics and incestuous relationships, they have little incentive to adapt. Even as new applications for training decline, as it becomes increasingly difficult to find training cases, as the motivation to seek advancement and assume leadership roles in our institutes fades, there is little capacity to think about adaptation and change. The system of social defenses I enumerated earlier is both sustained by this state of affairs but also contributes to it.

Frankly, though the situation is dire, I do not think it is hopeless. There is growing awareness of the stifling aspects of training. A number of books and articles have been published in recent years that call attention to the shortcomings of our traditional training systems: see, for example, Kernberg (1996, 2000), Casement (2005), Reeder (2004), Levine (2003), Berman (2004), Kirsner (2000). More importantly, there are actually some signs of change: in December 2007, the first in a series of conferences entitled "The Future of Psychoanalytic Education" was held in New York (www.international psychoanalysis. net; see also Kirsch & Spradlin, 2006).

Other disciplines are building upon our pioneering awareness of the role of the unconscious in mental life. The neurological and biological sciences are increasingly able to detail its functioning in ways that add to our clinical knowledge. We are no longer alone in asserting the persistent power of early, formative experience and of the irrational and the unknown (Westen, 1999).

Moreover, there is a growing awareness that the unconscious pervades all of contemporary life, not just our personal relationships but our work relationships as well, our organizations and governments, our schools and public institutions. Business leaders increasingly seek out the competitive advantage in learning about the limiting impact of their own unconscious assumptions as well as those of their competitors. Alas, it often takes enormous blunders on the part of our political leaders to highlight the role of the unconscious in their thinking, as illustrated by their wishful thinking about Iraq but also by their censorship of dissenting points of view. But this is increasingly being scrutinized. The American Senate's subcommittee investigating the intelligence "failure" with respect to WMD, for example, noted the role of "groupthink" in the Bush administration, the vulnerability of officials to compromise their capacity to think in the face of the pressure of conforming to group consensus (*The New York Times*, July 10, 2004, p. 1; Janis, 1986). We also see such processes at work in the stunning lapses of thought and judgment underlying such corporate scandals as Enron.

But even more important is the robust and growing demand for mental health services. To be sure, market forces are pushing prices down, taking control away from service providers, pressing for lesser levels of preparation and skill, disrupting traditional professional relationships – all the "evils" associated with our increasingly competitive global market, that is, the "evils" that balance the "benefits" of lower prices and greater access for consumers and increased profits for managers. Still, the demand is growing and new means of providing for that demand are growing as well.

But we have not worked very hard at adapting our skills to this new reality. Our focus is still the couch, our training still centers on frequent and prolonged treatments. By and large, we are training our candidates for careers that no longer exist.

For all the reasons enumerated in the discussion of the social defenses pervading institutes, we find it hard to change. Out faculties would have to give up some of their certainties and privileges. They would have to learn much about what they do not know.

Here is where the question of leadership and succession becomes extremely relevant, because it will take creative and daring leadership to push our institutions out of their established, entrenched ways. We will need leaders who are both alert to the profound changes that are occurring outside the walls of our inwardly focussed institutes but also alert to the Furies that will inevitably set upon them when they attempt to alter the status quo.

Oedipus had no help at all as he set about to lead the city he so proudly believed he had rescued. His individual destiny unfolded mercilessly, but he bequeathed the lesson of the unconscious: beware of believing that you know yourself. Orestes had far more help with the entanglements his quest led him into. Apollo and Pallas Athena cleared the way for him. But they are gone now, having bequeathed the lesson of the unconscious in our collective lives. We are now alone with each other, having to find our way together.

References

Arlow, J. (1972). Some dilemmas in psychoanalytic education. *Journal of the American Psychoanalytic Association* 20, 556–66.

Berman, E. (2004). *Impossible Training*. Hillsdale, NJ: The Analytic Press.

Bion, W. R. (1961). *Experiences in Groups*. London: Tavistock.

Cabernite, L. (1982). The selection and functions of the training analyst in analytic training. *IRPA* 9, 398–417.

Casement, P. (2005). The emperor's clothes. *International Journal of Psychoanalysis* 86, 1143–60.

240 Problems of Professionalization

Eisold, K. (1997). Freud as leader: the early years of the Viennese Society. *International Journal of Psychoanalysis* 78, 87–104.

Eisold, K. (2001). Institutional conflicts in Jungian analysis. *Journal of Analytical Psychology* 46, 335–53.

Eisold, K. (2004). Psychoanalytic training: the "faculty system." *Psychoanalytic Inquiry* 24, 51–70.

Eisold, K. (2007). The erosion of our profession. *Psychoanalytic Psychology* 24, 1–9.

Fordham, M. (1979). Analytical psychology in England. *Journal of Analytical Psychology* 24, 279–97.

Girard, R. (1977). *Violence and the Sacred*. Baltimore, MD: Johns Hopkins University Press.

Grosskurth, P. (1991). *The Secret Ring*. Reading, MA: Addison-Wesley.

Holt, R. R., & Luborsky, L. (1955). The selection of candidates for psychoanalytic training. *Journal of the American Psychoanalytic Association* 3, 666–81.

Janis, I. L. (1986). *Groupthink*. New York: Houghton Mifflin.

Jaques, E. (1955). Social systems as a defense against persecutory and depressive anxiety. In M. Klein, P. Heimann, & R. E. Money-Kyrle (eds.), *New Directions in Psycho-analysis*. London: Tavistock.

Kappelle, W. (1996). How useful is selection? *International Journal of Psycho-Analysis* 77, 1213–32.

Kernberg, O. F. (1996). Thirty methods to destroy the creativity of psychoanalytic candidates. *International Journal of Psycho-Analysis* 77, 1031–40.

Kernberg, O. F. (2000). A concerned critique of psychoanalytic education. *International Journal of Psycho-Analysis* 81(1), 97–120.

Kirsch, J., & Spradlin, S. (2006). Group process in Jungian analytic training and institute life. *Journal of Analytical Psychology*, 51(3).

Kirsner, D. (2000). *Unfree Associations*. London: Process Press.

Levine, F. J. (2003). The forbidden quest and the slippery slope: roots of authoritarianism in psychoanalysis. *Journal of the American Psychoanalytic Association* 51, 203–45.

Menzies, E. (1967). *The Functioning of Social Systems as Defense against Anxiety*. London: Tavistock Publications.

Reeder, J. (2004). *Hate and Love in Psychoanalytic Institutions*. New York: Other Press.

Weinshel, E. (1982). The functions of the training analysis and the selection of the training analyst. *IRPA* 9, 434–44.

Westen, D. (1999). The scientific status of unconscious process. *Journal of the American Psychoanalytic Association* 47, 1061–1106.

Chapter Eleven

Psychoanalytic Training

Then and Now, The Heroic Age, and the Domestic Era

[Originally published as Psychoanalytic Training: Then and Now, in *The Future of Psychoanalysis: The Debate about the Training Analyst System*, Psychoanalytic Ideas and Applications Series. Peter Zagermann, ed. London: Karnac, 2017, pp. 53–69.]

Looking at the landscape of psychoanalysis today, there are few signs remaining of the battles that swept across it until recently: the bitter schisms that rent many institutes, the proscribing of dissident ideas, banishment of colleagues, arrogant dismissals of alternative treatments, sharp competitive judgments of fellow analysts, as well as harsh attitudes toward outsiders. All of that characterized psychoanalysis in its "heroic" age, as it was struggling to establish itself as well as, in a period of decline, it was struggling to hold on to its self-image as the "gold standard" of psychotherapy.

Freud, a self-identified "conquistador" in his youth (Masson, 1985, p. 398), became in adulthood a "good hater" (Sachs, 1945, p. 117), surrounding himself with a band of "paladins" (Grosskurth, 1991). He demanded of his followers that they do battle with him against his enemies, and then there were colleagues who constituted in his eyes a particular danger to psychoanalysis because they had been disciples and followers at the start, Adler, and Jung, of course, then Ferenczi. Subsequently, conflicts in New York led to what Ernest Jones referred to as the "psychoanalytical civil wars," running roughly from 1931 to 1938 (Hale, 1995, p. 103; see also Frosch, 1991). This was followed by the outbreak of conflict in London between the local Kleinians and the émigré Freudians, intense infighting expressed, ultimately, in the "controversial discussions" that narrowly averted the splitting up of the British Society (see King & Steiner, 1991).

242 Problems of Professionalization

Moreover, after World War II, schisms occurred in Germany, Austria, France, Sweden, and Norway (Eckhardt, 1978). In France, the controversies surrounding Lacan produced at least four institutes: the Freudian School, the Fourth Group, the Paris Institute, and the French Psychoanalytic Association (Turkle, 1992). The record is not precise, but Gitelson (1983) also noted schisms in Spain, Brazil, Mexico, Argentina, and Venezuela, as well as in the United States, in Washington/Baltimore, Philadelphia, Boston, Cleveland, and Los Angeles. Arlow (1982) refers to half a dozen splits in the American Psychoanalytic Association, and adds Columbia and Australia to the census of splits in the International Psychoanalytic Association.

Now, we are in a relatively tranquil "domestic era." Institutes that split apart in the past are negotiating mergers. Strict standards are being relaxed, while alternative methods are increasingly tolerated or, even, affirmed. Virtually anyone seeking training can find it today.

To be sure, we are also in a period of contraction, as fewer patients seek psychoanalytic treatment, with many analysts subsisting on reduced practices and slender reimbursements from insurance companies. Institutes can no longer afford to be uncompromising, and, indeed, they are reaching out to a wider variety of mental health professionals than at any time in the past to fill their classes. This has led them to offer training in alternative therapies, though it has not led them to experiment much with alternative methods of training.

Each institute, as in the past, still has its own faculty, its own set of analysts or supervisors dedicated to training candidates who have come up through the ranks of that institute and been vetted for their training roles by their senior colleagues. Rarely do the faculty members of other institutes have a hand in that training, and faculty members seldom work with candidates outside their own institutes. Such isolated, independent organizational structures are often called "silos," as they are self-sufficient containers, isolated from each other.

Moreover, each institute, each "silo," is virtually identical to the others. Their autonomy – and their isolation – has not led them to deviate significantly from the basic training model established in Berlin almost one hundred years ago. Each candidate is required to undergo a "training analysis," to take courses offered by their own faculty, and to see patients under the supervision of designated senior colleagues.

Moreover, in addition to following this "hallowed tri-partite" model (Wallerstein, 1993, p. 175), each institute usually has a "training committee," sometimes called an "education committee," charged with evaluating candidates, approving courses, selecting faculty and frequently selecting training analysts (TAs) as well. Candidates are monitored as they "progress" through the stages of training, and they are usually required to present their work as they approach the end of their training after completing a set number of treatments (see Kachele & Thoma, 2000).

This may not strike most analysts as strange, and the paradox of uniformity may not strike them as troubling. For most of us, it is familiar and normal, the way things have always been.

But why is this so? Why have they not developed along different lines in response to differences in the composition of their members or cultural differences in their environment? If institutes do not interact with each other or exchange faculty, what has kept them so alike? Why have different theories of development or psychic structure not led to different forms of training? Is it possible that this basic model is the only conceivable one, and that it was born full blown in its current, perfected form?

To be sure, there are some differences among institutes, different courses candidates are required to take and different procedures for determining the selection of TAs. And some institutes are subject to the regulations and rules of umbrella associations, such as the IPA and APsaA, which set and monitor standards and strive to keep them uniform. But by and large this pattern of self-imposed uniformity is impressive – but it is also stifling, as Otto Kernberg noted in his classic paper published almost 20 years ago, "Thirty Methods to Destroy the Creativity of Psychoanalytic Candidates." When that paper was published, it elicited a buzz of recognition for his trenchant points. His spirit of irreverence was perhaps even more striking and a source of hope for reform. Little has changed, however, as a result.

The outstanding exception to this uniformity, of course, has been France, where Jacques Lacan, beginning by undermining the authority of the psychoanalytic fathers who "presume to know," went on to establish a radically different form of training based on the authority of candidates themselves – or, better, their need to establish themselves as authentic authorities in their own right. Within the French

Institute, struggling to conform to the requirements of the IPA, it became increasingly clear that Lacan's practices were at variance with the orthodoxy it required (see Turkle, 1978; Roudinesco, 1990).

However one views Lacan's innovations, sessions of variable length, his willingness to enlist analysands in fulfilling personal needs, impromptu sessions in the middle of the night, and so forth, it would be fair to say that this was a serious attempt to break with standardized rules and to relate psychoanalytic practice more closely to theory. But it was unacceptable to the commission charged with investigating the French Institute's suitability to become a component of the IPA, with the result that, eventually, Lacan was dropped from the list of training analysts (he referred to this as his "excommunication"), and it became clear that the French Institute would not be accepted so long as Lacan was associated with it.

The fall-out from the IPA's rejection of Lacan and his innovations led to creation of a number of other institutes and splinter groups, a chaotic situation, certainly chilling to any spirit of innovation. The subsequent conflicts may also suggest that the self-imposed uniformity of institutes had served the defensive function of keeping under control the latent competitiveness of analysts, who might otherwise have striven to depart from the standard model. At the very least, that uniformity can be seen as containing the anxiety inherent in deviation and experimentation.

There are other possible explanations. The uniformity can also be seen as the product of an "apostolic age" (Arlow, 1982), in which disciples of Freud spread throughout the world with word of his discoveries: the dynamic unconscious, transference, infantile sexuality, the Oedipus Complex, and so forth. This process, spurred on by the diaspora of analysts fleeing Nazi Germany, was informed by the desire of the refugee analysts to replicate the professional world they had lost, and so it was little surprise that they recreated the training model they knew.

But even before the diaspora, it was clear that Freud and his disciples had strenuously sought to control the movement and prevent alternative views from taking hold (Grosskurth, 1991). The "secret committee," formed after Jung's "defection," was designed, in part, to ensure that Freud's loyal sons would faithfully sustain his theories while monitoring and restraining their own competitiveness. And, arguably, when training was first set up in the 1920s, the institution of the training analysis incorporated that task as well.

The end of this embattled "Heroic Age" has brought with it the fear that psychoanalysis itself would die, and indeed the world of psychoanalysis is suffering a decline, at a time when psychotherapy and interest in mental health are growing. Indeed, the current decline of psychoanalysis (see Hale, 1995; Eisold, 2007) is all the more disturbing and poignant given the upsurge of interest in psychotherapy and the proliferation of other treatment methods.

But today, fewer candidates apply for training as fewer patients seek psychoanalytic treatment. Some institutes are chafing under the restrictions of traditional standards as the general decline of our field has exacerbated competition for members. The lowering tide is stranding many ships.

One response within many institutes has been the development of training programs in psychotherapy, informed by psychoanalytic thinking about transference and the layering of unconscious motivations. Another response has been to minimize the focus on training altogether, emphasizing the individual development of existing members through presenting papers and offering workshops – the new primary mission of the many other umbrella organizations that are proliferating in this pluralistic era: the Academy of Psychoanalysis, the Division of Psychoanalysis of the American Psychological Association (Division 39), the International Association for Relational Psychoanalysis and Psychotherapy (IARPP), the American Association for Psychoanalysis in Clinical Social Work (AAPCP), the International Association for Psychoanalytic Self Psychology (IAPSP), the International Federation of Psychoanalytic Societies (IFPS), the International Forum for Psychoanalytic Education (IFPE). This impressive array of professional associations primarily provides opportunities to present papers and panels, keeping analysts busy developing their ideas, talking to each other, and, I suspect, diverting their attention from the general decline of the field as a whole.

Increasingly, in the umbrella organizations that do focus on training – the IPA and APsaA – alternate "models" are being proposed and accepted. Moreover, one hears frequently that, at times, the "rules" are simply ignored as the component institutes and societies chafe under the restraints they impose while struggling to adapt to this new landscape.

Some of those umbrella organizations represent a further fragmentation of the field, being open only to sub-specializations in the field of mental health, such as psychologists, social workers, and such newly established categories as mental health workers. Increasingly, as the industry of mental health treatment has expanded, the state has stepped in to establish new forms of certification independent of what many institutes have established for themselves. Indeed, an inflection point of absurdity was reached recently when, at the behest of a non APsaA institute, New York State established a "certificate in psychoanalysis," reflecting requirements that vary from what most institutes in the state offer. That law pushed several institutes to set up parallel programs to help candidates qualify for this new certificate, forcing them to compete in effect with their own certificate granting programs.

Embedded as we are in this paradoxical system of training, we tend not to notice how strange this uniformity is. Indeed, as our institutes and associations adapt to changes induced by economic and social factors, our adherence to the standard model becomes even more fixed – and odd. We adapt but we don't seem to change. Moreover, there continues to be little research on training. Twenty years ago, a meeting of directors of training in APsaA concluded: "empirical research [about training] was not thought appropriate" (Ahmed, 1994) and that attitude persists. This stance reflects the virtual absence of any research on many of the factors that shape training: the effectiveness of the designated training or supervising analysts (SAs), the selection of candidates, or the difference that frequency makes in an analysis – two, three, four, or five times weekly – though rules on frequency have often been the defining feature of bitter disputes among psychoanalytic factions. The field does not seem to want to investigate or explore what unites or divides us.

The great benefit of having such uniformity and certainty is that it leaves little room for questions about what training should be. It becomes, clearly, the inevitably "right way" to train. As psychoanalysts, of course, we are trained to suspect that such certainty in an individual masks anxiety and perhaps even conflict. But on an institutional or group level, we are all too ready to accept such beliefs as normal and appropriate. This means that institutionally, though, we are less able to conceive improved forms of training. New ideas seldom have the opportunity to develop.

Obviously this institutional sclerosis must have consequences for those in training or those beyond training who rely on their institutes to do an effective job with candidates in order to replenish the field. And, indeed, there are some fairly objective signs of trouble, though they are not always linked to this paradox. Candidates do complain about their training, often particularly about the quality of the teaching to which they are exposed. Such complaints can sometimes be felt as too risky to voice loudly, but, then, graduates express their resentments in other ways: they often do not volunteer for committees or roles in training, or engage in institute affairs. They contribute less to fundraising and, even, sometimes fail to maintain their memberships in their institutes or graduate societies.

Data on this is hard to come by and is often murky, as alienation and disaffection are not easy to measure. Lack of participation in institute governance is sometimes explained away as practitioners being too busy to spare the time committee work demands or too financially strapped to give away the valuable time needed to make ends meet. And, to be sure, the traditional rewards of status and referrals that stemmed from taking such prominent roles in the governance of institutes are also in decline.

Indeed, the field is generally strapped for cash. Institutes struggle to cover expenses, seeking new ways to generate income. I mentioned above the proliferation of psychotherapy programs, and there are, in addition, specializations that are continually being designed and added to institute curriculums: workshops and programs in parenting, eating disorders, attention deficits, trauma, sexual abuse, the arts, etc. Institutes have a decided advantage here, as trainings in various forms of psychotherapy are not generally available elsewhere. Medical schools long since stopped training residents in psychotherapy, partly because they have shifted focus to medications, partly also because there is little demand. Graduate schools, in addition, seldom offer training, apart from the narrow focus on specific techniques whose outcomes and effectiveness individual academic psychologists seek to measure. That approach offers advancement in academic careers for those who develop such treatments, theorizing them and researching them with their students. In all these cases, however, training for the sake of providing a public service or meeting a social need seldom figures in the thinking of those providing service.

Here our institutes fill an important gap, fulfilling a need with which few others are concerned. Graduate programs in psychology as well as medical schools have priced themselves out of the market. They cannot afford to train students for psychotherapy practices, particularly in an era when insurers and providers are struggling to keep down the costs of medical care. The incentives are lacking.

What we have, then, is essentially a cottage industry of psychotherapy, centered around institutes that provide generally low-cost training, for practitioners subsisting on work that is no longer profitable for others to perform. It is up to each individual practitioner to make it work economically, to rent an office he or she can afford, to cover expenses, to create a niche that distinguishes them from others while promoting their services by word of mouth or social media, while the system keeps driving down the prices they can charge.

A sign of this is how, increasingly, institute listservs have turned into informal referral networks, as participants respond to requests for therapists who are on specific insurance panels, treating disorders in other neighborhoods or cities, or willing to work at unusual times or for low fees because the patient is interesting or deserving. They strive to join the network of "providers," even if they cannot provide the service themselves. To be sure, that could be seen as simply wanting to be helpful, and no doubt sometimes that is what it is. But it is also a way of promoting oneself as knowledgeable and potentially helpful, even when unable to participate directly. It is the generosity of the poor, while affirming the identity of a "provider."

To be sure, our field is somewhat more stratified than this overview suggests. The reputation and standing of institutes vary, allowing some graduates to charge higher fees or benefit from more robust referral networks. And generally, psychiatrists charge higher fees than psychologists, while social workers charge less, mental health workers even less than that. The more successful practitioners, by and large, are specialists who publish books on their area and offer talks and workshops.

If the analogy with eighteenth- and nineteenth-century weavers in England holds – the cottagers who held on to their livelihoods in the face of the Enclosure Acts, on the one hand, allowing landowners to confiscate the land on which their sheep grazed, and the mill owners, on the other, who built far more efficient equipment for weaving – we can be seen as awaiting a new technology that will finally put us out of business.

This is, of course, a considerable irony for psychoanalysts who not only once tried to distinguish the "pure gold" of psychoanalysis from the "alloy" of psychotherapy, as Freud once put it (Freud, 1919). Few patients today seek out three or four times weekly treatments, featuring the couch and free association, though some analysts strive to maintain such traditional practices by offering reduced fees. For candidates who need to find several analysands for training this is increasingly an obstacle. Time is in short supply in our work-driven culture, and patients find it difficult to make even their once or twice weekly psychotherapy appointments.

Apart from such problems that make it more and more difficult for institutes to offer their traditional training, there are more subtle problems that stem from our rigid training models and the ways in which we have been set up. One of the biggest is that our institutional "silos" trap practitioners within their institutes. There are two major costs of this. One is that they are deprived of the potential fertilization that comes from being exposed to different styles and practices. Those having developed within their own particular silos are conditioned to accept the status quo, including the idealizations sanctioned by the group mind. Existing practices are not challenged. Indeed, they are hardened.

An even greater problem, though, is that the interpersonal differences and difficulties, the transferences and conflicts that inevitably characterize organizations – and professional organizations in particular – have no outlet outside the institute. Internal politics can become more frustrating and bitter as individuals feel stuck in their organizations, unable to leave. Often in the past, those differences led to schisms or the establishment of alternative institutes, but as the field is contracting now, they lead to alienation and covert battles, political struggles, disaffection, and contempt. Unhappy teachers and supervisors often have little choice but to put up with those they do not like or respect, or with whom they disagree or of whom they do not approve.

Battered and beleaguered, our institutional silos have become prisons, in effect. We cling to them, but they offer us no security, and often even little advantage in the marketplace. To be sure, we can leave them, stop paying dues and stop attending meetings – and we often do just that – but there is no place else to go. Other institutes, by and large, will not take us in.

Meanwhile, stuck inside our organizational silos, the slights and disappointments that inevitably arise among institute members, the recognition that comes to some, but not to others, the intellectual and political differences, the alliances and friendships, the gossip, the favoritism, the slights, perceived and otherwise – all of these have no external outlet. This emotional "noise" is comparable to what occurs in academic departments, notoriously the site of such personal hatreds, jealousies, and resentments. The academic world, however, offers more individual opportunity. Professorships may not be easy to find today, but a successful scholar will expect to get offers from other universities or be able to renegotiate a teaching load. Academics are less embedded in their academies than analysts in their institutes, freer to roam. Universities and other schools do not depend on the willingness of faculty to volunteer themselves as institutes do, and they charge higher fees and pay better salaries.

The Future

Let me briefly summarize the dilemma. The numbers of those seeking psychoanalytic treatment as well as training in psychoanalysis are in decline, at a time when the demand for psychotherapy is rising and the need for mental health services is increasingly recognized. But our field seems unable to adapt to this change. We adhere to a "standard model" of training established one hundred years ago, and have not shown much capacity for significant change.

Institutes do add on services in psychotherapy as well as provide exposure to specific treatments for particular disorders, but at the core they remain committed primarily to turning out "psychoanalysts" who see patients three, four, or five times weekly for prolonged periods of time. The demand for this service no longer exists as it did, certainly not sufficiently to support the array of institutes that have come into existence over the years.

Let me make it clear that I am not implying that traditional psychoanalytic treatments are no longer valuable or effective. On the contrary, I believe that wonderful work is being done. Many of my colleagues are thoughtful and effective, and I myself continue to be grateful for the training I received. But as the management theorist Edward Deming (2013) once put it, "survival is not mandatory." Competition is putting more and more psychoanalysts out of work, as marketplace dynamics undermine the viability of our existing practices.

It might be argued that we should simply accept the fact that we will be working for fewer and fewer clients who will value our help and can pay for it. Under such circumstances, many institutes will go under, and the survivors will move on without being forced to compromise their integrity or modify their hard-won skills and identities.

The alternative argument is that we have something of great value that can be repackaged or repurposed. The unconscious, the repetition of old patterns of behavior, dissociation, and irrational beliefs, will not cease affecting human behavior – but they may not require psychoanalysis as currently practiced to unearth and change. Is there a way we could adapt that knowledge respectfully and without compromise?

Our history suggests a lack of flexibility in our methods of training. We may not be troubled by the bitter conflicts and schisms of the past, as the sources of our current discontents are more buried, but we appear to be encased in an identity that prescribes what and how we must work as well as organizational structures that resist alteration.

Yet necessity and opportunity can teach us, and our field has attracted brilliant and creative minds, many of whom could rise to the challenge. Let me propose some steps it might be possible to take.

1. Greater choice in the selection of TAs and SAs. At the core of the silo structure is the restrictions it imposes on choosing TAs, and it seems obvious that greater choice is desirable as well as greater separation between TAs and candidates.

This is actually more of a thorny problem than it may seem at first, but not for what is usually perceived to be the problem, the need to ensure quality. Existing systems for selecting TAs and SAs have not been rigorously evaluated. They are maintained, I believe, largely because they are familiar and sustain the illusion of control, not because they have proved more effective than "free markets."

The more troubling problem is that the TA system is a key element in developing and sustaining cohesiveness within institutes. Arguably it would be better for candidates to be free to choose their analysts from a wider pool, and that would also help institutes circumvent the incestuous conflicts and tensions that the current system inevitably arouses, along with the transferences and judgments that cloud perceptions on all sides. On the other hand, the intense analytic relationships formed in training between analysts and analysands, supervisors and supervisees, bind many members of institutes together emotionally, forming a nexus that often makes faculty members want to work together and willing to volunteer the time required for teaching and committee work. Without that, institutes might be weakened even further. (This bonding obviously exists in parallel with the negative dynamics created in the "silos," the disturbing "noise" that leads to alienation and disengagement for many.)

Some candidates actually prefer to "play" the system, currying favor and avoiding confrontation with their more blatant problems while planning their future advancement. This is not an argument for retaining the system, but it does suggest an additional difficulty in changing it.

2. Expansion of training in psychotherapy, essentially fewer sessions over shorter periods of time than in traditional psychoanalysis. Clearly, there is a market for this in today's world, and, as I pointed out, institutes have moved in to capitalize on this need. But they have been hamstrung in their willingness to take advantage of this opportunity, still viewing psychotherapy as the lesser form of treatment. Indeed, when they do set up such programs they often view them as feeders for psychoanalytic training, hoping that students once exposed to the benefits of dynamic psychotherapy will want to go on to the "superior" training offered in psychoanalysis. The success of such programs is often measured by the numbers recruited for psychoanalytic training. Understandable as that may be, it compromises the psychotherapy programs in several important ways.

If the faculty views psychotherapy training as second best, students inevitably will pick that up, and sense a lack of commitment to excellence. Secondly, it will be more difficult to recruit the best teachers and supervisors to participate, as they will be reluctant to embrace a second-class status. Finally, the energy required for innovation and experimentation in psychotherapy will be inhibited or drained off.

The great advantage psychoanalysis has had from the start was our recognition of the role the unconscious plays in human motivation. Even today in the psychotherapy programs that have been added on to institute offerings, those programs benefit from their proximity to a community of teachers, supervisors, and others steeped in an understanding of the unconscious. That would need to be a core element in the brands of dynamic psychotherapy we could develop and promote.

Our ability to do that would be profoundly enhanced by recent advances in neuroscience. Instead of viewing those discoveries as evidence that our theories have been correct all along, as we have tended to do, we might better mobilize them to develop new approaches that could be seen as more practical and scientific.

We would be aided in this immeasurably by the public knowledge that the existence of the unconscious is no longer just a theory but has scientific backing.

3. A second step could be institutes setting up alliances with other institutes, joint programs drawing on resources beyond what any one institute has on its own. In fact, a program in psychotherapy, such as I was suggesting above, might have a better chance to succeed if it were not tied to any one institute. A consortium could draw from a wider pool of faculty and supervisors than exists in any one. And it might stand a better chance of operating free from the internal political pressures that constrain planning and decision-making in particular institutes.

A consortium of institutes might also be able to set up programs focused on continuing professional development, courses that address specific clinical problems or new theoretical developments that other therapists want to learn about. And it might be able to draw on a greater concentration of recognized experts and outstanding clinical practitioners than any one institute could offer.

To be sure, in the beginning such consortiums would be seen to be in competition with comparable programs in individual institutes – and, indeed, they would be. Some institutes might be resistant to throwing in their lot with them if they think they might be more successful on their own or if they fear being associated with institutes of lesser status. But in the long run they would be more viable.

4. Applied psychoanalysis has been insufficiently explored by institutes, despite the fact that many individual practitioners have had significant success, and there is enormous opportunity. Many executives seek consultation, as they know the advantages of having help in seeing their blind spots and understanding more deeply their competitors' thinking. It gives them a significant advantage.

"Coaching," as this is sometimes called, has proliferated to the point that many businesses and other organizations routinely offer it to their top executives. But this is generally an unregulated and highly varied area, and takes many forms. Though often efforts are made to protect the confidentiality of the coaching relationship, many clients are wary of services offered by their organizations, preferring to hire outside coaches themselves where there is far less danger of information leaking to superiors. On the other hand, organizations are reluctant to pay for help with little control over the form it takes or guarantee of its benefits.

At the highest levels, though, superb advisory services are currently being offered by psychoanalysts, and they are being well compensated for it. This help requires not only the ability to understand unconscious motives or to discern obscure intentions – skills psychoanalysts are trained to develop – but also a grasp of organizations and the business dilemmas their leaders face.

Along those lines, institutes could offer training in organizational consultation, helping organizations face the hidden, unconscious obstacles they inevitably encounter. These are just a few of the many opportunities available to the institutes and practitioners who venture out beyond the realm of individual clinical work. Political candidates often use such help to decipher the messages of their opponents and their unconscious appeal; advertising agencies can use help understanding and crafting subliminal communications in the service of their clients; and diplomats can be helped in grasping the psychological profiles of their counterparts, or their vulnerabilities (see Eisold, 2010).

Whatever institutes do, however, whatever programs they offer in psychoanalysis, psychotherapy, or applied psychoanalysis, it is essential that evaluation and review are key components. Faced with a proposal to alter training, it is easy to imagine many of our colleagues saying, "If it ain't broke, don't fix it." I have heard that refrain all too frequently, suggesting how hard it is to see the degree to which our training programs have become ritualistic, impervious to change. But continuous assessment and evaluation does not require an admission of failure as a place to start, just a willingness to improve. And it could be the starting point for creative conversations among those of us interested in education and training. Possibly umbrella organizations like IPA and APsaA could institute annual reports on the state of psychoanalytic education as revealed by annual surveys, reports that could include information on innovations and experiments that some institutes have attempted.

Continuous evaluation has been established as an essential element in today's organizations. We see it reflected in the "learning objectives" we are now required to submit to our professional meetings along with our proposals. But rather than being annoying formulas with which we are obliged to comply, we could accept it in the spirit of actually wanting to know the impact of what we do.

Some final thoughts. Traditionally we have been preoccupied by theories of psychic structure and mental processes. We pay attention to the process of change and development in our patients, not so much in ourselves as professionals or in our organizations. It may be time to be broader and more inclusive in our thinking.

My own limited practice in organizational consultation has made me aware of how resistant to change organizations are, in general, as well as ingenious in subverting initiatives that require altering established practices. In this they are generally worse than individuals. And that is not to take into account the rigidities specific to psychoanalytic institutes.

So change would have to come slowly and in small increments. But new initiatives would not go unrecognized, especially if they succeeded in attracting candidates. Programs in applied psychoanalysis that meet a need will similarly attract attention.

Change must come, if only the slow change of decline and eventual failure.

References

Ahmed, J. (1994). Meeting of directors of training institutes. *Bulletin of the International Psycho-Analytical Association* 75, 184–5.

Arlow, J. A. (1982). Psychoanalytic education: a psychoanalytic perspective. *Annual of Psychoanalysis* 10, 5–20.

Deming, W. E. (2013). *The Essential Deming*. New York: McGraw Hill.

Eckhardt, M. H. (1978). Organizational schisms in American psychoanalysis. In J. M. Quen & E. T. Carlson (eds.), *American Psychoanalysis: Origins and Development*. New York: Brunner/Mazel.

Eisold, K. (1997). Freud as leader: the early years of the Viennese Society. *International Journal of Psychoanalysis* 78, 87–104.

Eisold, K. (2007). The erosion of our profession. *Psychoanalytic Psychology* 24, 1–9.

Eisold, K. (2010). *What You Don't Know You Know*. New York: Other Press.

Freud S. (1919). Lines of advances in psycho-analytic therapy. In J. Strachey (ed. and trans.), *The Standard Edition of the Complete Psychological Works of Sigmund Freud* (Vol. 17, pp. 157–68). London: Hogarth Press.

Frosch, J. (1991). The New York Psychoanalytic civil war. *Journal of the American Psychoanalytic Association* 39(4), 1037–64.

Gitelson, F. H. (1983). Identity crises: splits or compromises – adaptive or maladaptive. In E. D. Joseph & D. Widlocher (eds.), *The Identity of the Psychoanalyst* (pp. 157–79). New York: International Universities Press.

Grosskurth, P. (1991). *The Secret Ring*. Reading, MA: Addison-Wesley.

Hale, N. G. (1995). *The Rise and Crisis of Psychoanalysis in the United States*. New York: Oxford University Press.

Kachele, H., & Thoma, H. (2000). On the devaluation of the Eitingon-Freud model of psychoanalytic education. *International Journal of Psycho-Analysis* 81, 806–7.

Kernberg, O. F. (1996). Thirty methods to destroy the creativity of psychoanalytic candidates. *International Journal of Psycho-Analysis* 77, 1031–40.

King, P., & Steiner, R. (eds.) (1991). *The Freud–Klein Controversies*. London: Routledge.

Klauber, J. (1983). The identity of the psychoanalyst. In E. D. Joseph & D. Widlocher (eds.), *The Identity of the Psychoanalyst*. New York: International Universities Press.

Masson, J. M. (1985). *The Complete Letters of Sigmund Freud to Wilhelm Fliess, 1887–1904*. Cambridge, MA: Harvard University Press.

Rudinesco, E. (1990). *Jacques Lacan and Co.: A History of Psychoanalysis in France, 1925–1985*. Chicago: University of Chicago Press.

Roustang, F. (1982). *Dire Mastery: Discipleship from Freud to Lacan*. Baltimore: Johns Hopkins University Press.

Roustang, F. (1983). *Psychoanalysis Never Lets Go*. Trans. Ned Lukacher. Baltimore: Johns Hopkins University Press.

Sachs, H. (1945). *Freud: Master and Friend*. Cambridge, MA: Harvard University Press.

Turkle, S. (1992). *Psychoanalytic Politics*, 2nd edn. New York: Guilford Press.

Wallerstein, R. (1993). Between chaos and petrification: a summary of the Fifth IPA Conference on Training. *International Journal of Psychoanalysis* 74, 165–78.

Index

Abraham, Karl 6, 14, 26, 153
accountability, authority and 237
accreditation: psychoanalytic institutes 134, 144, 160, 226; training institutes 123
Adler, Alfred: Alfred Adler Institute in New York 144, 160; expulsion from Vienna Society 27, 132, 172; foundation of Association of Jungian Analysts (AJA) 139; foundation of new Vienna group 22, 27; and Freud, Sigmund 5, 7, 9, 15, 17, 20, 152, 153, 155, 241; as Freud's successor 132, 157; President of Vienna Society 16, 19; proposals on Vienna Society groups 14; proposals on Vienna Society meeting venue 11, 12, 13; resignation as President 18, 21; support for 130; support for Vienna Society independence 19, 26
adult development: Jung's work on 166; psychotherapy and 167
AJA *see* Association of Jungian Analysts (AJA) (UK)
Alexander, F. A. 60, 61
Alfred Adler Institute 144, 160
American Psychoanalytic Association (APA, APsaA): and Academy of Psychoanalysis 86; anti-trust suit 105; Board of Professional Standards 62, 116; committees 42, 45; component institutes 61, 119; development of 39; exclusion of psychologists from 186; inclusiveness 2; and International Psychoanalytic Association 86; marketing survey 64; meetings 59;

membership 34, 41, 61; President 38, 59, 64; splitting of 86, 186, 242; standards 243; study group 169; training 64, 76, 116, 245, 246, 255
analytic authority 95, 111
Association of Jungian Analysts (AJA) (UK) 139
authority: accountability and 237; analytic 95, 111; of candidates 243; centralized 97; Chairmen 11; collapse of 50; construction of 32; controversy about 34; Freud's 10, 12, 13, 42, 141, 226; Freud's attitude to 23; groups 12; IAAP 136, 139, 141; and illusion of certainty 116; investing of 124; Jung's 132, 136, 157; leaders 7; loss of established and traditional forms 236; medical profession 212; monolithic 97, 98; professional 37, 112, 122, 183, 185, 188, 200, 205; psychoanalytic institutes 34, 35; public authority of psychoanalysis 183; in relationships 127; of state 228; success of 45; succession and 231; transfer of 136; undermining of established 243; uniformity and 116; Zurich Jungians 138, 141

bias, analytical 92
Binswanger, Ludwig 6, 11
Bion, W. R. 8, 25, 26, 28, 49, 87, 96, 98, 106, 165, 170
Board of Professional Standards *see* American Psychoanalytic Association (APA, APsaA)
Boligningi, Stephano 1

Index 259

British Association of Psychotherapists (BAP) 72, 140
British Medical Society 138
British Psychoanalytical Society 72, 73, 137, 138, 159
British Psychological Society 138, 241

'candidate system' of training 112
candidates, authority of 243
Cassel Hospital (UK) 72
centralized authority 97
certainty, authority and illusion of 116
certification, training and 112
Chairmen, authority of 11
clinical skills in psychotherapy 124
collaboration, need for greater 146

Deutsche Psychoanalytische Gesellschaft (DPG) 70
Deutsche Psychoanalytische Vereinigung (DPV) 70
dreams and symbols, Jung's work on 163

England *see* United Kingdom

Ferenczi, Sándor 7, 14, 17, 85, 100, 241
Fordham, Michael 130, 133, 136, 143, 156, 159, 164, 226
Fourth Group (France) 86, 242
France: institutes 86, 186, 242; IPA's authority in 243; Lacanian school *see* Lacan, Jacques
French, T. M. 60
French Psychoanalytic Association 86, 242, 244
Freud, Sigmund: and Adler, Alfred 5, 7, 9, 15, 17, 20, 152, 153, 155, 241; Adler as successor to 132, 157; attitude to authority 23; authority of 10, 12, 13, 42, 141, 226; death 48; 'History of the Psychoanalytic Movement' 5; and Jung, Karl 6, 154; leadership 5; leadership assessed 27; 'ownership' of psychoanalysis 152; and Stekel, Wilhelm 11, 16, 20, 21, 85; and Vienna Psychoanalytic Society 6, 15, 17, 22, 27, 40, 100, 138
Freudian analysis: analytical bias 92; and Jungian analysis *see* Jungian analysis
Freudian School (France) 86, 242
Freudian teachings, dominance of 11

Germany: Deutsche Psychoanalytische Gesellschaft (DPG) 70; Deutsche Psychoanalytische Vereinigung (DPV) 70; IPA membership 71; psychiatry profession in 69, 212; training 70; UK developments compared 74
group authority: growth of 12; over leadership 8
group relationships within training institutes 95

Horney, Karen 32, 33, 34, 41, 43, 47, 58, 60, 155

Independent Group of Analytical Psychologists (IGAP) (UK) 139, 140
International Association for Analytical Psychology (IAAP): authority in United States 141; foundation of 136, 139; and Zurich Institute 130, 141
International Psychoanalytic Association (IPA): and American Psychoanalytic Association (APA) 86; component institutes 244; creation of 14, 15, 16, 17, 25, 153; and Deutsche Psychoanalytische Gesellschaft (DPG) 70; and Deutsche Psychoanalytische Vereinigung (DPV) 70; France, authority in 243; and International Federation of Psychoanalytic Societies 186; and Jung, Karl 134, 154; and Jung's 'Psychological Club' 133; and Lacan, Jacques Lacan 244; meetings 14; membership 34, 71; President 1, 19, 26, 154, 156; public face 100; rules 243, 244; splitting of 86, 132, 242; task force 64; training 70, 85, 114, 245, 255; United States, authority in 141
International Training Commission 42

Joint Committee of Higher Psychiatric Training (UK) 74
Jones, Ernest 6, 14, 25, 39, 59, 60, 72, 93, 100, 131, 132, 156, 164
Jung, Karl: adult development and identity, work on 166; authority of 132, 136, 157; and Freud, Sigmund 6, 154; symbols in dreams, work on 163; synchronicity, work on 168; and Zurich Psychoanalytic Society 133, 154

Jungian analysis: accreditation 134; analytical bias 92; Association of Jungian Analysts (AJA) 139; clubs 134; collaboration, need for greater 146; Freudian analysis, break from 152; Freudian analysis, coexistence with 170; Freudian analysis, conflicts with 130; Freudian analysis, distinction from 135; Freudian analysis, effects of exclusion from 161; Freudian analysis, potential links with 161; Freudian analysis, rejection of Jungian contribution to 162; institutional conflicts in 130; organization, avoidance of formal 156; professionalization of 141; sequence of splits in 142; training institutes 135, 139, 140, 158; in UK 136; Zurich Institute *see* Zurich Institute

Klein, Melanie 46, 48, 93, 155, 159, 164
Kleinian school 86, 91, 100, 139, 144, 185, 186, 241
Kubie, Lawrence 33, 35, 38, 39, 41, 42, 47, 59

Lacan, Jacques 86, 95, 111, 155, 186, 242, 243
leaders, authority of 7
leadership, group control over 8
licensing of US practitioners 76, 145, 185
Lincoln Institute (UK) 72, 73
London Centre for Psychotherapy 72
London Jungian club 135
London Society of Analytical Psychology *see* Society of Analytical Psychology of London (SAP)

Medical Society of Analytical Psychology (UK) 136
medicine: medical profession, authority of 212; medical schools, separation from psychoanalytic institutes 40; professional links with 216; psychotherapy within 210, 217; training institutes within 70
Menninger, William 59, 62, 64
Minutes of the Vienna Psychoanalytic Society 5
monolithic authority 97, 98

National Health Service (NHS) (UK) 72
New York Psychoanalytic Society, splitting of 32, 59, 85, 185
non-professionalization as alternative form of development 196

Oedipus myth as model of succession 225
Orestes myth as model of succession 227
organizations: psychodynamic forms of consulting to 125; psychodynamics of 76, 221
'ownership' of psychoanalysis 152

Paris Institute 86, 242
Portman Clinic (UK) 72
professional authority 37, 112, 122, 183, 185, 188, 200, 205
'professional system' of training 112
professionalization: aim of 192; antithesis of 196; authority *see* professional authority; benefits to practitioners 182; control of 141; fragmentation of profession 185; future of 181, 220; historical development 181; identity and status, challenges to 211; Jungian analysis 141; link with medical profession 216; new approach to 202; non-professionalization as alternative 196; other professions in relation 181, 211; perspectives on 179; problems of 210; process of 136; 'project' of 182; status as profession 211; training *see* training
professions, challenges to identity and status of 211
psychiatry: biological 76; psychodynamic 76
psychoanalysis: fragmentation of 185; Freudian *see* Freudian analysis; historical perspectives 3; Jungian *see* Jungian analysis; New York Psychoanalytic Society, splitting of 32; organizational perspectives 83; 'ownership' of 152; profession, erosion of 210; profession, past and future of 181; professionalization perspectives 179; psychoanalytic authority, construction of 32; psychoanalytic institutes, intolerance of diversity in 85; psychodynamic 60, 61, 62; psychotherapy and 55, 200, 204,

205, 216, 241, 245, 249, 253; succession to leadership of profession 225; training, 'faculty system' of 111; training, history of 241; Viennese Society, early years of 5
psychoanalytic culture 99
psychoanalytic institutes: accreditation as 144, 160; APA, APsaA *see* American Psychoanalytic Association (APA); authority and 34, 35; 'caste system' within 119; conflicts within 183; intolerance of diversity 34, 85, 104, 255; medical schools, separation from 40; membership of 93; psychoanalytic culture 99; redefinition as sites of learning 127; research and 71; training and 119, 123; work of 88
Psychoanalytic Society of Zurich *see* Zurich Psychoanalytic Society
psychoanalytically oriented psychotherapy 119, 125, 194, 210, 214, 235
psychodynamics: organizations 76, 125, 221; psychiatry 76; psychoanalysis 60, 61, 62; psychology 76; psychotherapy 60, 61, 72, 214
psychology: decline of 76; psychoanalytic 76; psychodynamic 76; training 76
psychotherapy: and adult development 167; careers in 158; clinical skills 124; combination with other clinical disciplines 221; competing methods of 103, 105; demand for 250; effectiveness of 190; future of 75; growth of interest in 245; IARPP 245; within medicine 210, 217; 'new thinking' about 148; Post-World War II 58; practice 214; practice, structure of 248; present-day 64; problems addressed by 218; professional position of 220; programs 247, 253, 255; psychoanalysis and 55, 200, 204, 205, 216, 241, 245, 249, 253; psychoanalysis as 200; psychoanalytically oriented 119, 125, 194, 210, 214, 235; psychodynamic 60, 61, 72, 214; qualification to practice 133, 135, 156; research on 45; service provision 221, 222, 250; training 247, 252; UK split 145; worldwide 69

public authority of psychoanalysis 183

qualification to practice psychotherapy 133, 135, 156

Rado, Sandor 32, 33, 34, 40, 41, 43, 45, 47, 58, 59
Rank, Otto 10, 11, 40, 85, 100, 165
relationships, authority in 127
research, psychoanalytic institutes and 71

Sachs, Hanns 11, 23, 25, 51, 241
Sadger, Isidor Isaak 11, 12, 13, 16, 23
Scottish Institute for Human Relations 73
Society of Analytical Psychology of London (SAP) 137, 138, 139, 140, 159, 165
standardization within training institutes 122
state, authority of the 228
Stekel, Wilhelm: and Adler, Alfred 13, 18, 19, 20, 21; and Ferenczi, Sándor 15; foundation of Vienna group 9; and Freud, Sigmund 11, 16, 20, 21, 85; resignation from Vienna Society 22; and Sadger, Isidor Isaak 13
succession: authority and 231; historical perspectives 226, 236; Oedipus myth as model of 225; Orestes myth as model of 227; process of 230; success of 225
Sullivan, Harry Stack 34, 39, 40, 41, 51, 59, 91, 155
supervision in training 113
symbols in dreams, Jung's work on 163
synchronicity, Jung's work on 168

Tausk, Victor 23
Tavistock Institute (UK) 72, 74, 138
Thompson, Clara 32, 96, 155
training: 'candidate system' 112; certification 112; faculty power 114, 115; 'faculty system' of 111; future of 122, 250; history of 241; institutes *see* training institutes; International Training Commission 42; model of 1, 116, 242, 244, 249, 250; 'professional system' 112; psychoanalytic institutes and 119, 123; psychology 76;

psychotherapy 247, 252; supervision 113; systems of 112
training institutes: accreditation 123; coherence within 130; conflicts between 140, 143; curricula 70; establishment of 135, 143, 158, 183; functioning of 66, 114; group relationships within 95; Jungian 135, 139, 140, 158; within medicine 70; standardization 122; task of 11; United Kingdom 72; vulnerability of 146

uniformity, authority and 116
United Kingdom: Association of Jungian Analysts (AJA) 139; British Association of Psychotherapists (BAP) 72, 140; British Medical Society 138; British Psychoanalytical Society 72, 73, 137, 138, 159; British Psychological Society 138, 241; Cassel Hospital 72; German developments compared 74; Independent Group of Analytical Psychologists (IGAP) 139, 140; Joint Committee of Higher Psychiatric Training 74; Jungian analysis in 136; Lincoln Institute 72, 73; links between psychoanalysis and psychiatry 72; London Centre for Psychotherapy 72; London Jungian club 135; London Society of Analytical Psychology 138; Medical Society of Analytical Psychology 136; National Health Service (NHS) 72; Portman Clinic 72; psychotherapy profession split 145; Scottish Institute for Human Relations 73; Society of Analytical Psychology of London (SAP) 137, 139, 140, 159, 165; Tavistock Institute 72, 74, 138;

training institutes 72, 135, 143, 145, 164
United States: Alfred Adler Institute in New York 144, 160; APA, APsaA *see* American Psychoanalytic Association (APA); Columbia Institute 59, 60; future of dynamic psychotherapy in 75; IAAP authority in 141; licensing of practitioners 76, 145, 185; psychiatry profession in 58; training 64

Vienna Psychoanalytic Society: Adler's two groups proposal 14; beginning of 9; and Freud, Sigmund 6, 15, 17, 22, 27, 40, 100, 138; independence from 58; and International Psychoanalytic Association (IPA) 16; meetings 9, 15, 18; *Minutes* 5; Nuremberg Congress 14; President 17; refugees from 44; training 32, 38, 135; and Zurich Institute 15, 18, 26, 139
Viennese Society: early years of 5; independence of 25; members of 16, 39

White, William Alanson 39, 40, 41, 59
William Alanson White Institute 34, 86, 95, 185

Zurich Institute: accreditation by 226; and AJA 139; authority of 138, 141; foundation of 15, 137, 159, 160; and IAAP 130, 141; importance of 137, 141, 160; and London Society of Analytical Psychology 138; training 134, 135, 137, 139, 141, 143, 158, 226; and US Jungians 140; and Vienna Psychoanalytic Society 15, 18, 26, 139
Zurich Psychoanalytic Society 133, 154